ANTIQUE FURNITURE
AND DECORATIVE ACCESSORIES

ANTIQUE FURNITURE
AND DECORATIVE ACCESSORIES
A Pictorial Archive with 3500 Illustrations

Thomas Arthur Strange

DOVER PUBLICATIONS, INC.
Mineola, New York

Bibliographical Note

This Dover edition, first published in 2000, is an unabridged reprint of *English Furniture, Decoration, Woodwork & Allied Arts,* originally published by the author, London, n.d.

DOVER *Pictorial Archive* SERIES

Library of Congress Cataloging-in-Publication Data

Strange, Thomas Arthur.
　[English furniture, decoration, woodwork & allied arts]
　Antique furniture and decorative accessories : a pictorial archive with 3500 illustrations / Thomas Arthur Strange.
　　　p. cm. — (Dover pictorial archive series)
　Originally published: English furniture, decoration, woodwork & allied arts. London : T.A. Strange, [18—?].
　　ISBN 0-486-41224-5 (pbk.)
　　1. Decoration and ornament—England. 2. Furniture—England. 3. Antiques—England. I. Title. II. Series.

NK2043 .S85 2000
749.22—dc21

00-034535

Manufactured in the United States of America
Dover Publications, Inc., 31 East 2nd Street, Mineola, N.Y. 11501

A GUIDE TO COLLECTORS.

3,500 ILLUSTRATIONS.

ENGLISH

Furniture, Decoration,

WOODWORK & ALLIED ARTS

DURING

The last half of the Seventeenth Century,

THE WHOLE OF THE

EIGHTEENTH CENTURY,

And the earlier part of the Nineteenth,

BY

THOMAS ARTHUR STRANGE.

Enlarged Edition : 368 Pages.

Published by the Author at 24, Christopher Street, Finsbury Square, London, E.C.

Price 12s. 6d. Nett.

ENTERED AT STATIONERS' HALL.

PREFACE.

ONE of the most noticeable features of Eighteenth Century Cabinet-work, etc., is the way the Master-men seemed to have combined a scholarly knowledge of design, etc., with a thorough knowledge of their craft, entering into the minutest details. Ruskin, in his "STONES OF VENICE," suggests a "consummation devoutly to be wished," and which must have been to a large extent practised by these old cabinet-makers, etc. Ruskin says, speaking of the great variety in the designs of Venetian Glass, with the absence of modern finish : "Now you cannot have the finish and the varied form too. If the workman is thinking about his edges, he cannot be thinking of his design ; if of his design, he cannot think of his edges. Choose whether you will pay for the lovely form or the perfect finish, and choose at the same moment whether you will make the worker a man or a grindstone.

"Nay, but the reader interrupts me—'If the workman can design beautifully, I would not have him kept at the furnace. Let him be taken away and made a gentleman, and have a studio, and design his glass there, and I will have it blown and cut for him by common workmen, and so I will have my design and my finish too."

"All ideas of this kind are founded upon two mistaken suppositions : the first, that one man's thoughts can be, or ought to be, executed by another man's hands ; the second, that manual labour is a degradation, when it is governed by intellect."

"On a large scale, and in work determinable by line and rule, it is indeed both possible and necessary that the thoughts of one man should be carried out by the labour of others ; in this sense I have already defined the best architecture to be the expression of the mind of manhood by the hands of childhood. But on a smaller scale, and in a design which cannot be mathematically defined, one man's thought can never be expressed by another : and the difference between the spirit of touch of the man who is inventing, and of the man who is obeying directions, is often all the difference between a great and a common work of art. How wide the separation is between original and second-hand execution, I shall endeavour to show elsewhere ; it is not so much to our purpose here as to mark the other and more fatal error of despising manual labour when governed by intellect ; for it is no less fatal an error to despise it when thus regulated by intellect, than to value it for its own sake. We are always in these days endeavouring to separate the two ; we want one man to be always thinking, and another to be always working, we call one a gentleman, and the other an operative ; whereas the workman ought often to be thinking, and the thinker often to be working, and both should be gentlemen in the best sense. As it is, we make both ungentle, the one envying, the other despising, his brother ; and the mass of society is made up of morbid thinkers and miserable workers. Now it is only by labour that thought can be made healthy, and only by thought that labour can be made happy, and the two cannot be separated with impunity. It would be well if all of us were good handicraftsmen in some kind, and the dishonour of manual labour done away with altogether ; so that though there should still be a trenchant distinction of race between nobles and commoners, there should not, among the latter, be a trenchant distinction of employment, as between idle and working men, or between liberal or illiberal professions. All professions should be liberal, and there should be less pride felt in peculiarity of employ-ment, and more in excellence of achievement. And yet more, in each several profession, no master should be too proud to do its hardest work. The painter should grind his own colours ; the architect work in the mason's yard with his men ; the master-manufacturer be himself a more skilful operative than any man in his mills ; and the distinction between one man and another be only in experience and skill, and the authority and wealth which these must naturally and justly obtain."

List of Architects, Designers, and Authors whose Works are illustrated in this Book.

SYNOPSIS.

INIGO JONES.

Inigo Jones
Born 1572 —
Died 1653

I HAVE thought it best to preface this work with a short account of the Renaissance of Architecture. Inigo Jones, who was born in 1573, during the reign of Queen Elizabeth, and died in 1653, was most probably the first English Architect who practised the Renaissance style free from any Gothic additions; his influence being felt right through the last half of the 17th century down to about the year 1800—in fact, he has been called the father of the English Classical Revival of Architecture. This is how Horace Walpole, in his "Anecdotes of Painting," prefaces the account of his life: "Inigo Jones who, if a table of fame like that in the 'Tatler' were to be formed for men of real and indisputable genius in every country, would save England from the disgrace of not having her representative among the arts. She adopted Holbein and Vandyck; she borrowed Rubens; she produced Inigo Jones. Vitruvius drew up his grammar, Palladio showed him his practice, Rome displayed a theatre worthy of his emulation, and King Charles I. was ready to encourage, employ, and reward his talents."

17th Century.

INIGO JONES.

Chimney-Piece.

His Majesty's Drawing Room at Greenwich.

Chimney-Piece.

Somerset House.

No 1.

No 2.

But some of my readers may ask (and this book is mainly written for those who cannot be expected to understand architectural terms) what is the meaning of the word Renaissance as applied to Architecture? I will endeavour, as briefly as possible, to explain. Nearly everyone knows that in ancient Greece, civilisation, and refinement were carried to a very high state of perfection. This was especially so as regards the Fine Arts. The great period

17th Century.

INIGO JONES.

of Greek Art began during the Fifth Century B.C. After the conquest of Greece by the Romans, the latter imported to Rome, Greek artists to build their temples, etc., and thus continued and considerably developed the Greek style; and this lasted until about the middle of the Third Century Anno Domini. The period embraced during these centuries is known as the Classic period of Antique Art. Architecture had been classified into the "Five Orders," the Doric, Ionic, Corinthian, Tuscan and Composite; the first three are Greek, the other two are Roman orders. The style which followed this period was called Byzantine, and was a sort of debased classic style influenced by Eastern Art. The Mediæval or Gothic style followed this and reached its greatest perfection during the Thirteenth and Fourteenth Centuries, but mostly in the churches and palaces—the only places where it could safely develop in those lawless times. Domestic Gothic Architecture developed during the Fifteenth Century.

About the end of the Fifteenth century in Italy, encouraged by more peaceful times, began what is called the Renaissance (meaning New Birth or Revival), that is, the students of those times, both in Literature and in the Arts, began to study the remains of the old Roman (and Greek) or Classic times; the Architects of this time not only imitating the ancient Roman buildings, but further developing the style. (It must not be forgotten that in Architecture the Revival in Italy was mainly based on the old Roman Ruins.) This was done not only in Architecture, but in Furniture, etc., some of the best artists of those days working thereon, and in their enthusiasm for the old style making their carved chests in the forms of the Roman sarcophagi, and giving the general outline an architectural character; and even a century later on, making the fronts of their cabinets imitate the elevations of ancient temples and house fronts. In the South Kensington Museum are to be seen many examples of these periods of Italian art.

17th Century.

INIGO JONES.

Chimney-Piece.

His Majesty's Drawing
Room, Greenwich.

Chimney-Piece.

His Majesty's Drawing Room,
Greenwich.

INIGO JONES. 17th Century.

Among the great Architects of the Renaissance in Italy were Bramante, Barbaro, Sansovino, Sangalla, Michael Angleo, Raphael, Urbin, Julio Romano, Serlio, Labaco, Scamozzi, but, above all, the great Palladio.

Inigo Jones was one of the first English Architects who studied in Italy the old Roman ruins, and the newer buildings erected by the above Architects. He says in the first part of his work, " Stonehenge Restored, 1655 "—" Being naturally inclined in my younger days to study the Art of Design, I passed into foreign parts to converse with the great Masters thereof in Italy, where I applied myself to search out the ruins of those ancient buildings, which, in despite of time itself and violence of barbarians, are yet remaining. Having satisfied myself in these, and returning to my native country, I applied my mind more particularly to the study of Architecture." He paid two visits to Italy, and he returned from his second visit filled with the very spirit of the great Italian artists of the Renaissance. From among the various buildings he erected I have taken and illustrated here some of the Chimney-pieces, etc., and readers will notice that they are of a free classic type. I have not attempted to thoroughly illustrate his work, but only so far as to enable me to get a proper sequence, so that my readers may be better able to understand the underlying feature which animated the Art workers of the Eighteenth century ; and which, as I have before observed, Inigo Jones was the first, or among the first, to start in this country. He was much employed by the Court, in conjunction with Ben Jonson, the poet, in the production of Masques ; Inigo Jones designing the scenery and Ben Jonson composing the verses. He is credited with completely revolutionizing the scenes of the stage by placing the stage itself at the back where it now is (it formerly being in the centre), and by that means having moveable scenery at the sides which he greatly developed by mechanical resources. After a while these joint authors fell out, and the following lines—among a lot of others—which Dryden called " dotages," were written by Ben Jonson about Inigo Jones, probably referring to his supposed mean birth :—

> " *Med.*—Indeed there is a woundly luck in names, sirs,
> And a vain mystery, an a man knew where
> To find it. My Godsire's name I tell you
> Was In-and-in Shuttle, and a weaver he was,
> And it did fit his craft ; for so his shuttle
> Went in-and-in still—this way and then that way.
> And he named me In-and-in Medley, which serves
> A *Joiner's* craft, because that we do lay
> Things in-and-in, in our work. But I am truly
> *Architectonicus Professor*, rather ;
> That is, as one would say, an Architect."
>
> *Tale of a Tub*, Act IV., Scene I.

His great work as an Architect, is the Banqueting Hall, Whitehall. He had a large number of pupils and many imitators. To John Webb and Edward Carter is due the credit of carrying out many of Inigo Jones' designs. Webb, who was his nephew and son-in-law, rebuilt the side of Wilton House and built Ashburnham House, among others, from the designs of Inigo Jones. Some of the Chimney-pieces were in marble, some in stone, or oak, and Italian workmen were brought to this country to carve them, although we had native talent—as is proved in the case of Nicholas Stone, who was much employed by the nobility and Architects of the time, Inigo Jones among others.

6

th Century.

INIGO JONES.

Chimney-Pieces Nos. 1, 3, 4, at Wilton. No. 6 Chimney-Piece in Ye Great Room at Lord Pembroke's at Wilton. No. 2 at the Earl of Shaftesbury at St. Giles. No. 5 in the Dining Room at Sir Mark Pleydell's, Coleshill, Berks.

Doorways by Inigo Jones.

Nicholas Stone was born at Woodbury, near Exeter, in 1586; was employed in making monuments for persons of the first distinction. He was employed by King James I. on various works, including the Banqueting Hall, Whitehall. He was appointed Master-Mason to Charles I., and this is the substance of his patent for same : " Charles, by the grace of God, King of England, Scotland, France and Ireland, Defender of the Faith, etc. To all whome these presents shall come, greeting. Knowe yee that wee, of our especiall grace, certeine knowledge and meere motion, and for divers other good causes and considerations us at this present moveing, have given and graunted, and by these presents, for us, our heirs and successors, doe give and graunte to our trusty and well-beloved servaunt Nicholas Stone, the office and place of our Master-Mason and Architeckt for all our buildings and reparations within our honour and Castle of Windsor, and him the said Nicholas Stone our said Master-Mason and Architeckt for all our said buildings and reparations within our honour and Castle of Windsor aforesaid, wee doe make, ordaine, constitute and appointe by these presents, for and dureing the terme of his natural life.   And further, wee doe give and graunt to the said Nicholas Stone for the executing of the said office and place the wages and fee of twelve pence of lawfull money of England by the day, in as large and ample manner as William Suthis, or any other person or persons heretofore, did enjoy.   A.D. 1626, April 21st."

Doorways by Inigo Jones.

INIGO JONES.

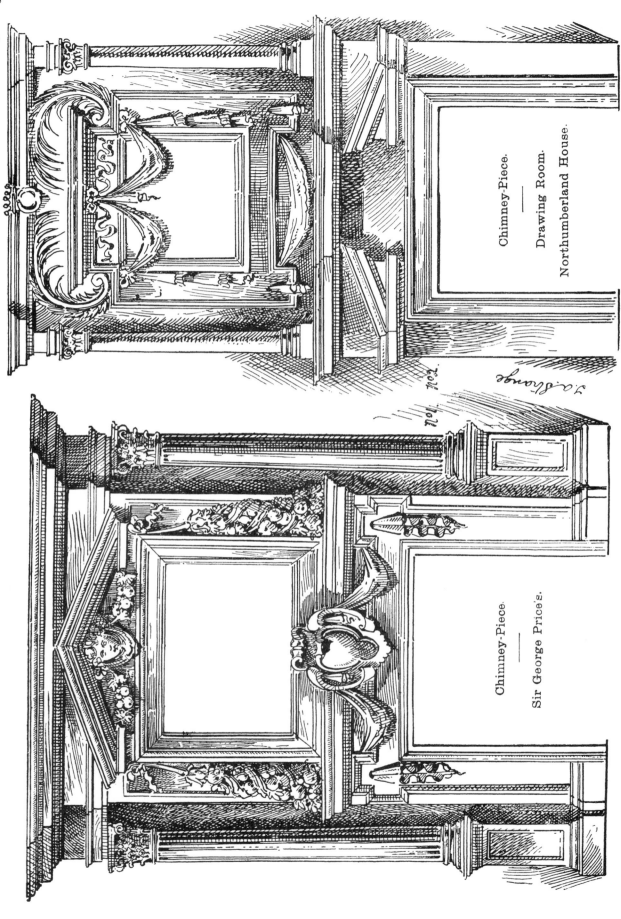

Chimney-Piece.

Drawing Room.
Northumberland House.

Chimney-Piece.

Sir George Price's.

He died in 1647. Among a great many other things that he did, he carved the Water Gate of Old York House (still existing in Gardens on Thames Embankment), and the Gateway of St. Mary's Church, Oxford. He also carved Chimney-pieces, etc. He worked in wainscot oak, white marble, alabaster, touchstone, and Portland stone, etc. Some of the marble and stone Chimney-pieces had parts like the centre medallions inlaid with various coloured marbles, and in some cases the marble Chimney-pieces were set off with elegantly chased brass mounts, examples of which can be seen at Hampton Court Palace

INIGO JONES.

17th Century.

In addition to having Italians working in this country, the Chimney-pieces and works of art were made in Italy and sent over here. This occurred in the case of some of the Chimney-pieces at Wilton, which were brought over together with Statues, Basso-Relievos, and other things of marble by the first Phillip Earl of Pembroke—Wilton being the ancient seat of the Earls of Pembroke and Montgomery. The nobility and gentry of those days were great admirers of the antique, and, in the course of their travels in Italy, bought or had copies made of rare examples, which were brought to England to adorn their mansions which they had built, or were having built after the style of the Italian Renaissance, so that the whole of the credit of the Renaissance in England does not belong to the architects of the period; for where the nobility made the "demand" for classic buildings, the "supply" naturally followed. Readers who are curious can turn up Colin Campbell's "Vitruvius Britanicus," and will there be able to see sides of rooms at Wilton (which space will not allow in this volume). The rooms have low dadoes, the walls above pannelled with full length portraits, enriched cornices, with very large cove leading up to ceiling of moulded classical design. In the Dining-room there is a very rich and magnificent doorway, or rather door case, on the inside. On each side of the Chimney-piece, and between panels, are heavy swags of carving in the Grinling Gibbons' style, but heavier and of a more conventionalized character.

Talman was another eminent architect of this period; he built "Chatsworth" for the Duke of Devonshire.

It has been mentioned that the Chimney-pieces were made of marble, among which were Common Statuary, which is rather soft, and Carrara, which is harder—both imported from Italy; Touch-stone is a black marble which comes from Namur in Belgium; Plymouth marble (Devonshire), hard, red and white—this is rather brittle, and, I believe, was used (Derbyshire marble was also used) about this time, Chimney-pieces of which can be seen at Hampton Court Palace, and in the Vestry Room at St. Lawrence, Old Jewry, next the Guildhall, London; Verde Antique (Egyptian marble), which is green with white veins; Alabaster (plain Alabaster), which is a white and glittering stone, like the finest Statuary marble

but more brittle; plain Yellow Alabaster, a very beautiful and the most transparent of all kinds: and Oriental Alabaster, a very beautiful stone of a yellowish colour, elegantly veined with a brown and reddish colour.

The ceilings of this period are a great feature of the Interior decoration, and were made in plaster. One very noticeable feature is the cove; the ceiling itself was divided into panels and circles, the borders of same being enriched, in some cases, with flowers and fruits of all descriptions—apples, marigolds, grapes, roses, tiger lilies, pomegranates, etc., etc., all mixed up together, and well raised and undercut. It must be remembered when noticing these naturalistic designs, that these modellers of ceilings were working side by side with carvers of the school of Grinling Gibbons, as it was the custom at that time for such workmen to carry out their work *in situ*, and not as it is often done now—in a workshop, perhaps, hundreds of miles away, and then workmen sent to fix them. A good example of this is illustrated a few pages further on—"Holme Lacy," in Herefordshire.

In other cases the borders had flat ornamentation of Greek or Roman design, and in others a flowing Italian Renaissance character. In many cases, both the naturalistic and geometric, etc., patterns were on the same ceiling, the flowers, etc., being on the border of the centre medallion. The panels of these ceilings were often painted with allegorical and other subjects; nymphs and cupids sprawling on clouds, etc. Nearly every artist of the Seventeenth century painted ceilings, staircases, etc.; even Rubens painted the ceiling of the Banqueting Hall, Whitehall.

No. 2 and 5 from the Duke of Northumberland's at Chiswick.

17th Century.

INIGO JONES.

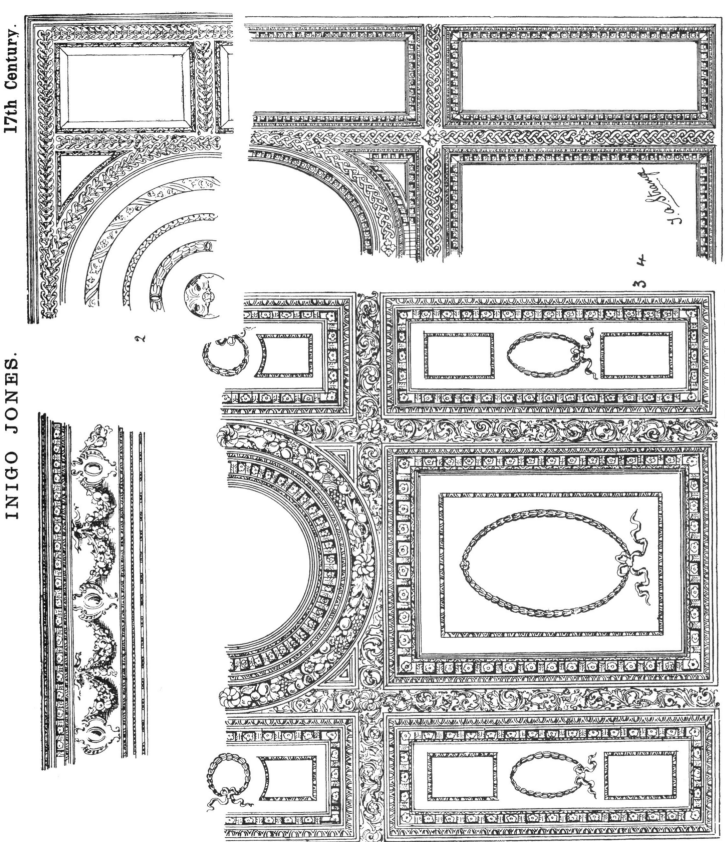

No. 1.—In the Cornice round room to match Ceiling No. 3, which is at Coleshill, in Berkshire.
No. 4 is the Ceiling of the Banqueting House, Whitehall; the Panels were painted by Rubens.
No. 2 is at Holland House.

FURNITURE.

17th Century.

Furniture, 2nd half of 17th Century.

SIR CHRISTOPHER WREN and GRINLING GIBBONS. 17th Century.

Carving over the Altar of St. James's Church, Piccadilly, London. By Grinling Gibbons.

Though Sir Christopher Wren and Grinling Gibbons can hardly be said to belong to the Eighteenth century, yet their work must be illustrated here, as it so greatly influenced the Architects and Art Workers of that century. Evelyn appears to claim the credit of "discovering" Grinling Gibbons. According to what he has left us in his famous diary, as he was out one day for a casual walk near his residence, Sayes Court, Deptford, he came near a solitary thatched house in a field, and upon looking in at the window saw Gibbons making a copy in wood of a large Cartoon or Crucifix of Tintoret's, and upon entering he was greatly impressed with the delicate workmanship—the best, he says, he had seen in all his travels. There was a regular colony of carvers at Deptford at that time, the decoration of the immense high decks of the old men-of-war affording ample employment for them. Some time after this Evelyn took Gibbons to Whitehall with some of his carvings, and introduced him to Charles II. who gave the artist a place in the Board of Works and employed his hand on the ornaments of the most taste in his palaces, particularly at Windsor Castle. He was also employed by Sir Christopher Wren on his various works, the Library at Trinity College, Oxford, being one of the first, and is justly considered one of his happiest works. He was also employed on such famous houses as Chatsworth, Petworth, Burghley, Houghton, Cassiobury, Blenheim, Belton House, etc. For the Choir of St. Paul's Cathedral he likewise did much of the foliage and festoons belonging to the stall work, and those in lime-tree which decorate the side aisles of the Choir. An immense number of designs of this period are attributed to him. Most all the City churches built by order of Queen Anne, the Act for which

String Course round St Paul's Cathedral, London.

Carved in Stone. From St. Paul's Cathedral, London.

was passed in 1708, to replace those destroyed by the Fire of London, claim to have carvings done by him. Sir Christopher Wren was commissioned to superintend their erection. He carved foliage, birds, fruit, flowers, shells, fishes, etc., in great variety—and as they are in nature, without any conventional treatment. Nothing can surpass the perfect mastery of execution. All the work is cut clean and sharp out of wood which admits of no tentative cuts, and requires no rubbing down with sand-paper, and in which errors are not to be repaired. Some good examples of his are to be seen at Hampton Court Palace—where visitors will notice groups of flowers, fruits, etc., surrounding portraits that are placed over the fireplaces, and one must confess to the added grandeur it gives to such pictures. They will also notice the carved mouldings of doorways as one goes from room to room—some of which are beautifully designed. Grinling Gibbons is supposed to have been born of Dutch parents; much controversy seems to have originated over the place where he was born, but as Horace Walpole justly observes: "When a man strikes out originality for himself, or in other words, is a genius, the place of his birth has little claim on his merit." From 1714 to 1721 he was appointed Master Carver in Wood to George I., with the magnificent salary of eighteen-pence a day. He died in 1721.

A great many mansions throughout the country, such as Lord Chesterfield's house, "Holme Lacy," in Herefordshire, have what they call his carvings; but it is well known he had a great number of assistants who worked under his supervision, and there were a great number of carvers who worked after his style. In fact he formed a School of Carvers. There is a Vestry Room and an Organ Loft in the Church of St.

**The Dean's Canopy, St. Paul's Cathedral, London.
Carved by Grinling Gibbons.**

SIR CHRISTOPHER WREN and GRINLING GIBBONS. 17th Century.

Carving from the Choir Stalls of St. Paul's Cathedral, London, by Grinling Gibbons.

Side Aisle of the Choir of St. Paul's Cathedral, London.

Lawrence Jewry, London, close to the Guildhall, that are known to be by his hand, and are well worth a visit.

We find his work principally on mirror frames, wall panels, chimney-pieces, and over Communion tables in churches. His materials are mostly lime-tree ; for church panels or mouldings he used principally oak ; and occasionally cedar for the architraves in large mansions. For medallion portraits he used pearwood or boxwood.

Sir Christopher Wren was born in 1632 and died in 1723, so that he lived from the reign of Charles I. well into the reign of George I. It is claimed for him that he succeeded Inigo Jones, although he was only about twenty when Jones died ; and it is well known he was not brought up as an Architect, his training for same being practically *nil*. But, as has already been suggested, it was thought necessary in those days for people in his position to have a general knowledge of Architecture, which is proven in the case of Wren's father, who was Dean of Windsor, and who is credited with having a good knowledge of same.

It is claimed for Wren, on account of the great quantity and quality of his finished works, that he established the Renaissance in this country in its natural form. As most readers are well aware, he built St. Paul's Cathedral, a large part of Greenwich Hospital, Hampton Court Palace, the great majority of the City churches built after the Fire of London, and other buildings and additions too numerous to mention. He was a great scholar, and one of the Founders of the Royal Society. He visited Paris during the building of the Louvre and was introduced to Bernini, the Architect, who, he says, showed him the designs for the Louvre, for which, he says, he would have given his skin, but the old reserved Italian gave him but a

THE LORD MAYOR'S STALL
ST. PAUL'S CATHEDRAL

Over North Inner Door of St. Paul's Cathedral, London.

Panel at Belton House, Grantham.   Grinling Gibbons.

Carving by Grinling Gibbons from the Choir Stalls, St. Paul's Cathedral, London.

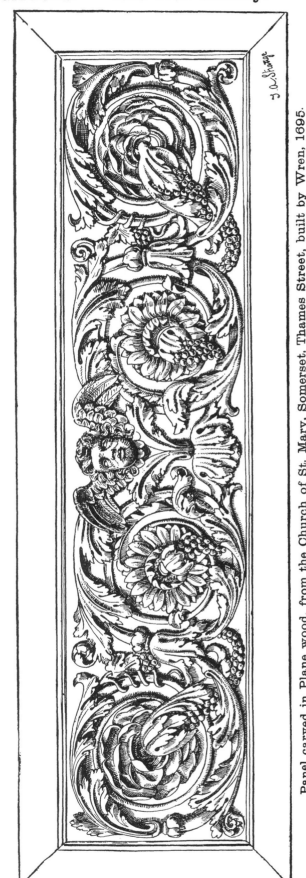

Panel carved in Plane wood, from the Church of St. Mary, Somerset, Thames Street, built by Wren, 1695.

18

Late 17th Century.

Sir CHRISTOPHER WREN and GRINLING GIBBONS.

Panels under the Great Windows of St. Paul's Cathedral, London. (On the South Side.)

Sir CHRISTOPHER WREN and GRINLING GIBBONS. Late 17th or early 18th Centuries.

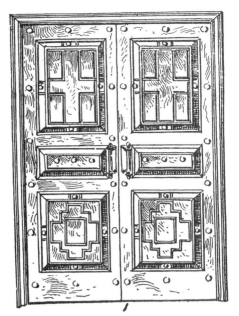

Doorway at Windsor Castle, by Grinling Gibbons.
No. 1—Doorway, St. Paul's Cathedral.
No. 2—Doorway, St. Stephen, Walbrook London.

Mantel-piece at Stoke Hall, by Grinling Gibbons.

Doorway, St. Nicholas Cole Abbey, Queen Victoria Street, London.

Sir CHRISTOPHER WREN and GRINLING GIBBONS.   Late 18th Century.

Panel at Belton House, Grantham, by Grinling Gibbons.

Panel at Belton House, Grantham, by Grinling Gibbons

Plaster Ceiling, Belton House, Grantham.

Plaster Ceiling, Belton House, Grantham.

few minutes' view. They were five little designs in paper, for which he received as many thousand pistoles; Wren had only time to copy it in his fancy and memory.

William and Mary commissioned Wren to build the existing suite of State apartments at Hampton Court Palace, in emulation of the splendour of Versailles. (It will be remembered that Louis XIV. was William III.'s great rival.) Wren not only rebuilt part of the palace, but superintended the decoration of the apartments for Queen Mary; and among others whom he employed in the latter work was Antonio Verrio, a Neapolitan, whose exuberant pencil was ready at pouring out gods, goddesses, cæsars, kings, emperors, and triumphs on the walls of ceilings and staircases. The New Testament and the Roman History were the main sources of his inspiration; so what with painted marble columns, nymphs, satyrs, muses, virtues, zephyrs, cupids, etc., etc., which all jostle each other in amazing confusion, he managed to produce something very gorgeous, and quite in the French taste. A specimen of his work on a large scale can be seen in the King's Great Staircase at Hampton Court Palace, which is the principal approach to William III.'s State Rooms. It appears that Charles II. having a mind to revive the manufacture of tapestry at Mortlake, sent for Verrio to England, but, changing his purpose, he employed him at Windsor Castle, where he did an enormous amount of decorative painting, for which he drew large sums. He does not appear to have been over modest in asking for money; it is recorded that once at Hampton Court, not being able to get near the King, he called out: "Sire, I desire the favour of speaking to your Majesty." "Well, Verrio," said the King, "what is your request?" "Money, sir, I am so short in cash, that I am not able to pay my workmen, and your Majesty and I have learned by experience that pedlars and painters cannot give credit long." The King smiled and said he had but lately ordered him a £1,000. "Yes sir," replied he, "but that was soon paid away, and I have no gold left." "At that rate," said the King, "you would spend more than I do to maintain my family." "True," answered Verrio, "but does your Majesty keep an open table as I do?" He was also employed at Burleigh and afterwards at Chatsworth. His performances were in his day

Sir CHRISTOPHER WREN and GRINLING GIBBONS.　Late 17th Century.

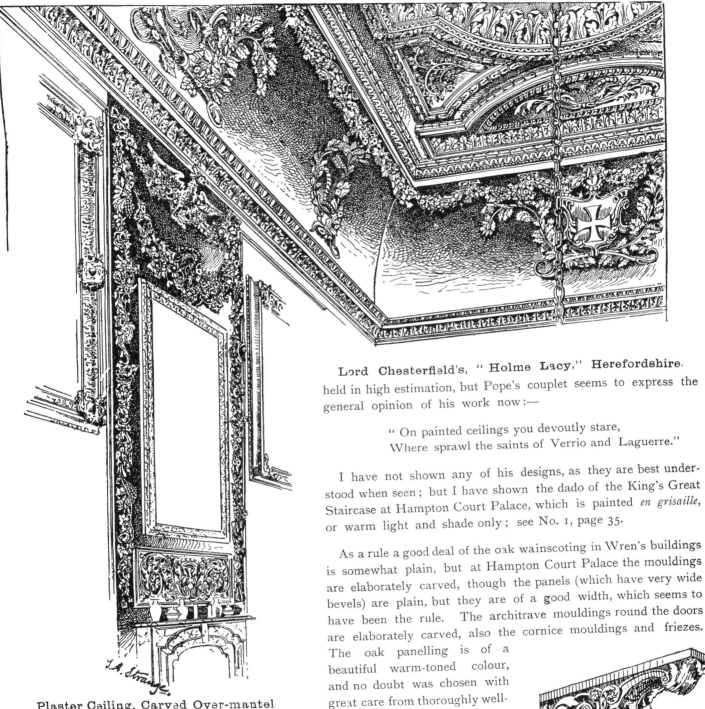

**Plaster Ceiling, Carved Over-mantel
by Grinling Gibbons.**

Lord Chesterfield's, " Holme Lacy," Herefordshire.

held in high estimation, but Pope's couplet seems to express the general opinion of his work now :—

> " On painted ceilings you devoutly stare,
> Where sprawl the saints of Verrio and Laguerre."

I have not shown any of his designs, as they are best understood when seen ; but I have shown the dado of the King's Great Staircase at Hampton Court Palace, which is painted *en grisaille*, or warm light and shade only ; see No. 1, page 35.

As a rule a good deal of the oak wainscoting in Wren's buildings is somewhat plain, but at Hampton Court Palace the mouldings are elaborately carved, though the panels (which have very wide bevels) are plain, but they are of a good width, which seems to have been the rule. The architrave mouldings round the doors are elaborately carved, also the cornice mouldings and friezes. The oak panelling is of a beautiful warm-toned colour, and no doubt was chosen with great care from thoroughly well-seasoned wood, and cut in such

a way as to show the largest amount of grain. It is known that Wren was largely influenced by the French style (Louis XIV.), and it is known he did not visit Italy, although he went to France, and returned to England with, as he says, " all France on paper." This feeling is certainly apparent in some of these carvings. The panelling in most of the City Churches is very plain, being an ovolo on edge, with large bevels and very wide panels. The cost was evidently a consideration. In some of the pulpits the plain panels were inlaid with a few simple geometric lines, etc. Doorways of rooms were made a

**Bracket, Library, St. Paul's
Cathedral, London.**

Sir CHRISTOPHER WREN and GRINLING GIBBONS. Late 17th Century.

At Lord Chesterfield's, "Holme Lacy," Herefordshire, Plaster Ceiling, Carved Over-mantel by Grinling Gibbons.

F. A. Strange

Carving from the Choir Stalls. St. Paul's Cathedral, London.

great feature in Wren's works, and he had in the best examples, rich architraves and pediments carried on beautifully carved brackets. The spaces over the doors were framed, and paintings of architectural ruins, with groups of shepherds, etc. Some of these (painted by J. Rousseau, born 1630, died 1723), to be seen at Hampton Court Palace, have swags of carvings each side by Grinling Gibbons. Rousseau painted these pieces expressly for the decoration of panels in these apartments, by order of William III. The Chandeliers of brass and silver, of this period, were made to carry twenty or thirty candles, and are well worth studying. I illustrate a few further on. The wrought iron work is also good. The cast-iron fire backs are full of interest, illustrating Coat-of-Arms, or such subjects as the Rape of Europa, Worship of the Brazen Serpent, Sacrifice of Isaac, and similar allegorical ideas. Ladies of the period were much given to embroidering curtains, etc., and some very beautiful examples remain.

The turning has the twist which was also in vogue during the Jacobean period. Among the coverings of this period were red, blue and green damask, which seem to have been common. Norwich damask, Spitalfields silk (sometimes richly embroidered and laced with gold) and velvet; Taffaty, which was sometimes painted; and tapestry on the walls, representing allegorical subjects such as the Loves of Venus and Adonis, etc.

There were alcoves in the Dining-room for sideboards and tables. Glasses and pier-glasses had the borders ornamented with blue glass, with the edge gently bevelled—sometimes they had double bevels—and were enclosed in carved and gilt frames of a Louis XIV. character. The glass was occasionally painted with festoons of flowers, etc. The bureau and furniture generally was in oak, veneered with Italian walnut and having Burr Walnut centres ; examples of the way they were veneered are shown on page 27, Nos. 15, 16, 17, and 18. The escutcheons and handles were often the Coat-of-Arms or the initials of the family. A great feature of the cabinet work was the number of secret drawers, etc. They were inlaid with marqueterie, after the Dutch style, of a large and naturalistic description, such as vases, tulips, birds, etc. The woodwork was sometimes swelled out into enormous proportions, wavy ebony mouldings being used in some cases, while the mouldings of panels were broken up, thus requiring a lot of mitreing. Ivory and mother-of-pearl are occasionally met with among the inlays

Sir CHRISTOPHER WREN and GRINLING GIBBONS. 17th and 18th Centuries.

Plaster Ceiling, Carved Over-Mantel, by Grinling Gibbons.

Carving by Grinling Gibbons, Belton House, Grantham.

At Lord Chesterfield's "Holme Lacy," Herefordshire. The feet of the bureaux were carved to represent claws, and the legs of stools, chairs, tables, etc., were often Cabriole. Silver furniture was occasionally made for the nobility, etc., examples of which from Windsor Castle, are shown in this book (see page 32, Nos. 11 and 12); they are embossed and *repoussé*, and are chased by the graver. Marble was extensively used for table-tops; sometimes the tops were inlaid with various coloured marbles, of a Florentine design, and placed on gilt stands. The plaster - work for ceilings, etc.,

was carried to a very high finish, and in the best rooms were painted. The chimney-pieces in some cases had receding shelves, to hold pieces of china, which were quite the rage at this time. There is a curious chimney-piece in Kensington Palace; over the fire-place is a map of North-west Europe, round the circumference of which are the points of the compass, with a dial-hand which was worked from a vane on the roof, so as to let people in the room know from which quarter the wind was blowing. It may interest readers to know what remuneration Sir Christopher Wren received for some of his works. As Comptroller of the Works he received £9 2s. 6d. per annum; and his stipend for rebuilding St. Paul's and all the City churches was fixed at £200 per annum. It has been remarked of Wren that "his knowledge had a right influence on the temper of his mind, which had all the humility, graceful modesty, goodness, calmness, strength and suavity of a sound and unaffected philosopher." He died at his house in St. James's, February 27th, 1723, in the 91st year of his age.

Plaster Ceiling, Carved Over·mantel by Grinling Gibbons at Lord Chesterfield's "Holme Lacy," Herefordshire.

Among the woods used during the last half of the Seventeenth century and first half of Eighteenth Century, were oak for wainscotting, and doors made of cedar ; but the doors, etc. about this time were also made of mahogany. Where the woodwork had to be painted or gilt, which was done extensively about this time, it was made of deal, even the carvings were painted or gilt, so that one wood was as good as another for that purpose, but deal was the most economical. Pear, cedar, and lime were much used by the carvers of this period, as they were more suitable for the tender work required for flowers, etc. Elm was sometimes used for various necessary articles about the house, such as dressers, and also ash, beech, birch and poplar of the three varieties, white, black, and aspen. Sycamore was much used ; in fact, in some old houses in the country the floors are of sycamore, and the wainscot of poplar. Walnut was extensively used—both English and Italian—effects being gained by contrasting the plain wood with "Burr" centres. Amboyna and rosewood were also used. Chestnut was, at an earlier date, used in the substantial parts of buildings, and, in old houses, is often mistaken, even by good workmen, for oak, which it so greatly resembles in colour and substance. Ebony mouldings were used by the Dutch cabinet-makers. Maple, yew, and cherry were also in use. Pear tree was cut into boards, and occasionally took the place of oak, while veneers of pollard oak were used in centres of panels.

It must be mentioned that in the country districts in the olden time, gentlemen building residences used the wood that grew on the estate, other woods not always being available.

There was a fashion about this time of painting the leather of the backs and seats of chairs. The edges of chairs covered with tapestry, woollen work, or figured velvet, etc., had, in most cases, an edging of fringe. The seats were often moveable. The chairs were sometimes caned, and the seats stuffed with horsehair, etc.

Screen, St. Nicholas Cole Abbey, Queen Victoria Street, London. Out through and Carved Fret.

Panel, St. Paul's Cathedral London, by Grinling Gibbons

Sir CHRISTOPHER WREN and GRINLING GIBBONS.   Late 17th or early 18th Century.

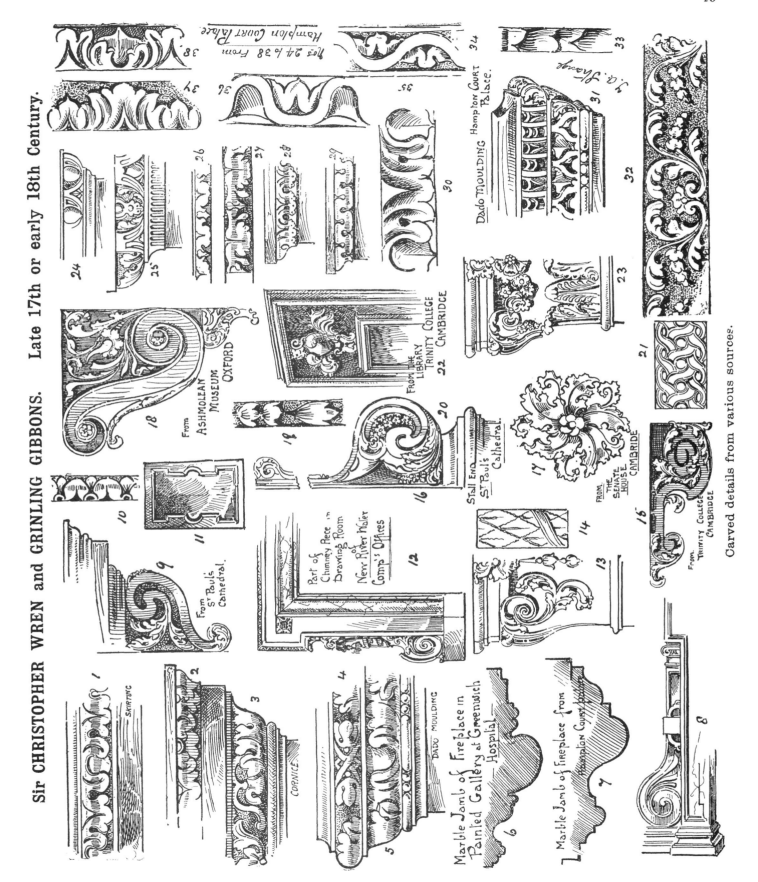

Carved details from various sources.

Sir CHRISTOPHER WREN and GRINLING GIBBONS. Late 17th or early 18th Centuries.

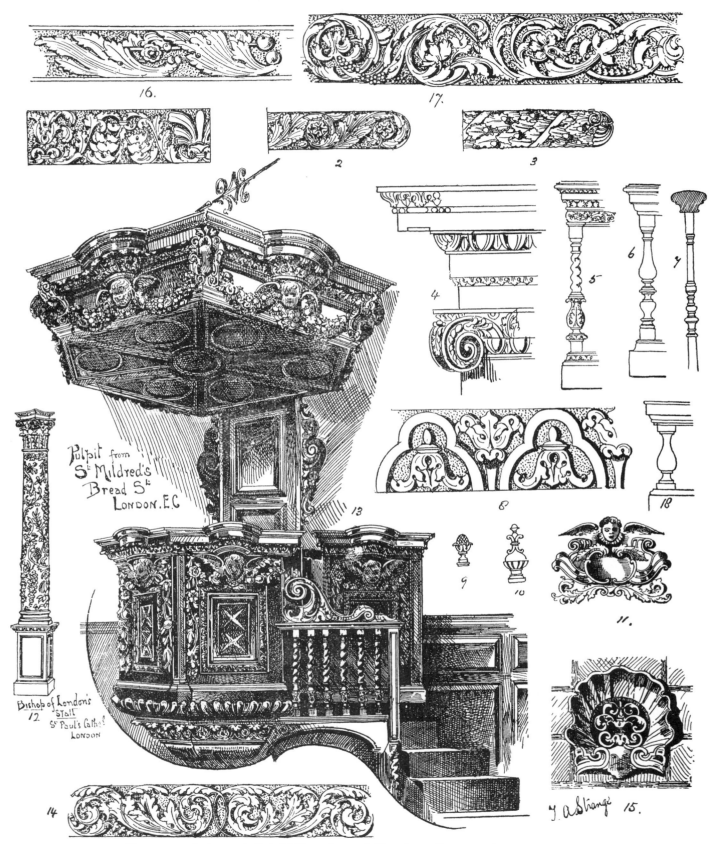

16.

17.

1

2

3

4

5

6

7

8

18

Pulpit from St Mildred's Bread St LONDON. E.C

13

9

10

11

Bishop of London's Stall St Paul's Cathl LONDON

12

14

J. A. Strange *15.*

Carved Oak Pulpit, Inlaid Panels, and Carvings from various sources.

Sir CHRISTOPHER WREN and GRINLING GIBBONS. Late 17th or early 18th Centuries.

Memorial Tablet to Sir Christopher Wren and Family, St. Paul's Cathedral, London.

Memorial Tablet, St. Paul's Cathedral, London.

Another great Architect of this period was Sir John Vanbrugh. Alan Cunningham, in his " Lives of British Architects," says " no man who has been satirized by Swift and praised by Reynolds could have much chance of being forgotten ; but the fame of him who was at once the author of ' The Relapse ' and ' The Provoked Wife ' and the architect of Castle Howard and Blenheim, stands independent of even such subsidiaries." He was born in the parish of St. Stephen, Walbrook, in the year 1666. In his younger days he seems to have met with misfortune, being at one time imprisoned in the Bastille. Castle Howard—one of the noblest mansions in England—was designed by him in 1702 for the Duke of Carlisle ; it has been greatly praised for its picturesque and varied beauty. In 1706 Parliament resolved to raise a

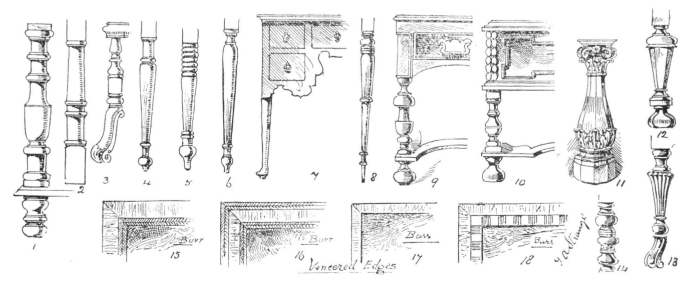

Examples of Turning, etc., of the last half of the 17th Century.

28

Sir CHRISTOPHER WREN, GRINLING GIBBONS, etc. Late 17th or early 18th Centuries.

Pulpit, St. Mary Aldermary, Queen Victoria Street, London, E.C.

public monument to the illustrious John, Duke of Marlborough, and voted a mansion, and Sir John Vanbrugh was appointed architect—this building is Blenheim. Among other buildings of his are Eastbury in Dorsetshire; King's Weston, near Bristol; Easton Neston in Northamptonshire; Oulton Hall, Cheshire, and Seaton Delaval in Northumberland. It is said by Walpole "if Vanbrugh had borrowed from Vitrurius as happily as from Dancour, Inigo Jones would not be the first architect of Britain." He died March 26th, 1726. In his character of architect, Dr. Evans bestowed on him this epitaph :—

"Lay heavy on him, earth, for he
Laid many a heavy load on thee,"

referring to the stupendous piles of Blenheim and Castle Howard.

James Gibbs, another eminent architect of this period, was born in Aberdeen about the year 1674. Gibbs decided early in life to study abroad, and went into Holland in the year 1694. His progress was rapid, and his abilities attracted the notice of the Earl of Mar, who assisted him to travel in Italy, in order to pursue his studies, correct his taste, and expand his views. It appears after the Mar family fell into disgrace, Gibbs remembered him in his will, and left to the only son of his first benefactor, £1,000 in money, all his plate, and an estate of £280 a year.

Font, Cover, and Doorway, St. Stephen, Walbrook, London, E.C.

After ten years in Rome, Gibbs appeared in London, and set up as an architect. The first building he completed was King's College, Cambridge. The first edifice which he erected in London was St. Martin's Church, the next was St. Mary's in the Strand. He was great in designing public monuments, and readers will find a good deal of his work illustrated, such as memorial tablets, urns, doors, windows, escutcheons, etc. He also built the Senate House at Cambridge.

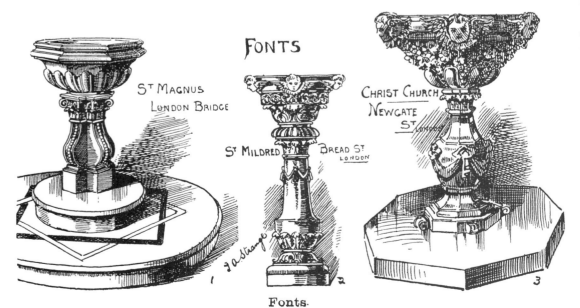

FONTS

St MAGNUS LONDON BRIDGE

St MILDRED BREAD St LONDON

CHRIST CHURCH NEWGATE St LONDON

Fonts.

Pulpit of St. Mary, Woolnough.

The church of St. Mary, Woolnough, was built by Nicholas Hawksmoor (1666-1736), who was one of Wren's pupils, and the only one that attained to any eminence. He assisted Wren in the building of St. Paul's Cathedral to its finish. He was Clerk of the Works at Greenwich Hospital, also at Kensington Palace, Whitehall, and St. James's Palace. He built, besides the above church, Christ Church, Spitalfields; St. George's, Middlesex; St. Anne's, Limehouse, and St. George's, Bloomsbury, the steeple of which consists of an obelisk, crowned with the statue of George I., and hugged by the royal supporters. Walpole says "a lion, a unicorn, and a king on such an eminence are very surprising."

"The things, we know, are neither rich nor rare,
But wonder how the devil they got there."

At Blenheim and Castle Howard he was associated with Vanbrugh.

Late 17th Century and early 18th Century.

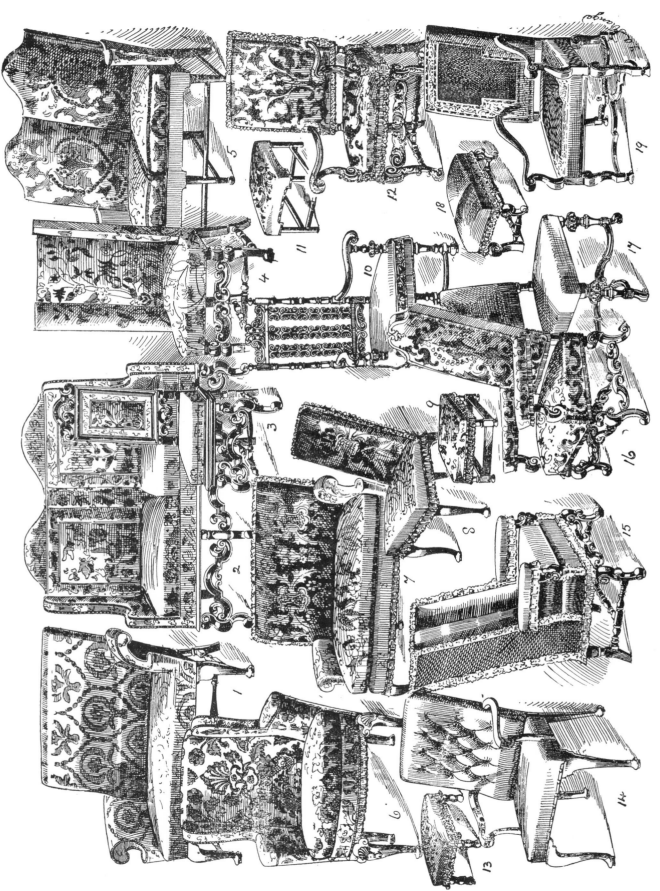

(For description see page 33.)

For description see page 33.

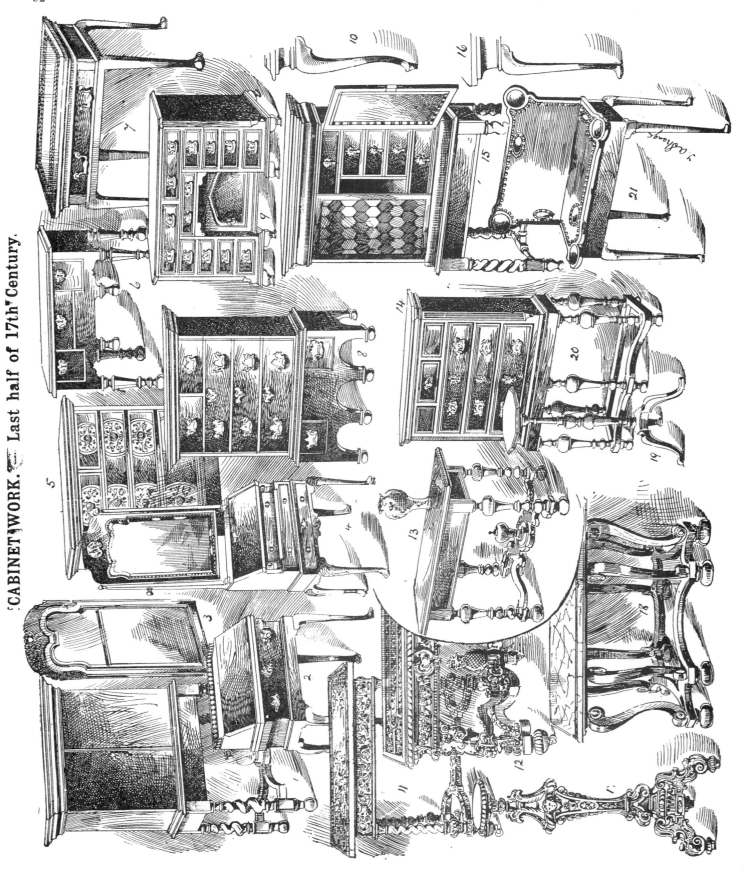

CABINET WORK. Last half of 17th Century.

Description of Settees, Chairs, Stools, and Seats on Pages 30 31, & 36,

PAGE 30.—

No. 1 is a small Settee of a typical Queen Anne design.

Nos. 2 and 3, Settee and small Chair, at Forde Abbey, are in oak, painted black, and covered with Mortlake tapestry representing sprays of cut flowers ; the arms are covered partly with tapestry, and partly with woollen work on canvas, which work was done extensively by ladies of the period—late half of the 17th Century.

No. 4 is from Broughton Castle, and

„ 5 from Knole Park, Sevenoaks, the residence of Lord Sackville, G.C.M.G., which is noted for its collection of old furniture, etc.

„ 6, period of Queen Anne, has the loose down cushions so much in use at that time.

„ 7, 8, 9, 10, and 11 are from Knole Park.

„ 12, also from Knole Park, is in walnut, covered with silk damask, and fringe on edge which was fashionable during the Queen Anne period—to which the chair belongs.

„ 15, 16, and 18 are from the same mansion.

„ 17 is from Broughton Castle, and

„ 19 from Hampton Court Palace.

PAGE 31.—

No. 1.—Chair in walnut, has a moveable seat ; about 1700.

„ 2.—Chair in chestnut, from Felding, Dorking ; about 1690.

„ 3.—Chair in walnut, moveable seat ; about 1700.

„ 4.—Chair in walnut, closely caned seat and back, from Montacute ; about 1690.

„ 5.—Chair in walnut, the front and back legs are similar, the seat covered with pile needlework, from Parham, Pulborough ; about 1710.

„ 6.—Chair in walnut, covered with tapestry, close brass nails, from Belton, Grantham.

„ 7.—Chair in walnut, covered with woollen work on canvas, from Parham, Pulborough.

„ 8.—Chair in walnut, covered with figured velvet, from Knole Park ; about 1710.

„ 9.—Settee in maple, covered in cut crimson velvet, from Brympton, Yeovil ; about 1710.

„ 10.—Chair in walnut, from Claydon House, Winslow.

„ 11.—Chair in oak, rush seat, from Hampton Court Palace.

„ 12.—Chair in mahogany, horsehair seating, period Queen Anne, from Claydon House, Winslow.

„ 14.—Chair, from Broughton Castle.

„ 15.—Chair in walnut, from Hampton Court Palace.

„ 17 and 19.—Stools in walnut, from Hampton Court Palace.

„ 18.—Stool, from Locock Abbey ; about 1710.

PAGE 36.—

Nos. 1, 2, 3, 4, 5, 7, 8, 9, 10, 11, 13, 14, and 18 are all from Knole Park.

„ 6.—Gilt, period early Georgian, from Hampton Court Palace.

„ 12.—Organ Stool, covered with velvet, from Belton, Grantham.

„ 15.—Mahogany ; about 1710.

„ 16.—Walnut Sofa, covered with pale blue damask, from Belton, Grantham ; about 1710.

34

FIREPLACES & FIRE-DOGS from Hampton Court Palace. Late 17th or early 18th Century.

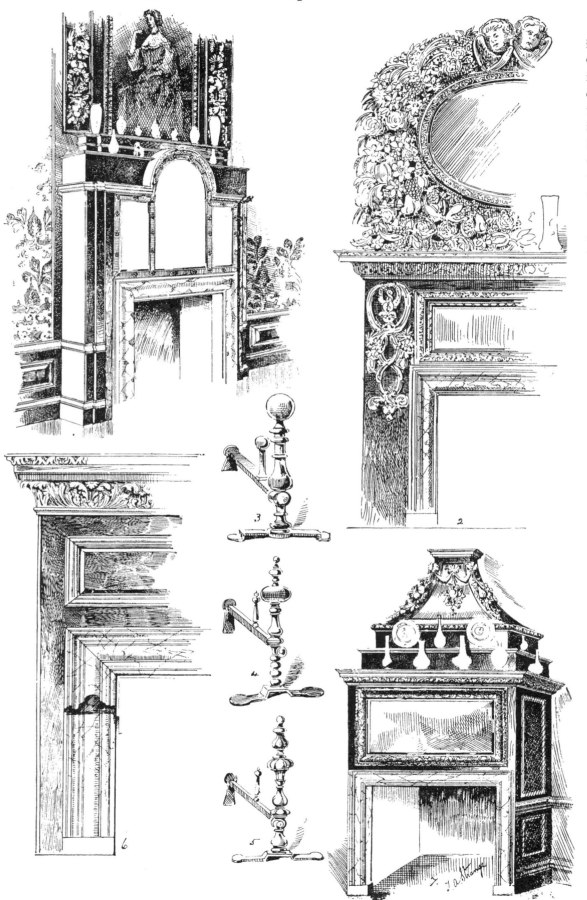

No. 1 on this page is from Hampton Court Palace, and is in oak. It has a border of blue glass round the silvered plate. It is in William III's State Bedroom. It is claimed that Sir Christopher Wren specially designed this room.

No. 2 is a rough idea of a Chimney-piece in the King's Private Dressing-room.

No. 6 is in the King's First Presence Chamber. It is in oak, with black-veined marble round the opening. These boldly moulded marble surrounds are a feature of this style.

No. 7, a corner fireplace in the King's Dressing-room.

Nos. 3, 4, and 5 are Fire-dogs in steel from Hampton Court.

No. 1 on Page 35 is a rough sketch of the panels on the King's Great Staircase, Hampton Court Palace, painted by Verrio. See Page 21.

Nos. 2, 3 and 5 on Page 35 are Carvings from the Palace.

No. 4 is a Table from the Victoria and Albert Museum, and is made of pine veneered with lignum vitæ, amboyna, and other woods, and black and white composition. Made about 1700

FURNITURE, etc., from Hampton Court Palace. Late 17th or early 18th Century.

STOOLS, last half of 17th Century and first half of 18th Century.

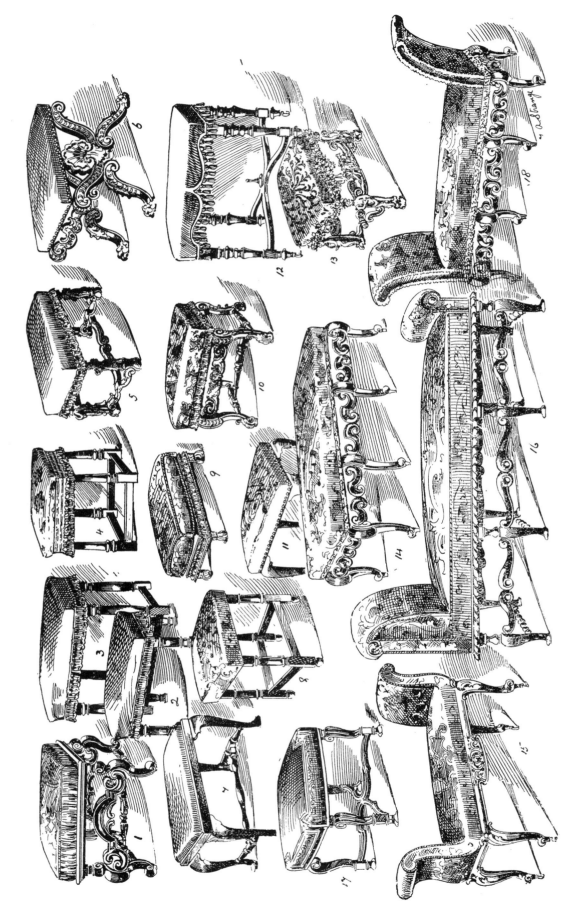

See Page 33 for particulars.

BED HANGINGS, last half of 17th and first half of 18th Centuries.

No. 1.—From Knole Park.

No 2.—From Knole Park, Sevenoaks.

Nos. 4 and 5 are old State Beds ; No. 5 being Queen Mary's, wife of William III. It is in crimson velvet.

No. 4, Queen Anne's bed. The hangings are of fine silk velvet, worked with an elaborate pattern of architectural designs and conventional vases and flowers, in orange and crimson on a white ground; it is said to have come from Spitalfields. Another old State bed at Hampton Court Palace is that of Queen Charlotte, wife of George III. The embroidery, on lilac ground, is said to be an exceedingly fine specimen of English needlework.

No. 3.—From Knole Park.

Nos. 4 and 5.—From Hampton Court Palace

GRATES & FIRE DOGS from Hampton Court Palace. Late 17th or early 18th Century.

No. 6 on Page 35 is a Cabinet of about the period 1700. Nos. 7 and 8 are gilt Girandoles from Hampton Court Palace. No. 9 is a Canopy from the King's First Presence Chamber, and is in two shades of crimson damask.

CANDELABRA. Late 17th or early 18th Century.

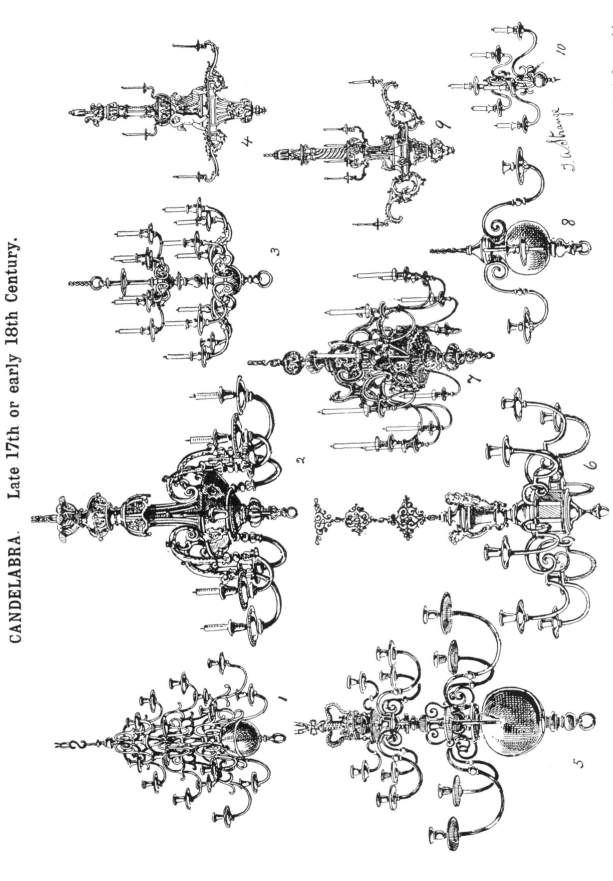

Nos. 10 and 11 on Page 35 are gilt Pedestals from Hampton Court Palace. In No. 11 is to be traced the style of Louis XIV., but clearly influenced by the Italian Renaissance. Nos. 7, 11, and 15 on Page 38 are from Hampton Court Palace, and the Fire-dogs are from various contemporary sources. Of the Candelabra above, No. 5 is from Hampton Court Palace; No. 8 from the Library of St. Paul's Cathedral, and the rest from various contemporary sources. The rounded shapes in these Candelabra are the ones traceable to the Jacobean period, and in the others Louis XIV. style is discernible.

A great many fine examples of Candelabra can be seen at Knole Park, Sevenoaks, and other mansions throughout the country, such as Broughton Castle, etc., etc., but the limited space prevents me from illustrating them.

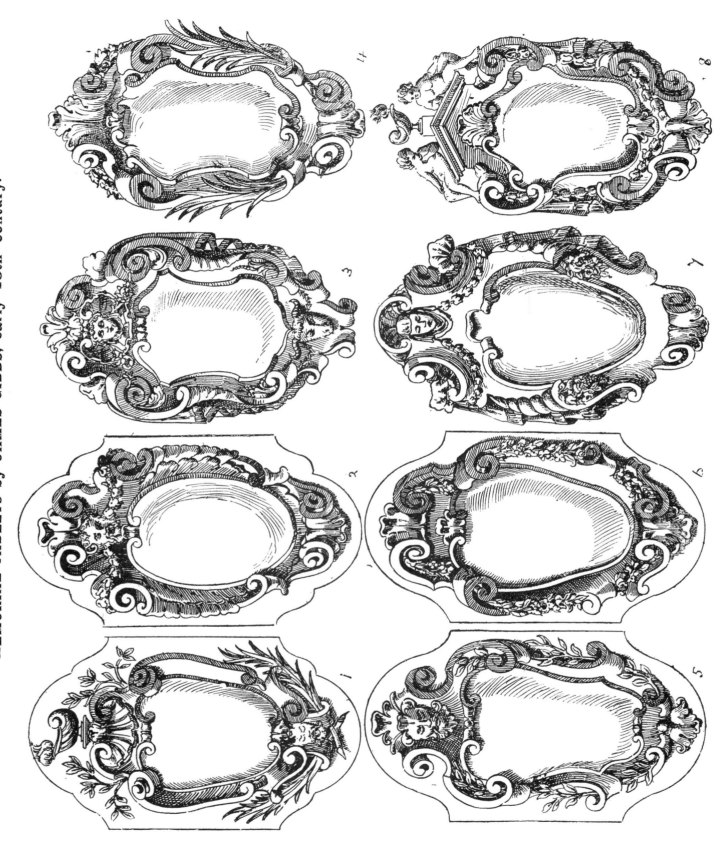

40

MEMORIAL TABLETS by JAMES GIBBS, early 18th Century.

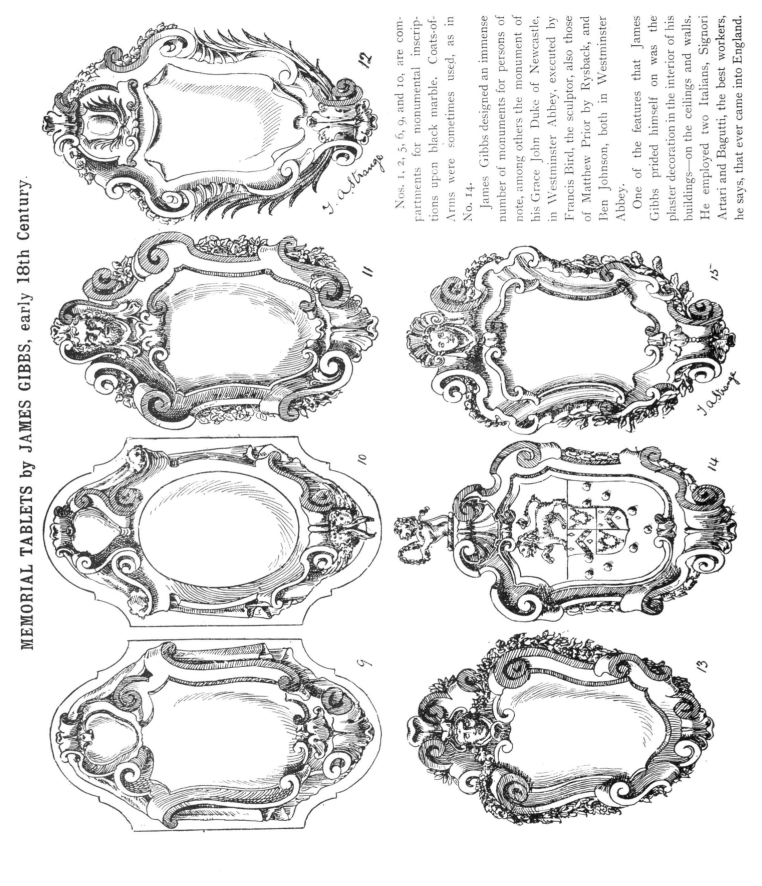

MEMORIAL TABLETS by JAMES GIBBS, early 18th Century.

Nos. 1, 2, 5, 6, 9, and 10, are compartments for monumental inscriptions upon black marble. Coats-of-Arms were sometimes used, as in No. 14.

James Gibbs designed an immense number of monuments for persons of note, among others the monument of his Grace John Duke of Newcastle, in Westminster Abbey, executed by Francis Bird, the sculptor, also those of Matthew Prior by Rysback, and Ben Johnson, both in Westminster Abbey.

One of the features that James Gibbs prided himself on was the plaster decoration in the interior of his buildings—on the ceilings and walls. He employed two Italians, Signori Artari and Bagutti, the best workers, he says, that ever came into England.

SARCOPHAGI, JAMES GIBBS. Early 18th Century.

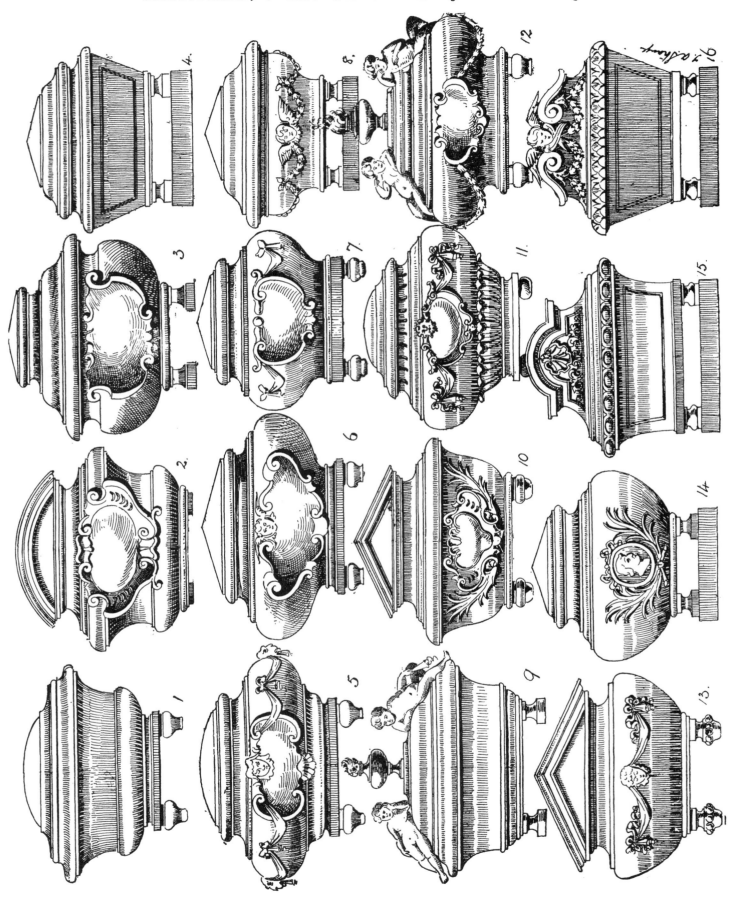

MEMORIAL TABLETS. JAMES GIBBS. Early 18th Century.

The Sarcophagi or Monumental Urns on Page 42 are in what Gibbs calls the "Antique Taste." They are mainly based or traceable to designs he had seen in Italy, where he studied for some considerable time. As has already been mentioned, he was eminent for his designs for Monuments, or Memorial Tablets to go in churches, of which there are several in Westminster Abbey, London. The above Memorial Tablets he calls "Twelve small compartments for monumental inscriptions."

Of course, some of the designs are extravagant, but could easily be simplified : they are certainly full of suggestive ideas to the experienced designer.

44

VASES designed by JAMES GIBBS.　Early 18th Century.

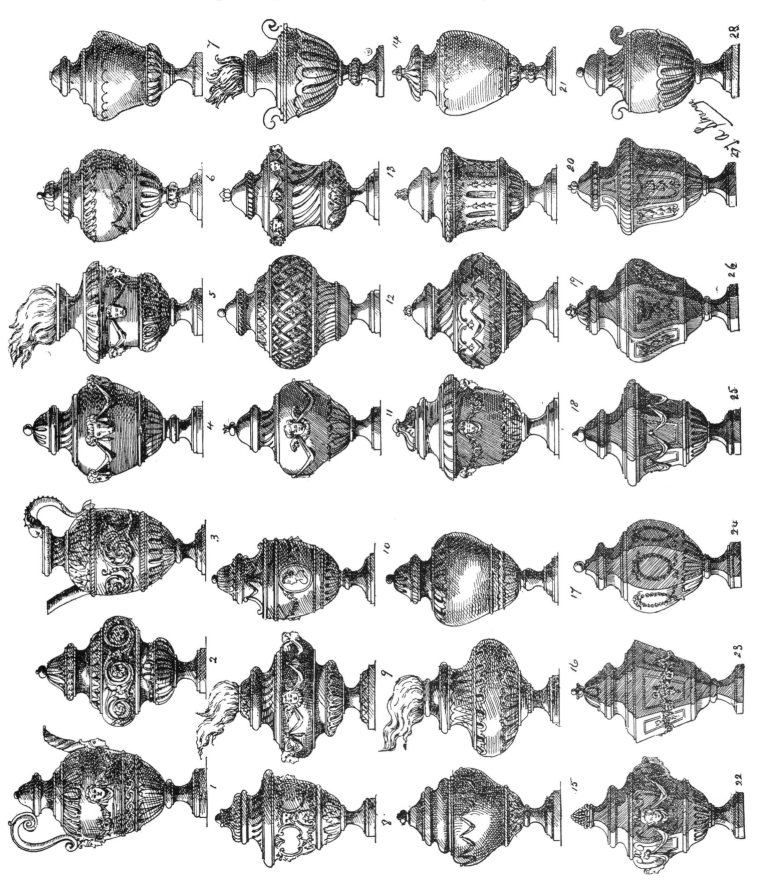

VASES designed by JAMES GIBBS.   Early 18th Century.

PAGES 44 and 45.—Fifty-four Designs of Vases, etc., in the Italian Renaissance style, executed in marble and lead.   These leaden Vases were very fashionable at this period, and are still to be seen in the gardens of old country houses.   I purpose later on in this book to give some further illustrations of lead-work.   James Gibbs studied in Italy, and the bent of his genius is distinctly traceable in these designs.   The taste for these ornaments was derived, as mentioned above, from the ancient Roman villas.   They were extensively used in decorating the gardens of Versailles and other palaces of the time of Louis XIV. and his contemporaries.   As the majority of readers already know, these vases were used to decorate the tops of pedestals, where the balustrades end, either on garden terraces, on the upper parts of buildings, or on the piers which carry large iron gates.   They were also placed on pedestals in gardens.

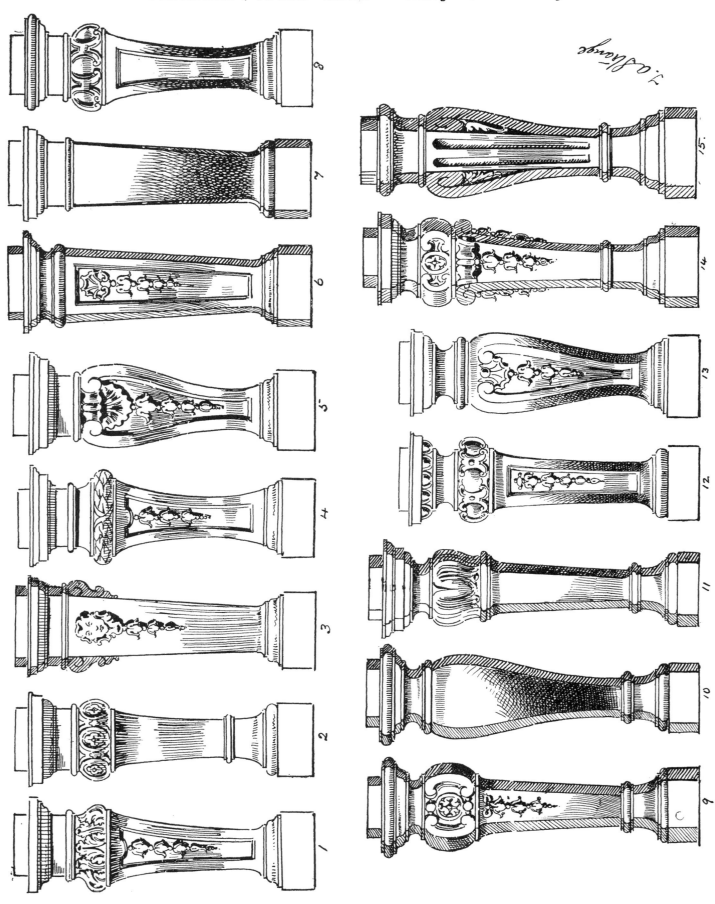

Two round Windows designed for the Pediments of St. Martin's Church, the lower one executed.

Eighteen designs for Dials. In my opinion it is much better for gentlemen to have pedestals of this sort than to have Dials supported by Figures, unless they are very well executed. These may be done by a common workman, and are equally useful and less expensive.

The Pedestals on Page 46 should be useful to designers, as they are all practical, and could be made at a moderate cost. The reason why I have shewn so much of Gibbs' work is that he gives a good deal of the details used about that time, and also that they are classified into groups, and are, therefore, easy for reference.

Cisterns placed upon pedestals, that may also serve for fonts.

STONE TABLES, CISTERNS and VASES by JAMES GIBBS, early 18th Century.

Nos. 1 to 8 on left hand are designs for Marble of Stone Tables for Gardens
    or Summer-houses.

Nos. 9, 10, 11, 12 are Cisterns, which can also be used as Fonts.

Nos. 1 to 8 on right hand are Marble Cisterns for Buffets.

Nos. 1 to 3 are Vases designed for the Right Honourable the Earl of Oxford.
    The centre one, executed in Portland Stone, is in the Garden of
    Wimpole, in Cambridgeshire.

JAMES GIBBS. CHIMNEY-PIECES. Early 18th Century.

JAMES GIBBS, TOPS OF CHIMNEY-PIECES and DOORS.   Early 18th Century.

1   2   3   4   5   6   7   8   9   10

JAMES GIBBS, CHIMNEY-PIECES and DOORS. Early 18th Century.

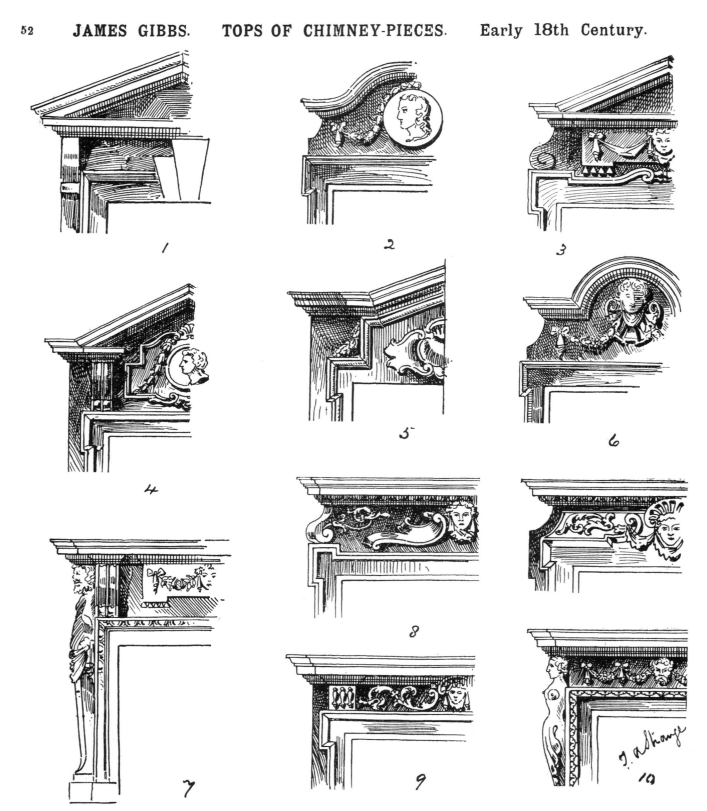

James Gibbs says of Ceilings in General and their Ornaments: There are different ways of adorning Ceilings. I have given here three different ways (not shewn in this book); one with large square panels; another with large octagon panels and squares, and the third with large hexagons and rhombs; all with roses in the middle of their panels, and bordered with fret and guilochis. The proportions of each are figured on their profiles on the left hand. These may serve either for curvilinear or flat ceilings. By curvilinear I mean either semi-circular or elliptical. I have made the ceilings of the church of St. Mary-le-Strand with squares and rhombs, and the elliptical ceiling of St. Martin's-in-the-Fields with large squares, the angles taken off, with roses in them; both which ceilings have a very good effect."

IRONWORK. Late 17th or early 18th Century.

No. 1 on this Page is from St. Paul's Cathedral, London; it shows great variety, and the contrast of the foliage with the stepwork seems most happy.

No. 3 on Page 54 is from Ragley.

No. 6 is from Church Street, Stoke Newington London.

No. 7 is from Abney Park Gates.

No. 10 is from Enfield, Middlesex.

No. 11 is from Church Street, Stoke Newington, London.

No. 13 is the Altar Rail of St. John's Church, Westminster, London.

No. 20 is from Huntercombe Manor.

The first illustration on Page 55 is the so-called "Lion Gates" at Hampton Court Palace. These were erected in the reign of Queen Anne. Sir Christopher Wren is credited with the design of these gates, but he probably designed the piers, etc., while Jean Tijou designed the ironwork.

The second large illustration on Page 55 is also from Hampton Court Palace.

The illustration to the right of the above is from the Geometrical Staircase in St. Paul's Cathedral.

The Proportions of Rooms, and the Coving of their Ceilings.—The rule for finding the height of rooms of these sorts is this: let the length and breadth of them be added together, half the sum is the height of the room. These are the just proportions of rooms as handed down to us by the greatest masters, if their ceilings are coved or arched; but if they are flat, their height will be agreeable if made equal to their breadth, as for example, a room thirty feet long and twenty feet broad should be twenty feet high; and even rooms of this proportion are often coved, and that sometimes one-quarter and one-fifth. But in the common buildings in England we are forced to give rooms a lower proportion in regard to the coldness of the climate and the expense of building, so that the height is sometimes one-fifth less than the breadth, as twenty feet broad by sixteen feet high, and sometimes less, as twenty feet broad by fifteen feet high, which is the lowest proportion they should have.

IRONWORK. Late 17th or early 18th Century.

The second large illustration on centre of this page is one of a series of thirteen at Hampton Court Palace. They were removed to the South Kensington Museum, but have lately been returned to the Palace. Each screen is 13 feet 2 inches wide, and 10 feet 6 inches high. They were designed by Jean Tijou, a Frenchman.

The Lion Gates at Hampton Court Palace.

Centres of Gates from Hampton Court Palace.

(They go with centre design.)

The Lion Gates at Hampton Court Palace.

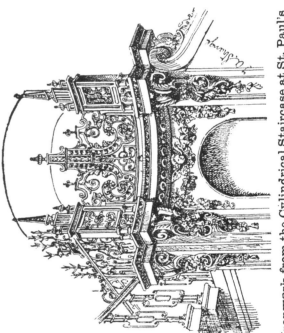

Ironwork from the Cylindrical Staircase at St. Paul's Cathedral, London.

IRONWORK. Late 17th or early 18th Century.

Walople House, Chiswick Mall.
London.

Gates of St. Paul's Cathedral, London.

Bulwick Hall.

Nos. 4 and 6 on lower line of Page 55 are from the Dining Hall, Trinity College, Dublin.

The third illustration on Page 56 is from Bulwick Hall.

The first illustration is from Walpole House, Chiswick Mall, London.

The second illustration is one of the Screens separating the choir aisles from the apse at St. Paul's Cathedral, London.

Nos. 1 to 6 on Page 57 are from Enfield, Middlesex.

No. 7 on same page is from Church Street, Stoke Newington, London.

57

IRONWORK. Late 17th or early 18th Century.

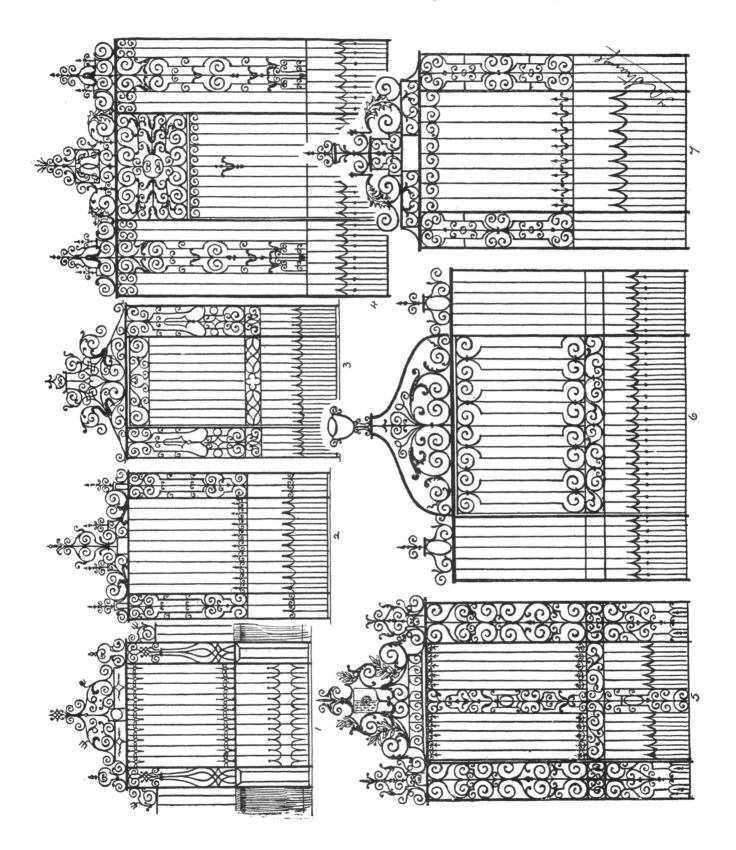

58

Sir JOHN VANBRUGH Late 17th or early 18th Century.

Chimney-pieces from Castle Howard, Yorkshire. (Built 1701-1714.)

ISAAC WARE. Early 18th Century.

Chimney-piece from Chesterfield House, Mayfair, London.

ISAAC WARE.   Early 18th Century.

Chesterfield House, Mayfair, London.

These Columns and Stairs came from a Mansion called 'Canons.''

ISAAC WARE. Early 18th Century.

Library at Chesterfield House, Mayfair, London.

Isaac Ware was an architect who held a good many official appointments. The story goes that, when very young he was a chimney-sweeper. He was at that time seen drawing with chalk the front of Whitehall, and then appears to have found a patron who sent him to Italy, and upon his return employed him as an architect. He was appointed Clerk of the Works of the Tower of London, 1728, and also at Windsor Castle in the same year. He published a large work called the "Complete Body of Architecture," which gives plates of Chesterfield House, Mayfair, which he built for Philip Earl of Chesterfield in 1749. "In 1763 he was Master of the Carpenters' Company, London. In the above book he says, speaking of interior decoration:—"Paper has in a great

measure taken the place of sculpture. The decorations of the inside of rooms may be reduced to three kinds: first, those in which the wall itself is properly finished for elegance; that is where the materials of its last covering are of the finest kind, and it is wrought into ornaments, plain or uncovered; secondly, where the walls are covered with wainscot; and thirdly, when they are hung; this last article comprehending paper, silk, tapestry, and every other decoration of this kind." He made the drawings, in conjunction with William Kent, for Thomas Ripley's book on "Houghton," in Norfolk, which Ripley built for Robert Walpole, 1722-1735. This book gives some extremely interesting details of interior decoration, etc. Mahogany seems to have been extensively used. It shews how the walls are decorated. He and Kent appear to have made the designs for the chimney-pieces, ceilings, etc., at "Houghton,"

ISAAC WARE and WILLIAM KENT.   Early 18th Century.

Side of Room by Isaac Ware.

Describing the Library at Houghton, Ripley says:—"This room is wainscotted with mahogany; and the bed, which is of painted taffety, stands in an alcove of the same wood."

Blue Damask Bed Chamber—hung with tapestry.

The Drawing-room hung with yellow caffory.

The Saloon is hung with crimson flowered velvet. The ceiling painted by W. Kent, who designed all the ornaments throughout the house. The chimney-piece is of black and gold marble, and so are the tables. In the broken pediment of the chimney stands a small antique bust of a Venus, and over the garden door is a large antique bust.

The Carlo Maratt Room has hangings of green velvet. The table is of lapis lazuli, at each end are two sconces of massive silver.

Breakfast-room.—Over the chimney-piece is a very good picture of hounds by Wooton.

Supping Parlour.—Over the chimney-piece is a portrait of Horace Walpole by Richardson.

Coffee-room.—Over the chimney-piece is a landscape with figures dancing by Swanivet.

The Great Staircase is painted in chiaro oscuro by W. Kent.

Common Parlour.—Over the chimney-piece is some fine pear-tree carving by Gibbons, and in the middle of it hangs a portrait of him by Sir Godfrey Kneller.

Velvet Bed Chamber.—The bed is of green velvet, richly embroidered and laced with gold. The hangings are tapestry, representing the Loves of Venus and Adonis. Over one of the doors is a seaport by old Griffier, a landscape over the other door.

The Dressing-room is hung with very fine gold tapestry after pictures by Vandyke.

The Embroidered Bed Chamber has the bed of the finest Indian needlework. The hangings are tapestry; over the doors two pieces of cattle.

The Cabinet-room is hung with green velvet.

The Marble Parlour.—One entire side of the room is of marble, with alcoves for sideboards, supplied with columns of Plymouth marble; over the chimney-piece is an alto-relievo in statuary marble, after the antique, by Rysback; and before one of the tables is a large granite cistern; two fruit pieces in panels over the doors.

The Hall.—The ceiling and frieze of Boys are by Altari. The basso-relievos over the chimney-pieces are from the antique.

The Long Gallery is hung with Norwich Damask.

William Kent was born in the North Riding of Yorkshire in 1684. He was apprenticed to a coach-builder, but according to Walpole, "having felt the emotions of genius," he left his master when he was nineteen and came to London. His early paintings, again according to Walpole, "excited a generous patronage in some gentlemen of his own country, who raised a contribution

Chimney-piece in the Dining-room at Wrotham Park.

HOGARTH CHAIRS.   Early 18th Century.

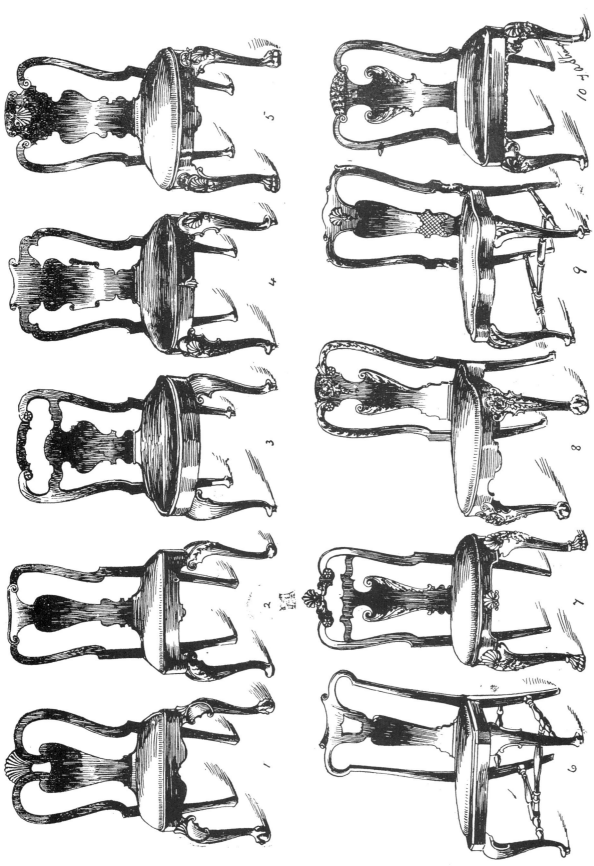

sufficient to send him to Rome in the year 1710." While there he appears to have attracted the attention of the young Lord Burlington, "whose sagacity," says Walpole, "discovered the rich vein of genius which had been hidden from the artist himself." Kent returned with him to England, where his lordship used his influence to promote his interests on all occasions. He was employed a good deal on painting ceilings, staircases, etc., dealing in allegorical subjects. He appears to have become quite the "rage" as a designer of interior decoration, furniture, silversmiths' work, etc., etc. There seems to have been much controversy as to Kent's ability. On Page 235 of this book will be found some very laudatory remarks by Robert Adam; but Alan Cunningham in his "Lives of British Architects," says: "William Kent is to be numbered among those fortunate men, who, without high qualities of mind, or force of imagination, obtain wealth and distinction through good sense, easy assurance, and that happy boldness of manner which goes rejoicing along the way where original merit often hesitates and stumbles." He is also known as a great landscape gardener. He died in 1748.

KENT. CHIMNEY-PIECES. Early 18th Century.

Comparing Kent to Wren, Ernest Law, in his "Guide to Kensington Palace," says of Kent:—"How very mediocre were his talents, this room will ever remain a palpable proof (Queen Caroline's Drawing-room, Kensington Palace); it exhibits all his false ideas of pseudo-classicism developed, as we shall see, to a most extravagant extent in the adjoining 'Cube or Cupola Room.' Examining the decoration in detail, we perceive everywhere evidences of his awkward, graceless style. The doorways for instance, are unnecessarily lofty and gaunt, and with their heavy cumbrous architraves, flat moulded with little light and shade, greatly impair the proportions of the room. Even in such details as the mouldings of the panelling, and of the framing of the doors, and the flatness of the raised panels, and their relative sizes to the width of the rails and 'stiles,' we detect the marked inferiority to Wren in the designing of such fitments."

CHAIRS, etc.   First half 18th Century.

William Jones, architect, published in 1739, "The Gentlemen's or Builders' Companion," which comprises chimney-pieces, slab-tables, pier-glasses, or tabernacle frames, ceilings, etc. They are mostly of a classical character. This seems to be one of the first books published in this country on Furniture.

BATTY and THOMAS LANGLEY, BOOKCASES. First half 18th Century.

BATTY and THOMAS LANGLEY, PIER-TABLES.　　First half 18th Century.

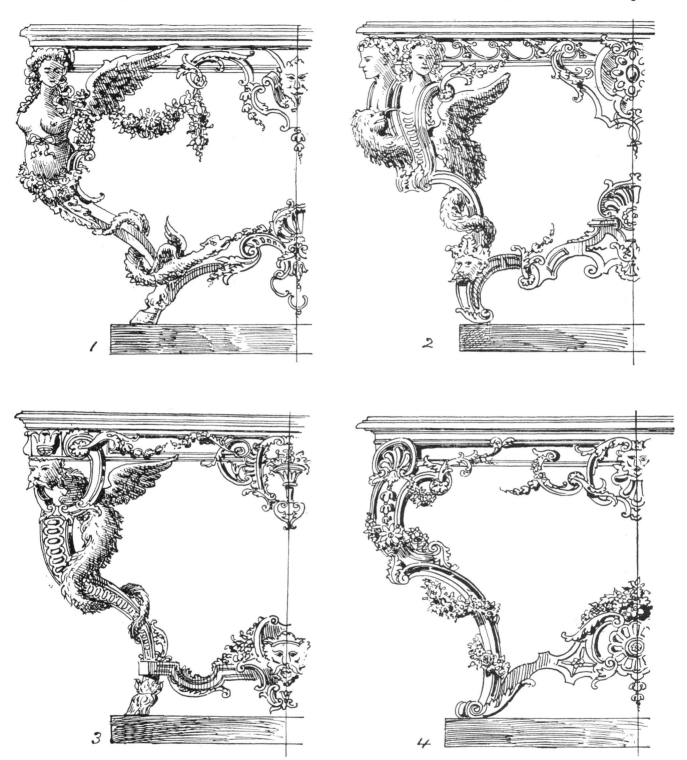

Adam, in his " Works of Architecture," says : " The Tabernacle Frame, almost the only species of ornament (in an apartment) formerly known in this country, now universally exploded." It is explained as "a collective term made use of by English artists to express the whole dressing of a door, window, niche, or chimney, when the dressing consists of columns or pilasters, with an entablature and pediment over them." There is a continual reference to Tabernacle Frames in Works published during the first half of the century, so I have thought it best to give Robert Adams' definition of same.

ABRAHAM SWAN, CHIMNEY-PIECES. First half 18th Century.

"The City and Country Builder's and Workman's Treasury of Designs," by Batty and Thomas Langley, contains examples of piers, gates, doors, windows, niches, buffets, cisterns, chimney-pieces, tabernacle frames, pavements, frets, gulochis, pulpits, types, altar pieces, monuments, fonts, obelisques, pedestals, sun-dials, busts and stone tables, bookcases, ceilings, and ironwork; but it must be confessed that they deliberately copied the designs of Inigo Jones and others, without acknowledging it in their book.

Abraham Swan published in 1745 a Work called "The British Architect: or, The Builder's Treasury of Staircases," containing, firstly, an easier, more intelligible, and expeditious method of drawing the Five Orders than had hitherto been published, by a scale of twelve equal parts, free from those troublesome divisions called "aliquot parts." Shewing also how to glue up their

ABRAHAM SWAN, CHIMNEY-PIECES.   First half 18th Century.

Columns and Capitals. Secondly, likewise Stair-cases (those most useful, ornamental, and necessary parts of a building, though never before sufficiently described in any book, ancient or modern) ; shewing their most convenient situation, and the form of their ascending in the most grand manner : with a great variety of curious ornaments, whereby any gentleman may fix on what will suit him best, there being examples of all kinds ; and necessary directions for such persons as are unacquainted with that branch.   Thirdly, designs of Arches, Doors, and Windows. Fourthly, a great variety of new and curious Chimney-pieces, in the most elegant and modern taste. Fifthly, Corbels, Shields, and other beautiful decorations. Lastly, several useful and necessary Rules

ABRAHAM SWAN, BALUSTERS and BRACKETS. First half 18th Century.

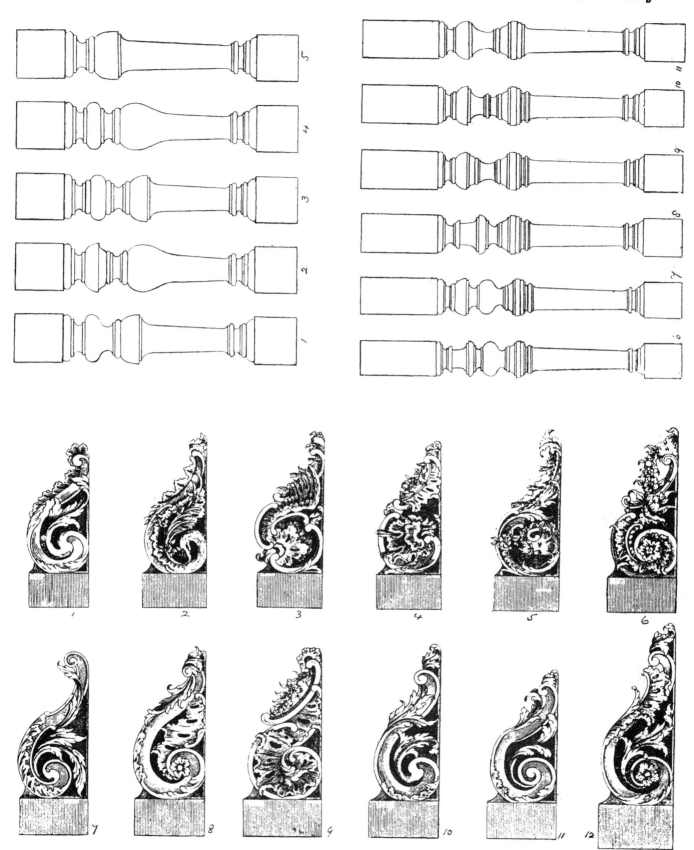

ABRAHAM SWAN, STAIRCASES.   First half 18th Century.

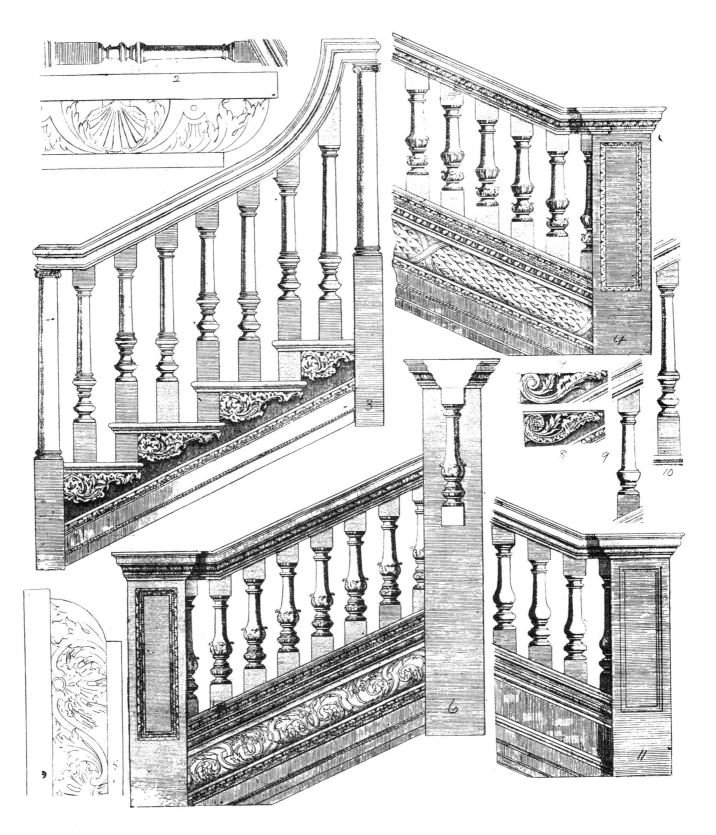

CHIMNEY-PIECE, etc.   First half 18th Century.

EDWARDS and DARLEY, "CHINESE" ORNAMENTS, etc. Middle 18th Century.

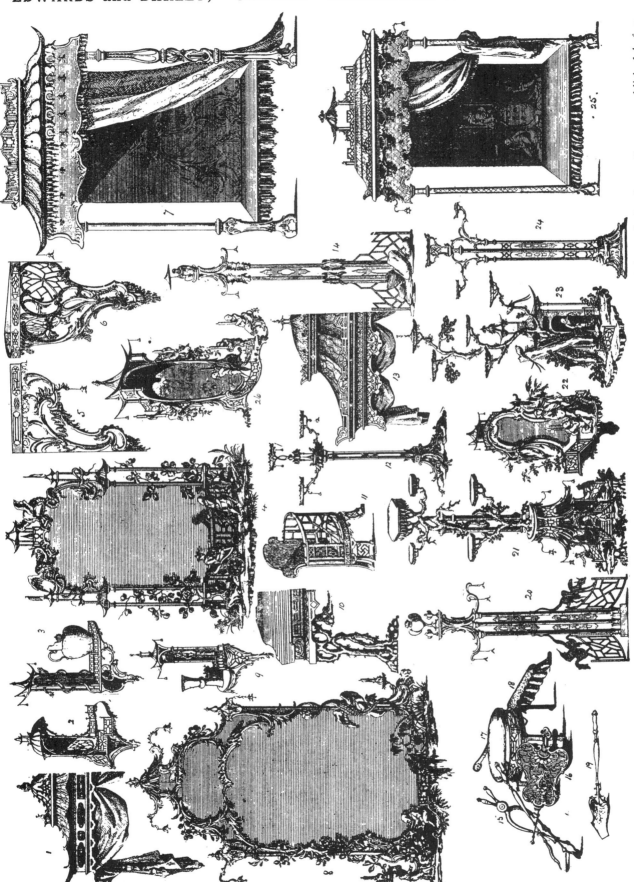

of Carpentry; with the manner of Trussed Roofs, and the nature of a displayed circular Soffit both in a straight and circular wall, never published before.

Together with Raking Cornices, Groins, and Angle Brackets described.

There are three different rules for proportioning Mouldings for Frames; one is to divide the whole width of the Frame into seven equal parts, and take one for the Moulding; the next is to divide it into fifteen parts, and take two for the Moulding; and the last is to divide it into eight equal parts, one of which is

EDWARDS and DARLEY, "CHINESE" ORNAMENTS, etc. Middle 18th Century.

given to the Moulding. Having thus found the width, you may divide it into three equal parts, and one of them into nine; then dispose these parts to the height and projection of each Moulding, as shewn in the design.

A Chimney-piece, with a frame over it, for a Picture or Panel.—The opening of this Chimney is a perfect square, which is certainly a very good proportion,

EDWARDS and DARLEY, "CHINESE" ORNAMENTS, etc. Middle 18th Century.

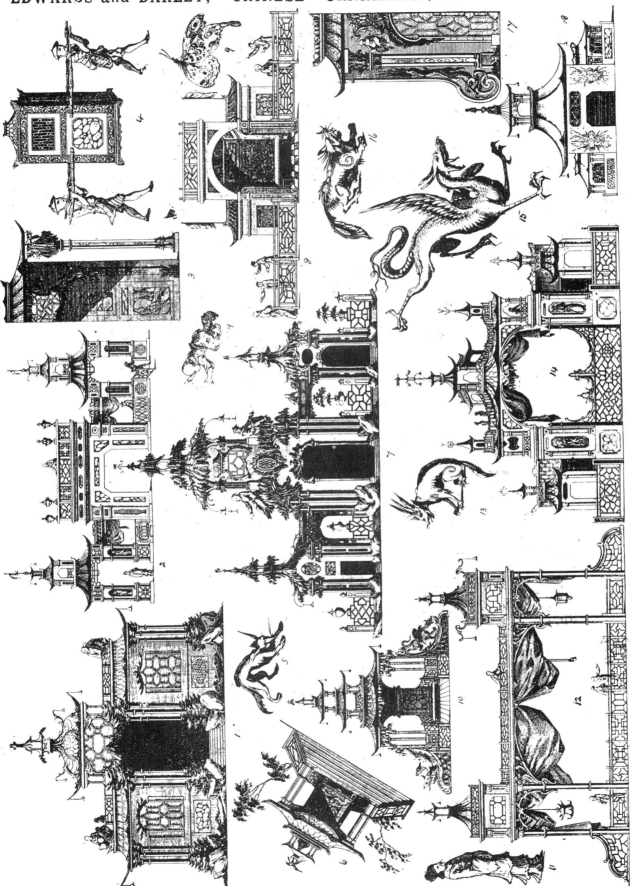

except when they run to a great extent; then the width of the Chimney may be divided into thirteen parts, twelve of which may be the height; or into seven parts, and take six for the height; or into fifteen, and assign thirteen for the height. Whichsoever proportion you follow, it makes no alteration in the ornaments. The architrave is one-sixth, as usual; the width of the architrave, and one-third part more, gives the height of the frieze. Over this Chimney-piece

76

EDWARDS and DARLEY, "CHINESE" ORNAMENTS, etc.   Middle 18th Century.

is a very rich Frame for a picture or panel. To proportion which—divide the width within into eight parts, seven of these parts will be the height within, and one of them is the width of the Moulding ; as is shewn at large in the design. The Knees at the corners are to be made of different lengths, according to the ornaments which are intended to be put in.

A great deal of the work about the middle of the Eighteenth century was influenced by the so-called "Chinese Taste," and no doubt such a book as that of Edwards and Darley had great influence on the said taste. Of the many things illustrated in their book, the following list will shew the great variety of

77

EDWARDS and DARLEY, "CHINESE" ORNAMENTS, etc.　Middle 18th Century.

articles or subjects that employed their attentions:—Temple, terminary, bridge, orchestra, alcove, summer-house, hermitage, water summer-house, embrasured rails, porticos, regular rails, windows, varied panels, palisades, doors, columns for lamps, varied rails, panels, oval landscapes, landscape with arches, water-piece, budgrow, fishing with birds, fishing with nets, dragon boat, pleasure boats, various birds, various beasts, borders, grand bed, girandoles, candlestands, chariot, glass frame, chimney furniture, palanquins, arm-chair, bed, brackets, canopy, garden chair, tables, philosopher; Figures—mandarin and soldier, mandarin and fakir, procession, heads, tea drinking; Flowers—water anemone, althea and reeds, water rose and thorn, double althea, etc., etc.

THOMAS JOHNSON, GIRANDOLES.   Middle 18th Century.

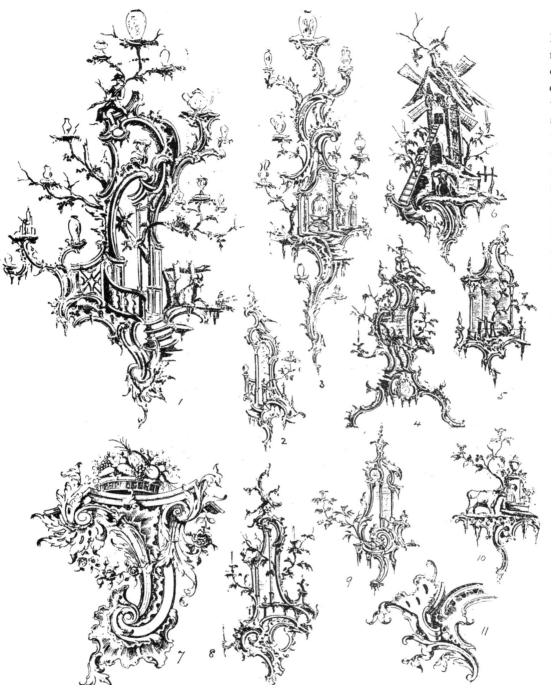

Thomas Johnson, published a Work about the middle of the Eighteenth century, in which the designs are all of an extravagant character, being a mixture of the Gothic, Chinese, and Louis XV. styles, with the further addition of all sorts of grotesque figures of men, animals, birds, etc., all mixed up in amazing confusion, comprising, among other things, as follows: Stands for candle-stands, kettle stands, overdoors of Watteau landscape, mirrors, picture frames, ovals (mirrors), slab-frames (consoles), side of room, organ, ceilings, lanthorns, overmantels, chimney-pieces, brackets for figures, clock cases, girandoles, stands for silversmiths' work, table brackets, stone grates, watch cases, etc.

Matthias Lock published several Works from about the year 1740, one of which he dedicated to the Right Honourable Lord Blakeney, Grand President of the Antigallican Association, and the rest of the brethren of that Most Honourable Order. He also published the following Works: "A New Book of Foliage for instruction of young Artists," 1769; "A New Book of Pier Frames, Oval Girandoles, Tables, etc.," 1769; in conjunction with H. Copeland, "A New Book of Ornaments," 1752 and 1768; "A New Drawing Book of Ornamental Shields," and "Six Sconces," in 1768. Although his first designs are all in the style of Thomas Johnson, later he designed furniture of a more classic type—more after the Adam style. It appears from a note he has left in a Design Book, that five shillings per day was the average wage paid in 1743 to operative carvers in London.

Speaking of Looking-glasses, Hungerford Pollen in his "Furniture and Woodwork"—one of the South Kensington Art Handbooks—says: "The Looking-glasses made in the Seventeenth and Eighteenth centuries by colonies of Venetian workmen in England and France, had the plates finished by an edge gently bevelled of an inch in width, following the form of the frame whether square or shaped in curves." The bevels were not always as

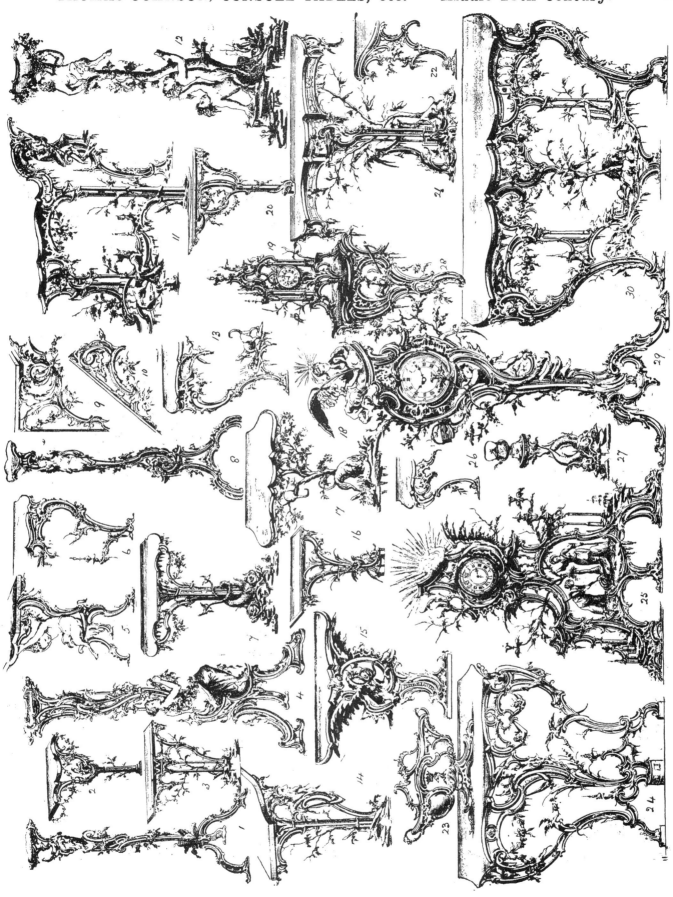

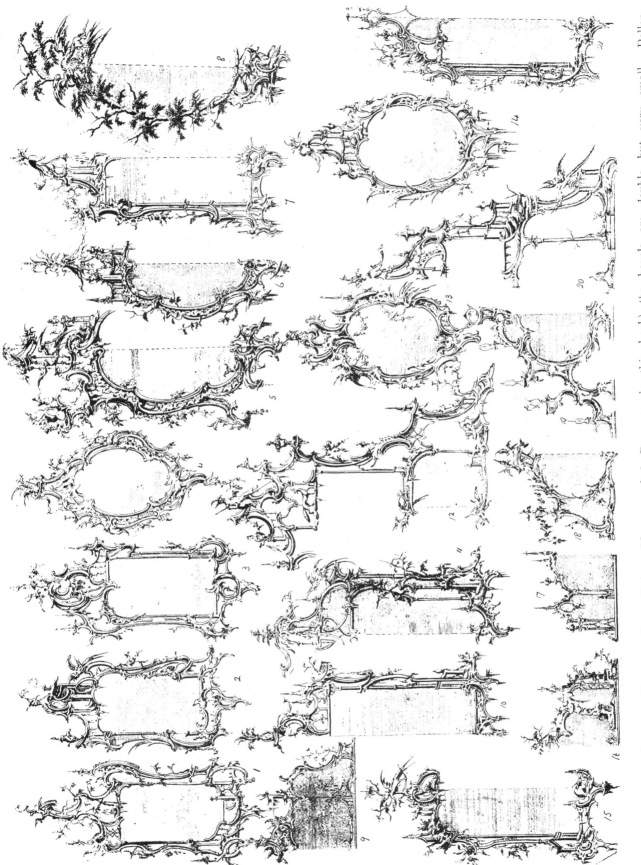

wide, and in the mirrors at Hampton Court Palace (Nos. 7 and 8, Page 35 in this book) the bevels are double, but very small. Pollen further adds: "This gives preciousness and prismatic light to the whole glass. It is of great difficulty in execution, the plate being held by the workman over his head, and the edges are cut by grinding. The feats of skill of this kind, in the form of interrupted curves, and short lines and angles, are rarely accomplished by modern workmen, and the angle of the bevel itself is generally too acute, whereby the

82

THOMAS JOHNSON, GIRANDOLES, OVERDOORS, etc.   Middle 18th Century

prismatic light produced by this portion of the mirror is in violent and too showy contrast to the remainder. In England, looking-glasses came into general use soon after the Restoration. In the Eighteenth century figures were sunk in the style of Intaglio, or gem cutting, on the back of the glass and left with a dead surface, the silver surface of the mercury showing through as the mirror is seen from the front." The figures on Nos. 2 and 3 on Page 80 were sometimes treated in this manner. Pollen also mentions that "Sir Samuel Morland built a fine room at Vauxhall

THOMAS JOHNSON, CHIMNEY-PIECES. Middle 18th Century.

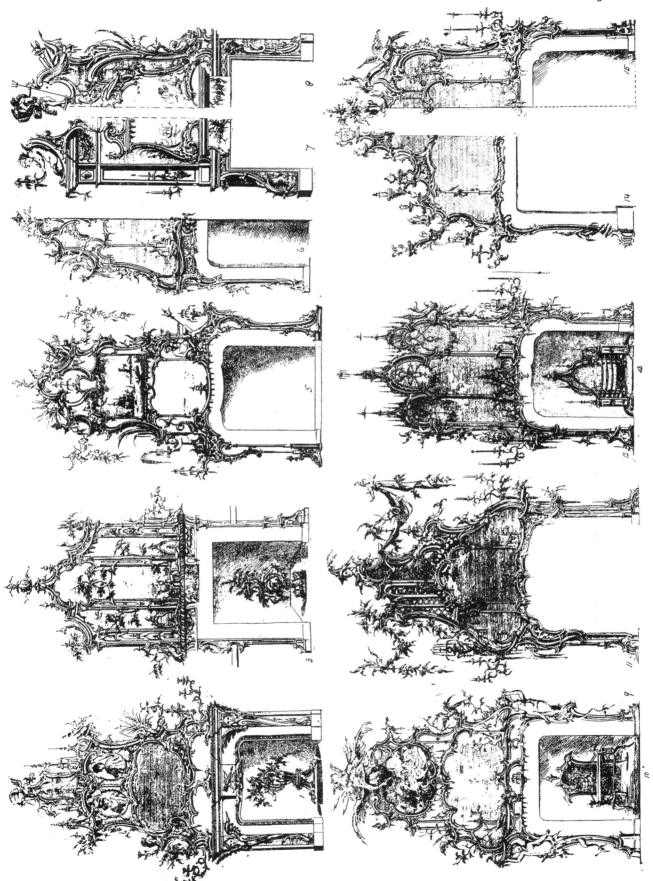

in 1667, the inside all of looking-glass, and fountains, very beautiful to behold." At about this period the house of Nell Gwynne, "the first good one as we enter St. James's Square from Pall Mall, had the back room on the ground floor entirely lined with looking-glass." These Pier Glasses and Girandoles often had painted panels inserted in them, as shewn herein. This idea was copied from France, where a school of painters had arisen who dedicated themselves to

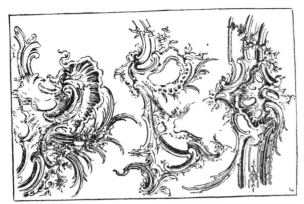

interior decoration. These painted panels were carried right on through the eighteenth century, even after the time that the "Rococo" work went out of fashion, which change was no doubt due to the discoveries made at Pompeii, etc., which had the effect of turning the attention of designers to the beauties of the old classical style.

James Paine (see Page 86) was born in 1725. He published in 1751 his designs for Doncaster Mansion House—the design here shown is from that book, the drawings for which he made in 1745-48. He also published "Plans, etc., of Noblemen's and Gentlemen's Houses executed in various countries in 1767." He used Adam's stucco in his later buildings. Of his designs for Ceilings and Chimney-pieces, one of the latter was for Sir Joshua Reynolds, Leicester Square, London. In 1783, he designed the bridges for Chertsey, Walton, and Kew, in Surrey. Gwilt mentions that Paine and Sir R. Taylor divided the practice of the profession between them until Robert Adam entered the list. He lived for some time at Sayes Court, Addlestone, near Chertsey, Surrey. He died in France in 1789.

JAMES PAINE.   Middle 18th Century.

" The Universal System of Household Furnishing," by Ince and Mayhew, Cabinet-makers and Upholsterers, contains upwards of three hundred designs—both useful and ornamental—in the most elegant taste; finely engraved, in which the nature of ornament and perspective is accurately exemplified. This Work was made convenient to the nobility and gentry in their choice, and comprehensive to the workman by directions for executing the several designs; together with specimens of ornaments for young practitioners of drawing. It is dedicated to the Most Noble George Spencer, Duke of Marlborough. The furniture was designed by Ince, Mayhew evidently being the business man. Their Lanthorns are similar to Chippendale's (Page 106), as are also their Terms for busts or lamps (Page 185), Sideboard Tables (Pages 148 and 149), Bookcases (Pages 158 and 159), and Bookcase Doors (Pages 152, 153, 154, and 155). The most fashionable Beds during the last half of the century were called Sofa beds, Field beds, Beds for Alcoves, French beds, Dome beds, and State beds. On Page 136 are some Chairs by Ince and Mayhew, which, in error, have been attributed to Chippendale. Ladies' toilets were draped, including the glass as on Page 109. Toilet Tables—which they call " Toilet Apparatus "—were also similar to Chippendale's (Page 207), having all the combinations there shewn. They had a decided preference for frets (Pages 156 and 157) coupled with a strong Chinese and Gothic taste. Their furniture was also like Chippendale's, but more extravagant, see Clothes-chests (Page 160), as were also the China shelves (Pages 181 and 182) and the China and Chinese Cases

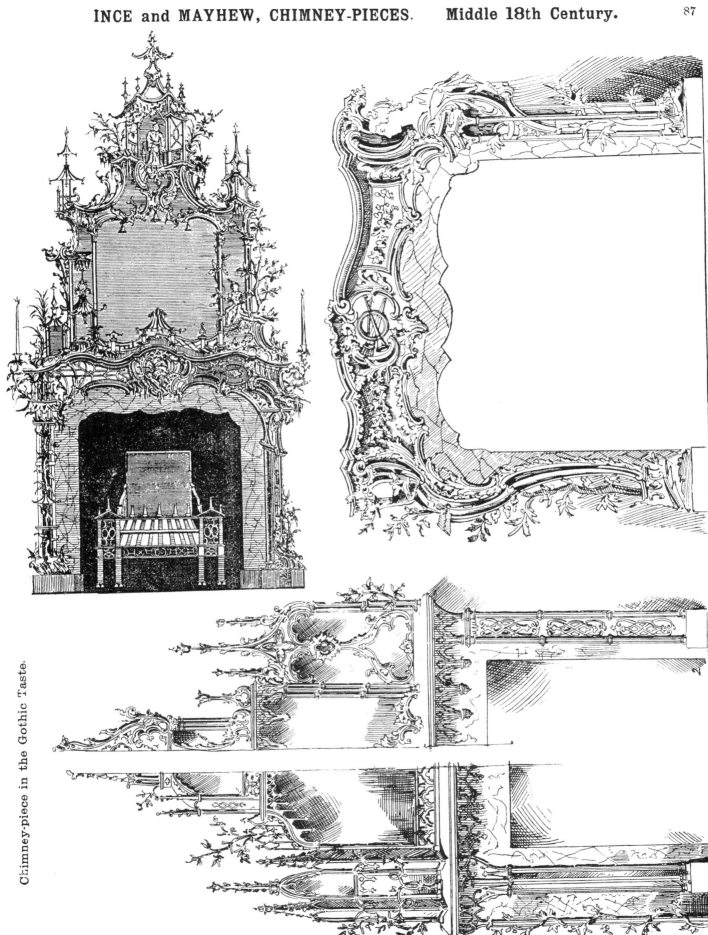

Chimney-piece in the Gothic Taste.

(Pages 187 and 188).　Back Stools were made in burnished gold covered in blue damask.　For French Chairs similar to Chippendale's, see Page 130.　Girandoles, Slab-frames, Pier-Glasses and Tables are similar to those of Johnson or M. Lock. Their designs of Fenders will be found on Page 206; Brackets for Marble Slabs (Page 186).　See Page 111 for Hand-rail for Balcony, Staircase Railing, and Brackets for Lanthorns.　If readers will turn up to the pages above mentioned they will find some of Ince and Mayhew's various designs—which in some cases have been grouped with other makers' designs—for the sake of easy comparison and reference.

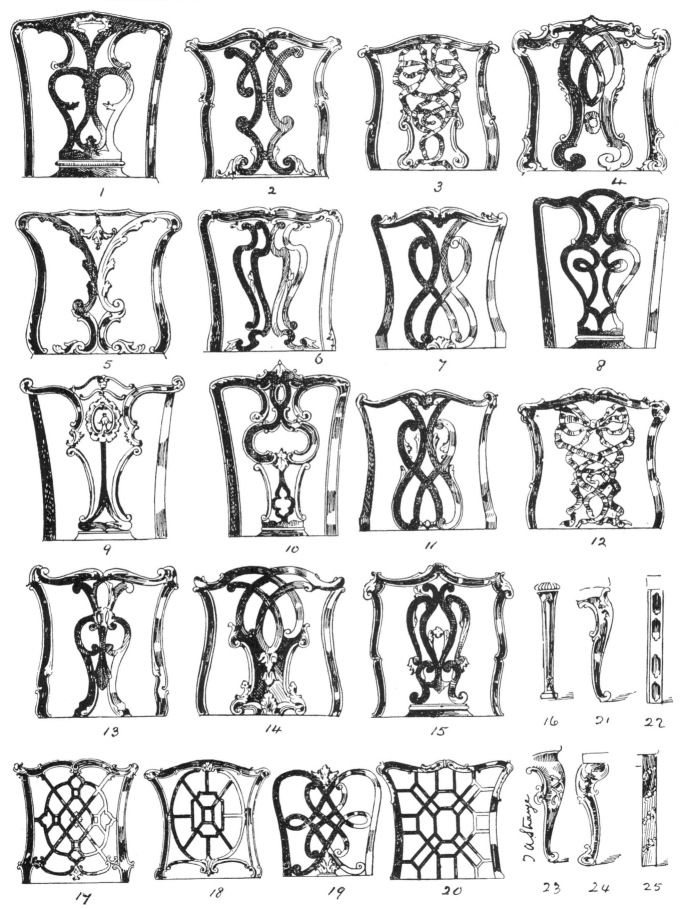

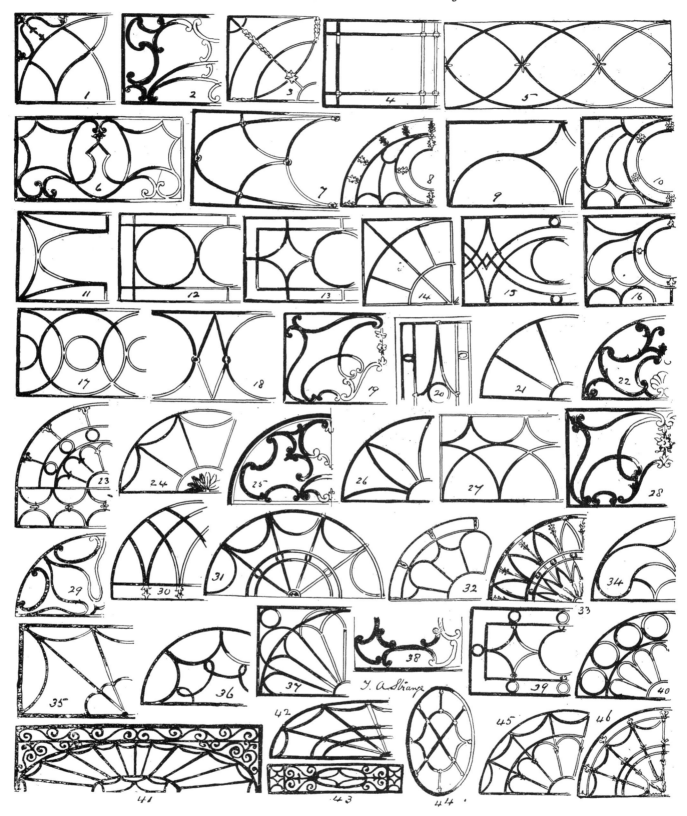

The Overdoors above are of various periods during the Eighteenth century, from the time of Queen Anne up to the end of the century. The fan shaped ones belong to the last half of the century. The Chinese Railings on Page 93 are from the books of Chippendale, Robert Manwaring, Ince and Mayhew, and other contemporary sources. Among the designs for Silversmiths' work on Page 95, are to be found some of the designs of the Adam Brothers, who designed a great deal of this class of work. (See Nos. 24, 28, 30, etc.)

CHINESE RAILINGS.   Middle 18th Century.

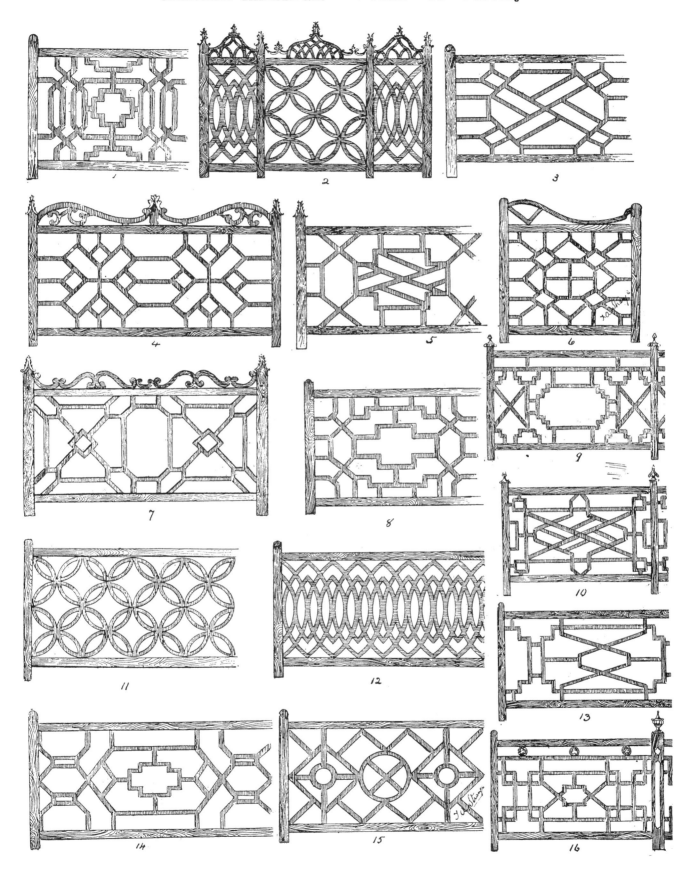

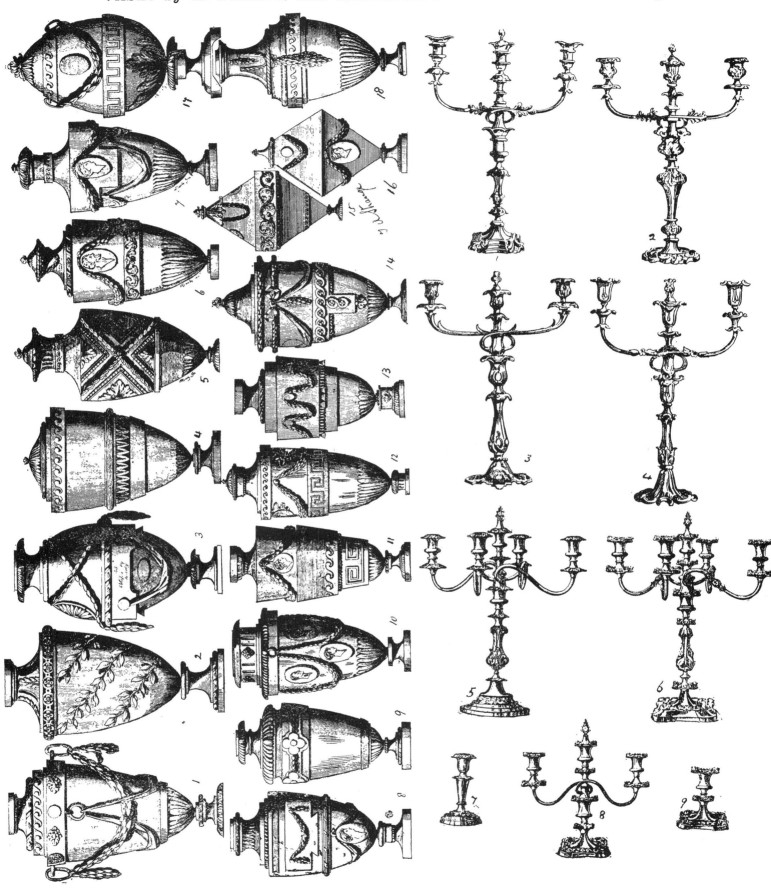

SILVERSMITHS' WORK.   18th Century.

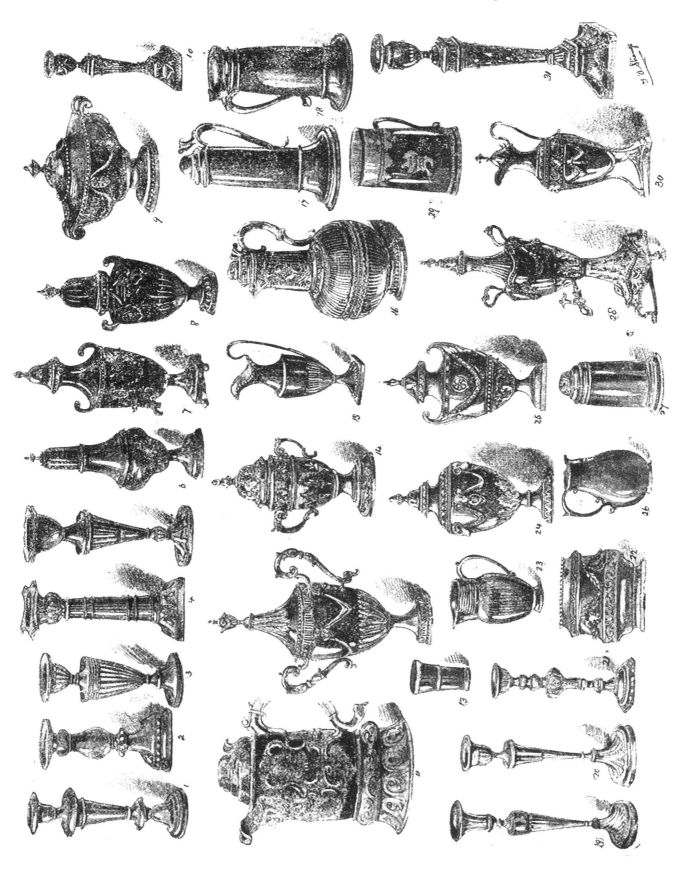

ESCUTCHEONS, HANDLES, FENDERS, etc., etc.   18th Century.

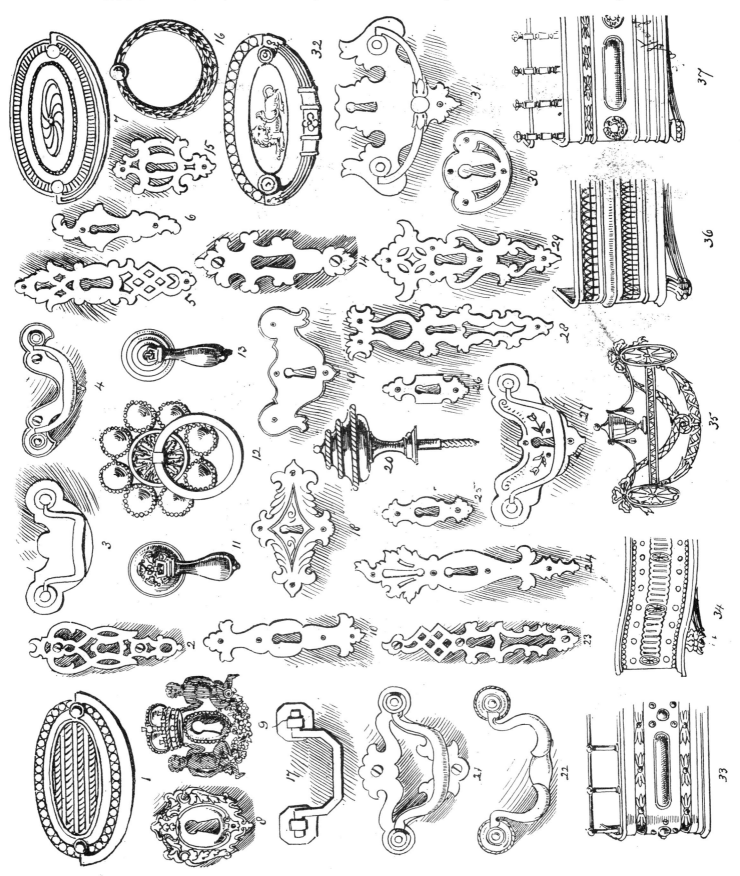

W. and J. HALFPENNY, DESIGN FOR CEILING.   Middle 18th Century.

W. and J. HALFPENNY, SIDE OF ROOM.   Middle 18th Century.

Here we have a classical Doorway with Louis XIV. carved panels; with Louis XIV. carved panels; with Louis XV. enrichments above and on the frieze; the low carved dado, so much in vogue during the latter half of the 17th and the earlier part of the 18th Century; also with tapestry panels of a Louis XIV. character.   The design might well belong to an earlier part of the Century.

W. and J. HALFPENNY, DESIGNS FOR CEILINGS.   Middle 18th Century.

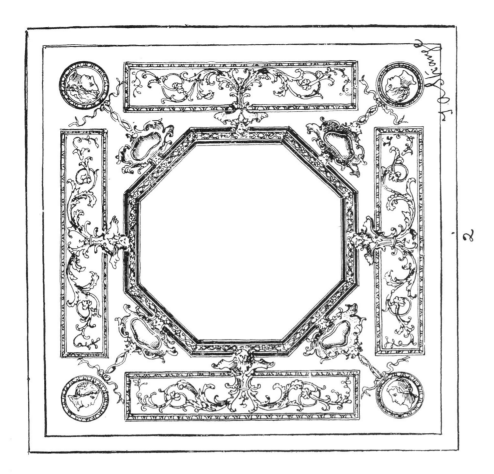

William Half-penny, " Carpenter and Architect," by himself, and later, in conjunction with his son, published a good many works on architecture during the first half of the 18th Century. The designs of his in this book are taken from " The Modern Builder's Assistant." Another work of theirs, " New designs for Chinese Temples, Triumphal Arches, Garden Seats, Palings, etc., published in 1750-52, contains designs of some monstrous absurdities for what they call " Chinese " Bridges, Temples, Triumphal Arches, Garden Seats, Palings, Obelisks, Termini, " Chinese " Doors, Windows, Piers, Summer-houses, etc.

Describing one of their designs entitled a " Chinese Alcove Seat, fronting four ways," they mention that " above the crown of the cove may be a room wherein musicians may be secreted and play soft music to the agreeable surprise of strangers, the performers going in by a subterranean passage, and a broad step ladder, between the back of the seats, lighted by

Among the works that W. and J. Halfpenny published are the following :—

"A New and Complete System of Architecture," 1719;

"Magnum in Parvo; or, The Marrow of Architecture," 1728;

"Art of Sound Building," 1725;

"Six New Designs for Convenient Farm-houses";

"New Designs for Chinese Temples";

"Geometry; Theoretical and Practical";

"Rural Architecture in the Gothic Taste";

"Useful Architecture for Erecting Parsonage-houses, Farmhouses, and Inns";

"Twenty New Designs of Chinese Lattice and other Works for Staircases, Gates, Pailings, etc.;"

"Chinese & Gothic Architecture";

"The Country Gentleman's Pocket Companion and Builder's Assistant for Decorative Architecture"; and

"The Modern Builder's Assistant."

small windows in the roof concealed from without." This building will be agreeably situated on a grand amphitheatre of green slopes. Summer-houses at the end of long walks, of a fanciful, and sometimes of a classical design, are to be seen in the grounds of 18th Century mansions. The Halfpennys seem to have been great exponents of the "Chinese Taste," and seem rarely to have missed an opportunity of introducing Chinese figures and ornaments wherever they could do so. Instances will be noticed in the designs shown here; in the corners of the Ceiling shown on Page 97; in the cove of Side of Room on Page 100; in Chimney-piece on Page 101; on Side of Room on Page 103, etc.; otherwise, their style for interior decorations seems based on the Louis XV.

W. and J. HALFPENNY, FIREPLACE and "CHINESE" PALINGS.

No. 1 is a Chinese Single-braced Paling.
No. 2 is a Chinese Double-braced Paling.
No. 3 is a Chinese Acute-angular Paling.
No. 4 is a Chinese Obtuse and Diamond Paling.
No. 5 is a Chinese Half-diamond Braced Paling.
No. 6 is a Chinese Diamond-braced-Paling.

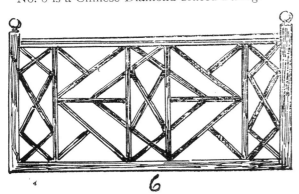

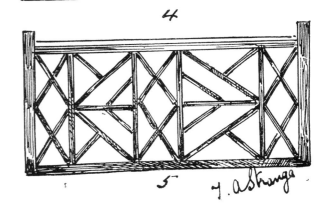

W. and J. HALFPENNY, SIDE OF ROOM, FIREPLACE and WINDOWS.

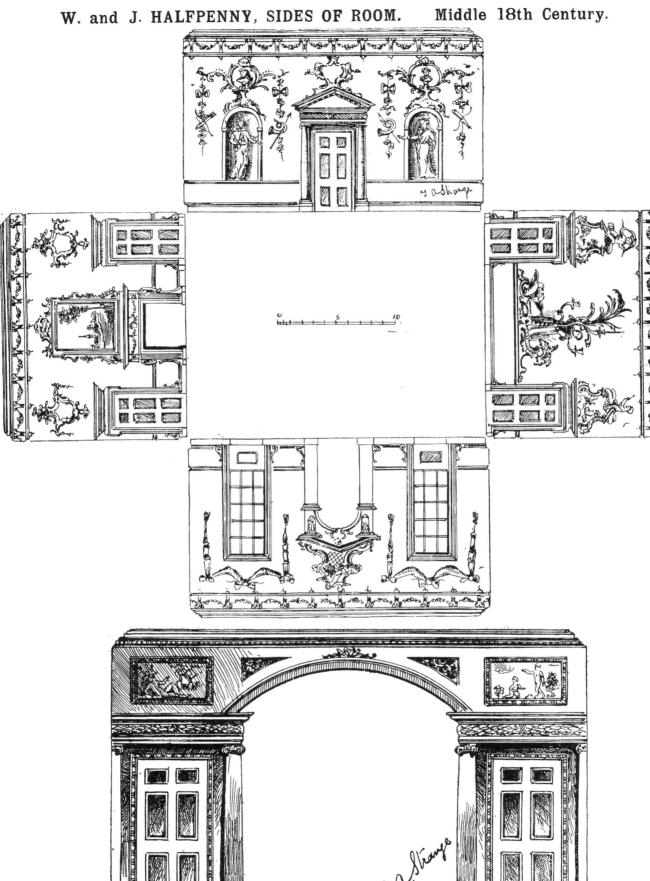

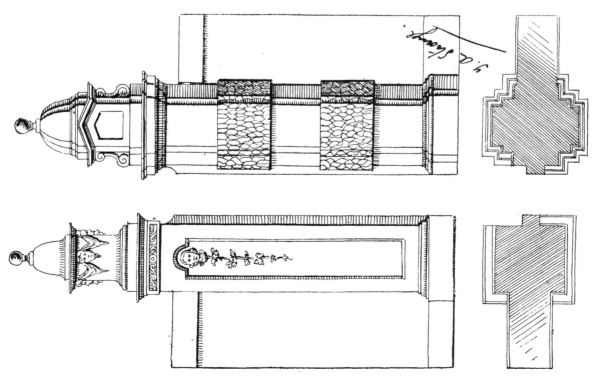

I may mention some of the ways of decorating rooms about this time.

An ordinary living room had a dado of wainscot, the height of a chair; the upper part had a wall-paper, which latter mode came into fashion about the year 1700, and was usual about this time (1750). This room would have a plain plastered cornice, the chimney-piece round the opening having a marble slab, or sometimes a slab of Portland stone. The rest of the chimney-piece would be of wood—more or less carved according to the means of the owner. A better room would be wainscotted right the way up to the cornice, with quarter-round and flat panels, and the chimney-piece with plain marble slabs round the opening, with ornaments in wood.

Another way for a best room, say a saloond would be to have a wainscot, chair high, and the remaining height to be stuccoed in panels with enriched ornaments and cornice; the chimney-piece of marble enriched (carved) in wood with flowers and festoons.

The hall was still paved, as in earlier times, with Portland stone and black marble planned out in diamonds, etc.

The floors in the saloon would be wainscot or best deal, dowelled.

The library was wainscotted to the top, with wood cornice.

Some of the best rooms were wainscotted dado height, and battened for hangings—that is for wall-papers, tapestry, or silk panels.

Billiard rooms had second - best deal floors; the walls wainscotted dado height, and stuccoed with black modillion plaster cornice.

Mahogany was mostly used about this time for handrails of stairs, and sometimes for the balusters of same.

It was the school of Chippendale that used mahogany so extensively.

Of course, exceptions must be made in the case of mansions of wealthy noblemen, etc., where mahogany was more extensively used, but the exceptions are rare.

CHIPPENDALE'S TITLE PAGE.

Borders for Paperhangings.

THE

GENTLEMAN AND CABINET-MAKER's

DIRECTOR:

BEING A LARGE COLLECTION OF THE

MOST ELEGANT AND USEFUL DESIGNS

OF

HOUSEHOLD FURNITURE,

IN THE MOST FASHIONABLE TASTE.

INCLUDING A GREAT VARIETY OF

Chairs, Sofas, Beds, and Couches ; China - Tables, Dressing-Tables, Shaving-Tables, Bason-Stands, Teakettle Stands ; Frames for Marble Slabs, Bureau Dressing-Tables, and Commodes ; Writing-Tables and Library-Tables ; Library Book-Cases, Organ-Cases for private rooms or churches, Desks, and Book-Cases ; Dressing and Writing-Tables, with Book-Cases, Toilets, Cabinets, and Cloaths-Presses ; China Cases, China Shelves, and Book Shelves, Candle-Stands, Terms for Busts, Stands for China Jars, and Pedestals ; Cisterns for Water, Lanthorns, and Chandeliers, Fire-Screens, Brackets, and Clock Cases, Pier Glasses, and Tables, Frames ; Girandoles, Chimney-Pieces, and Picture-Frames, Stove-Grates, Boarders, Frets, Chinese Railing, and Brass Work, for Furniture.

AND OTHER ORNAMENTS,

TO WHICH IS PREFIXED

A SHORT EXPLANATION OF THE FIVE
ORDERS OF ARCHITECTURE ;

WITH

PROPER DIRECTIONS FOR EXECUTING THE MOST
DIFFICULT PIECES,

THE MOULDINGS BEING EXHIBITED AT LARGE,

AND THE DIMENSIONS OF EACH DESIGN
SPECIFIED.

THE WHOLE COMPREHENDED IN TWO HUNDRED
COPPER PLATES, NEATLY ENGRAVED.

CALCULATED TO IMPROVE AND REFINE THE PRESENT
TASTE, AND SUITED TO THE FANCY AND
CIRCUMSTANCES OF ALL PERSONS IN ALL DEGREES OF LIFE.

BY THOMAS CHIPPENDALE,

CABINET-MAKER AND UPHOLSTERER, IN
ST. MARTIN'S LANE, LONDON.

THE THIRD EDITION.

LONDON :

PRINTED FOR THE AUTHOR AND SOLD AT HIS HOUSE,
IN ST. MARTIN'S LANE ; ALSO BY
T. BECKET AND P. A. DE HONDT, IN THE STRAND.

MDCCLXII.

The title page has already called the following Work "The Gentleman and Cabinet-Maker's Director," as being calculated to assist the one in the Choice, and the other in the Execution of the Designs ; which are so contrived, that if no one drawing should singly answer the Gentleman's Taste, there will yet be found a Variety of Hints, sufficient to construct a new one.

D

E

2

5

3

4

6

C

A

B

10

11

F

12

C

A

B

13

See Page 108.

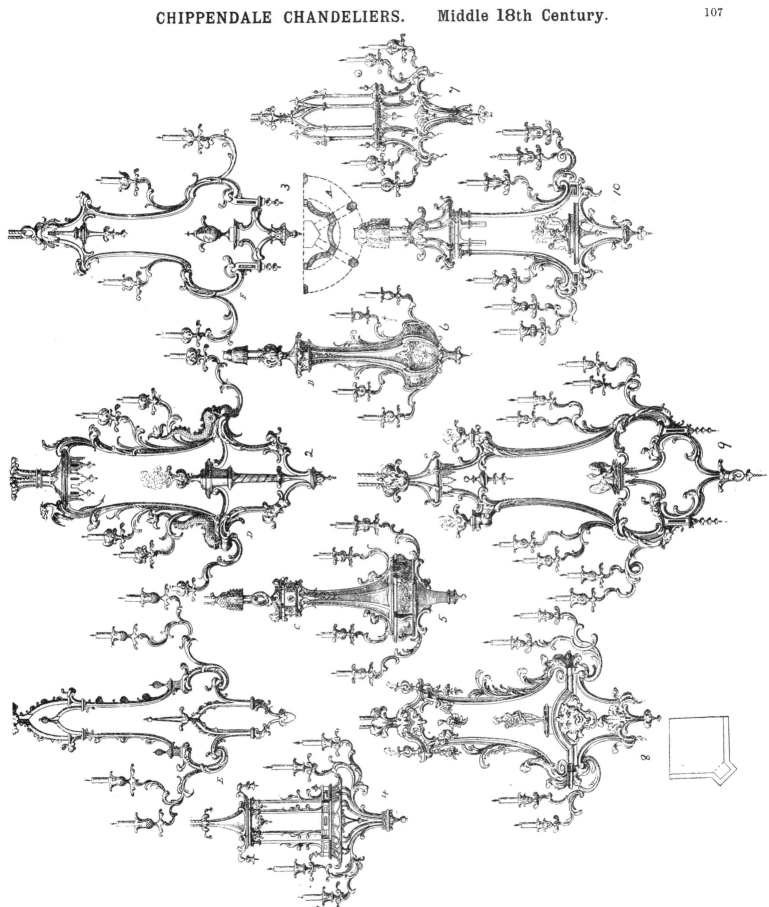

See Page 108.

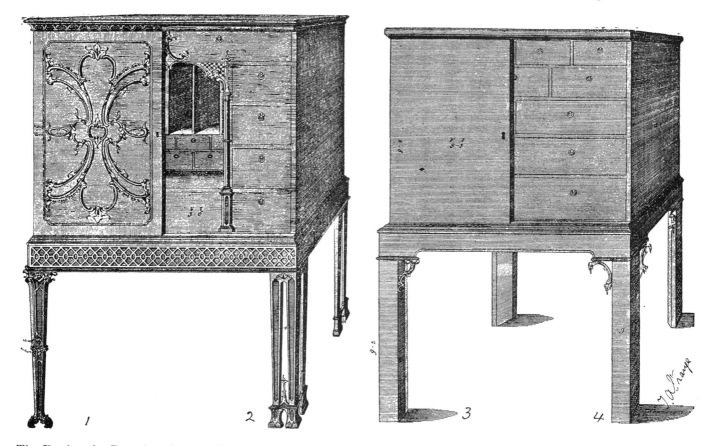

The Borders for Paperhangings on Page 105 should be useful for a variety of other purposes.

The Lanterns on Page 106 are for halls, passages and staircases. Some are square, and some have six sides. They are generally made of brass, cast from wooden moulds.

Of the Chandeliers on Page 107 some have four sides, others six. Both Nos. 5 and 6 are solid, but I think the open ones preferable. They are generally made of glass, and sometimes of brass, but if neatly done in wood, and gilt with burnished gold, would look better and come much cheaper.

The two Cabinets on Page 108 are made in mahogany.

Nos. 3 and 4 on Page 108 are designs for Breakfast-tables. One has a stretching-rail, and the feet are canted and sunk in. The other has a shelf inclosed with fret work; sometimes they are inclosed with brass wire-work. In the front is a recess for the knees, etc. No. 5 is a design of Table for holding a set of china, and may be used as a Tea-table. A shows the plan of the top; B is a fret to go round rim of top; and C is an ornament to go between the feet.

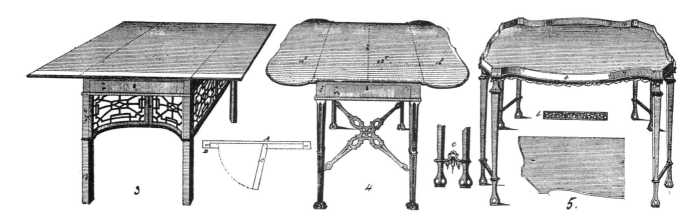

CHIPPENDALE DRESSING-TABLES and BUREAUX.   Middle 18th Century.

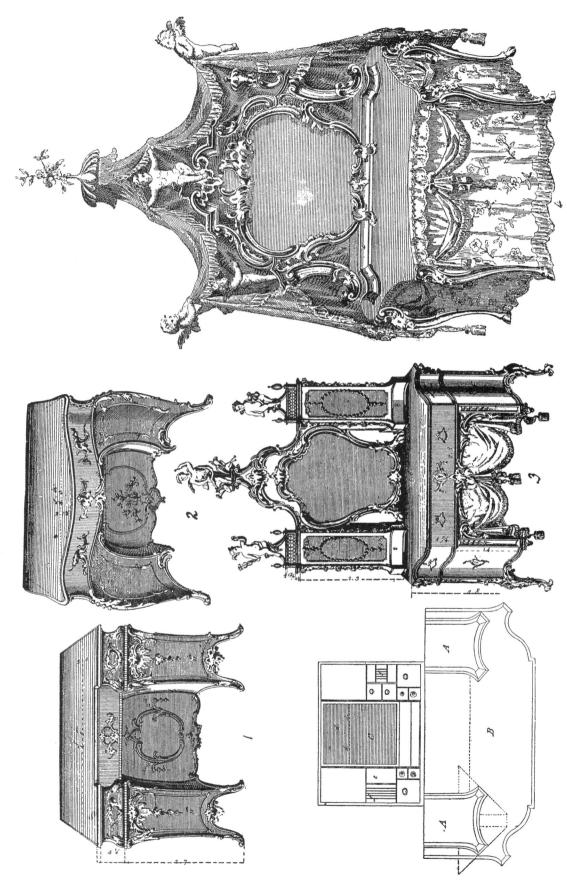

Nos. 1 and 2 on Page 109 are designs for two Bureau Dressing-tables. The upper drawers may be divided in like manner as the plan at side of No. 3. The ornamental parts are intended for brass-work, which, I should advise, should be modelled in wax, and then cast from these models. The under part may be made into drawers instead of cupboards. No. 3 on Page 109 is a design of a Lady's Dressing-table; the draw above the recess has all conveniences for dressing, and the top of it is a Dressing-glass which comes forward with folding hinges. On each side is a cupboard with glass doors, which may be either transparent or silvered; and inside, drawers or pigeon-holes. This design has been made in rosewood and gave entire satisfaction; all the ornaments are gilt. B is the plan of the under part; A, A, the plan of the cupboards; C, the plan of the dressing drawer; d, d, a glass made to rise and hung with hinges; f, f, places for combs, rings, bottles, boxes, etc. The dimensions are on the design.

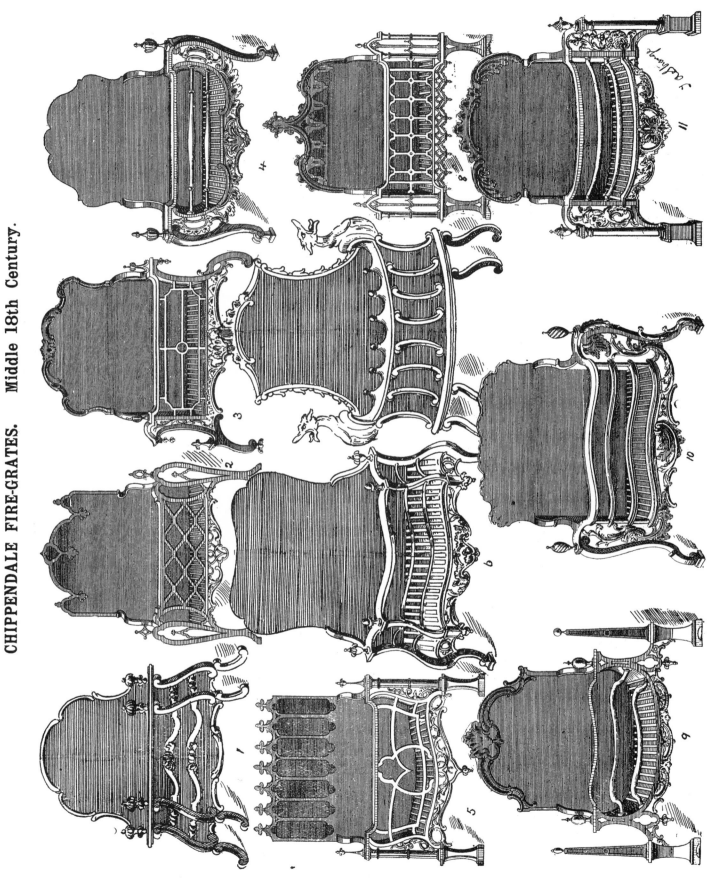

IRONWORK from Various Sources.   Middle 18th Century.

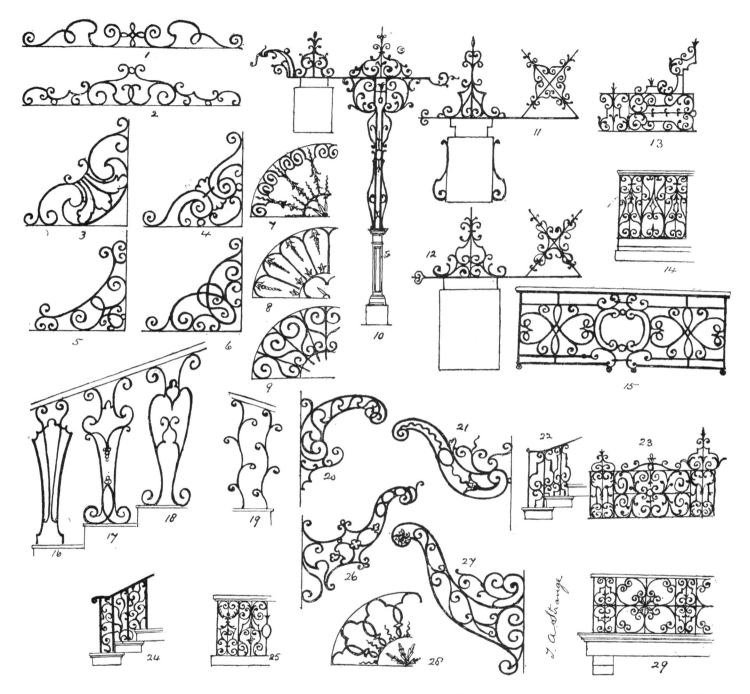

No. 4 on Page 109 is a design for a Toilet or Dressing-Table for a lady   The glass, made to come forward with folding hinges, is in a carved frame, and stands in a compartment that rests upon a plinth, between which are small drawers. The drapery is supported by cupids, and the petticoat goes behind the feet of the table, which looks better. The ornamental part may be in burnished gold or japanned. The drapery may be silk damask, with gold fringes and tassels.

The designs for Fire-grates on Page 110 may have the ornamental parts in wrought brass, and made to take off, and so be easily cleaned.

The designs for ornamental Ironwork on Page 111 are from various sources, and represent iron uprights for signs, balconies, overdoors, stair balusters, brackets for lanterns, etc., and are designs from Manwaring, Crunden, Ince and Mayhew, and other contemporary sources. In nearly every instance they betray the French Louis XV. style.

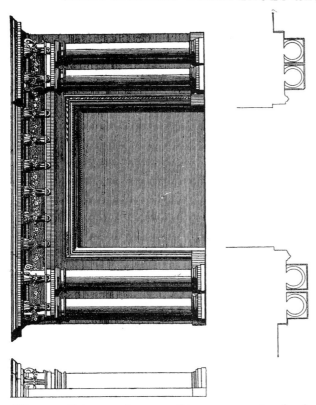

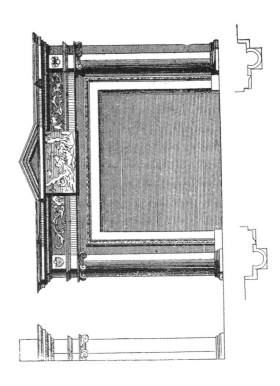

The two Chimney-pieces on this page are of a classical design, suitable for marble. The columns may be whole, the plans of which are given above. The four cisterns, also shewn on this page, should be in brass. No. 4 should be made of wood or marble, and cut out of the solid; the others may be made in parts, and joined with brass-work.

Chippendale says, in the Preface of his work, that "The Correction of the Judicious and Impartial I shall always receive with Diffidence in my own Abilities, and Respect to theirs. But though the following Designs were more perfect than my Fondness for my own Offspring could ever suppose them, I should yet be far from expecting the united Approbation of ALL those whose Sentiments have an undoubted Claim to be regarded; for a thousand accidental Circumstances may concur in dividing the Opinions of the most improved Judges, and the most unprejudiced will find it difficult to disengage himself from a partial Affection to some particular Beauties, of which the general Course of his Studies, or the peculiar Cast of his Temper may have rendered him most sensible. The Mind, when pronouncing Judgment upon any Work of Taste and Genius, is apt to decide of its Merit according as those Circumstances which she most admires either prevail or are deficient.

"Upon the whole I have here given no Design but what may be executed with Advantage by the Hands of a skilful Workman, though some of the Profession have been diligent enough to represent them (especially those after the Gothic and Chinese Manner) as so many specious Drawings, impossible to be worked off by any Mechanic whatsoever. I will not scruple to attribute this to Malice, Ignorance and Inability, and I am confident I can convince all Noblemen, Gentlemen, or others, who will honour me with their Commands, that every Design in the Book can be improved, both as to Beauty and Enrichment, in the Execution of them."

Chippendale further says, "Of all the ARTS which are either improved or ornamented by Architecture, that of CABINET-MAKING is not only the most useful and ornamental, but capable of receiving as great Assistance from it as any whatever. I have therefore prefixed to the following Designs a short Explanation of the Five Orders. Without an Acquaintance with this Science, and some Knowledge of the Rules of Perspective, the Cabinet Maker cannot make the Designs of his Work intelligible, nor shew, in a little Compass, the whole Conduct and Effect of the Piece. These, therefore, ought to be carefully studied by everyone who would excel in this Branch, since they are the very Soul and Basis of his Art." I have thought it best to include his Five Orders, also a Parallel of the Ancient Architecture with the Modern.

THE FIVE ORDERS OF ARCHITECTURE FROM CHIPPENDALE'S BOOK.

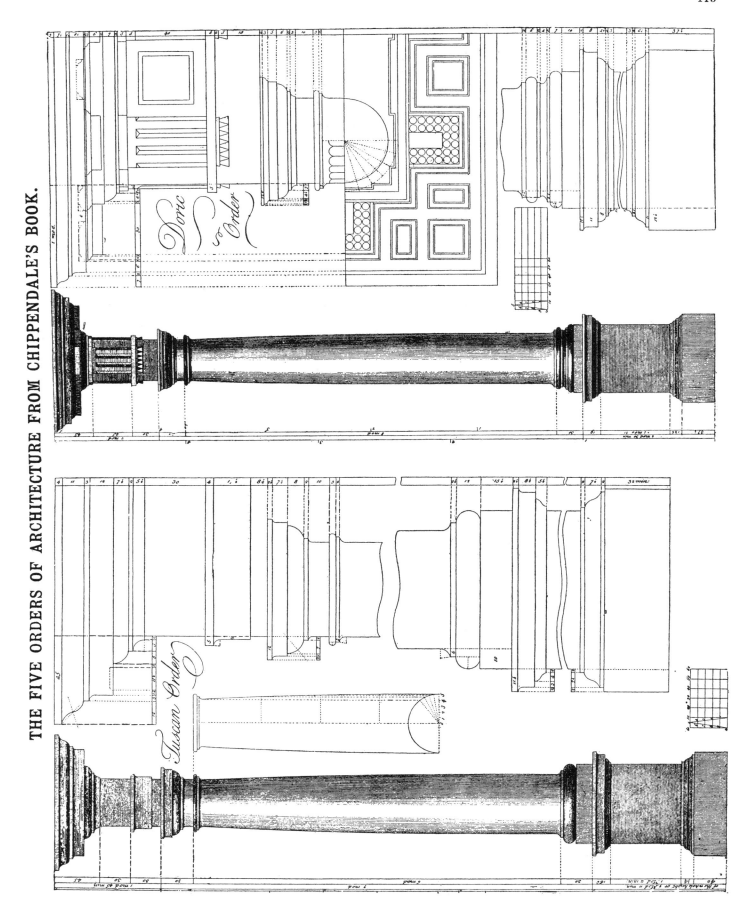

Doric Order

Tuscan Order

THE FIVE ORDERS OF ARCHITECTURE FROM CHIPPENDALE'S BOOK.

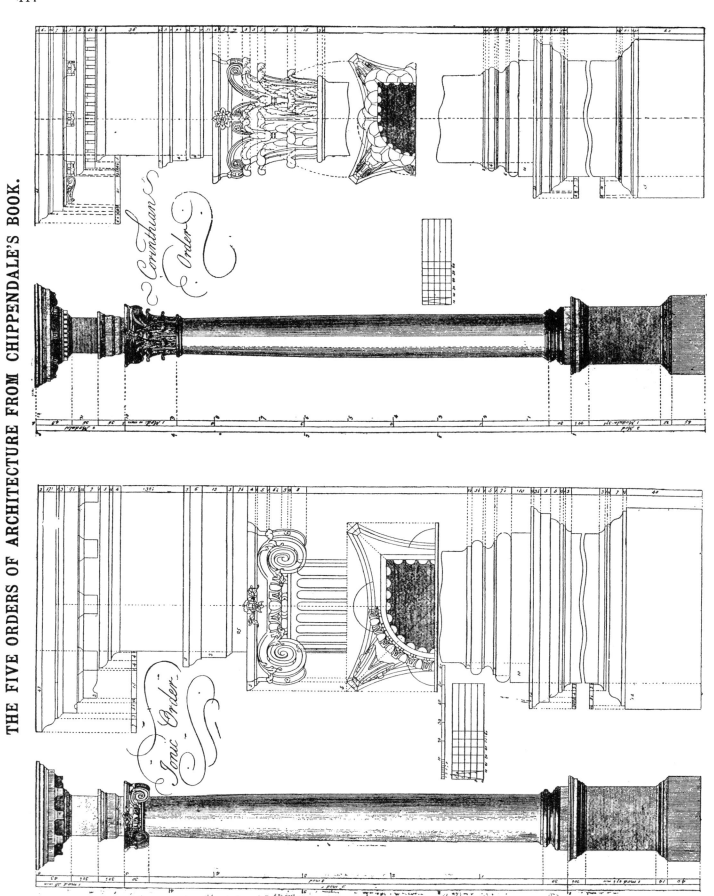

THE FIVE ORDERS OF ARCHITECTURE FROM CHIPPENDALE'S BOOK.

THE GENERAL PROPORTIONS OF THE TUSCAN ORDER.

PLATE I.

Take any Height proposed for this Order, and divide it into five equal Parts; one of those Parts shall be the Height of the Pedestal according to the small Division of the Scale, on the left Hand; the other four Parts above must be divided into five Parts, according to the outmost Line on the left Hand; the upper fifth Part shall be the Height of the Entablature, and the other four Parts betwixt the Pedestal and Entablature, shall be the Height of the Column, including its Base and Capital: and this Height being divided into seven Parts, one of those Parts will be the Diameter of the Column, which Diameter is divided into sixty equal Parts, and is called a Module; and this will serve to set off all the Mouldings for this Order. You have all the Particulars of the Mouldings at large on the right Hand; the Base and Capital are each in Height a Semi-diameter of the Column; the Column must be divided into three equal Parts betwixt the Capital and the Base, and from the top of the lower Division it is diminished one-fifth of its Semi-diameter on each Side. The Method of diminishing the Column is explained in the middle Scheme; the Breadth of the Die of the Pedestal is determined by the Projection of the Base of the Column.

THE GENERAL PROPORTIONS OF THE DORIC ORDER.

PLATE II.

Take any Height upon a straight Line, as in the TUSCAN Order, and divide it into five equal Parts; one of them shall be the Height of the Pedestal; the other four Parts must be divided into five Parts, one of them which is the Height of the Entablature; the remaining four Parts must be divided into eight Parts; one of them is the Diameter of the Column, or Module, which divide into sixty equal Parts, as in the TUSCAN Order, to set off all the mouldings, as you will see on the right Hand, where you have the Plan of the Cornice. The Column diminishes one-sixth of its Semi-diameter on each Side, from one-third Part of its Height, to the Top of the Capital. The Base and Capital are each in Height a Semi-diameter.

THE GENERAL PROPORTIONS OF THE IONIC ORDER.

PLATE III.

Take any Height, as in the foregoing Orders, and divide it into five equal Parts, one of these parts is the Height of the Pedestal; the other four being divided into six Parts, one of them is the Height of the Entablature; the remaining five Parts must be divided into nine equal Parts; one of them is the Diameter of the Column or Module, which is divided into sixty equal Parts as before; the Mouldings are at large, with a Scale or Module to draw them. The Column is diminished one-sixth on each Side, from one-third Part of its Height. The Base and Capital are each in Height a Semi-diameter.

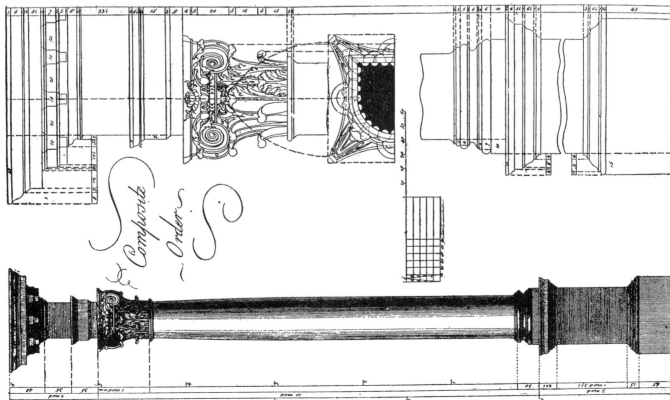

The Bases for the Columns of each Order.

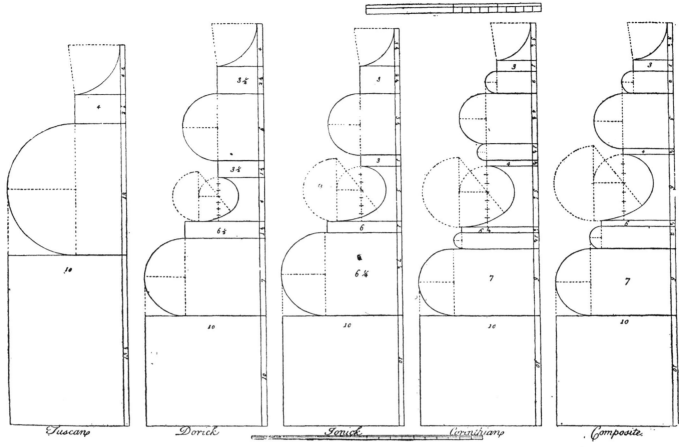

Tuscan   Dorick   Ionick   Corinthian   Composite

The Bases and the Caps of the Pedestals of each Order.

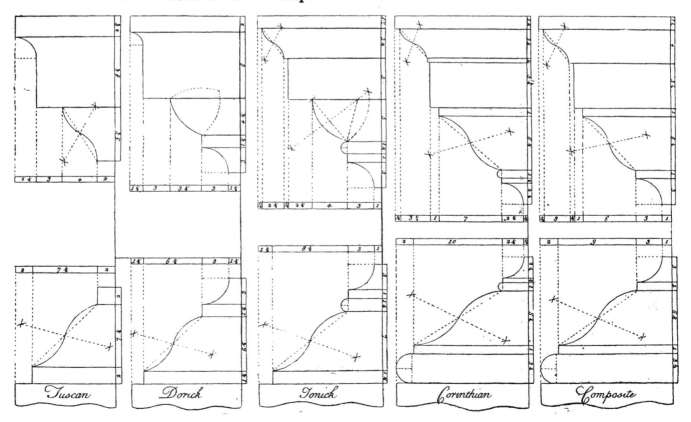

Tuscan   Dorick   Ionick   Corinthian   Composite

THE VOLUTE OF THE IONIC ORDER.

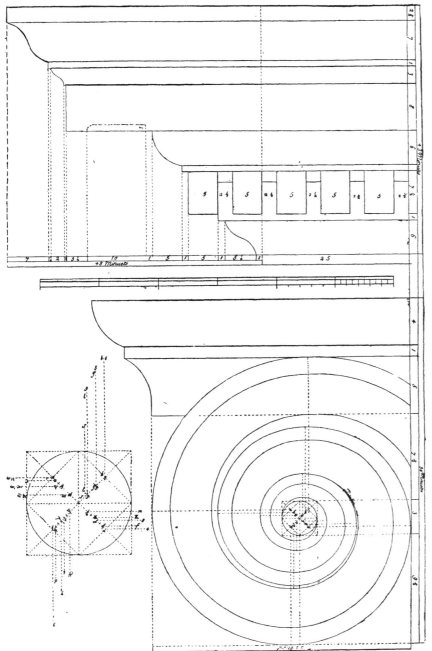

THE GENERAL PROPORTIONS OF THE CORINTHIAN ORDER.
PLATE IV.

The whole Height is divided into five Parts; one of them must be for the Pedestal, the other four remaining Parts must be divided into six; one of them will give the Height of the Entablature, the other five, betwixt the Pedestal and Entablature, must be divided into ten Parts, one of which is the Diameter of the Column, or Module, which divide into sixty equal Parts as before; the Base is in Height a Semi-diameter of the Column; the Capital is one Module, and ten Parts, in Height. The other Dimensions are as in the IONIC Order.

THE GENERAL PROPORTIONS OF THE COMPOSITE ORDER.
PLATE V.

Take any determined Height, as in the CORINTHIAN Order, and divide it into five Parts, one Part shall be the Height of the Pedestal, the other four Parts must be divided again into six Parts as before; one of them is the Height of the Entablature; The Height of the Capital is one Module, and ten Parts; The Column diminishes one-sixth of its Semi-diameter on each Side, from one-third Part of the Height. The Dimensions are as in the CORINTHIAN Order.

THE BASES FOR THE COLUMNS OF EACH ORDER.
PLATE VI.

The Bases are in Height a Semi-diameter of the Column; their Projections are one-third of the Height; their Members are of an easy Form, being most of them a Semi-circular, except the Scotia, which is a Mixtilinear drawn from two Centers, in this Manner, as in the IONIC Base. Having drawn and divided the Bigness of each Member, and the Centers of the upper and lower Torus, then let fall a Perpendicular from the Center of the upper Torus, and divide it within the Space of the Scotia into seven Parts, the three uppermost will be the Segment of the Circle drawn to the oblique Line; The other Segment is drawn by fixing the Center where the Oblique cuts the Perpendicular; the other Scotias are drawn in the same Manner. The Mouldings are all the same as pricked or marked in the Orders.

THE BASES AND CAPS OF THE PEDESTALS OF EACH ORDER.
PLATE VII.

The Projection of the Base of the Pedestal is equal to its Height, and the Caps project the same; the Mouldings are pricked off as they are drawn in the Order before.

See Page 120 re Ionic Volute.

A PARALLEL OF THE ANCIENT ARCHITECTURE WITH THE MODERN. [DORIC ORDER.

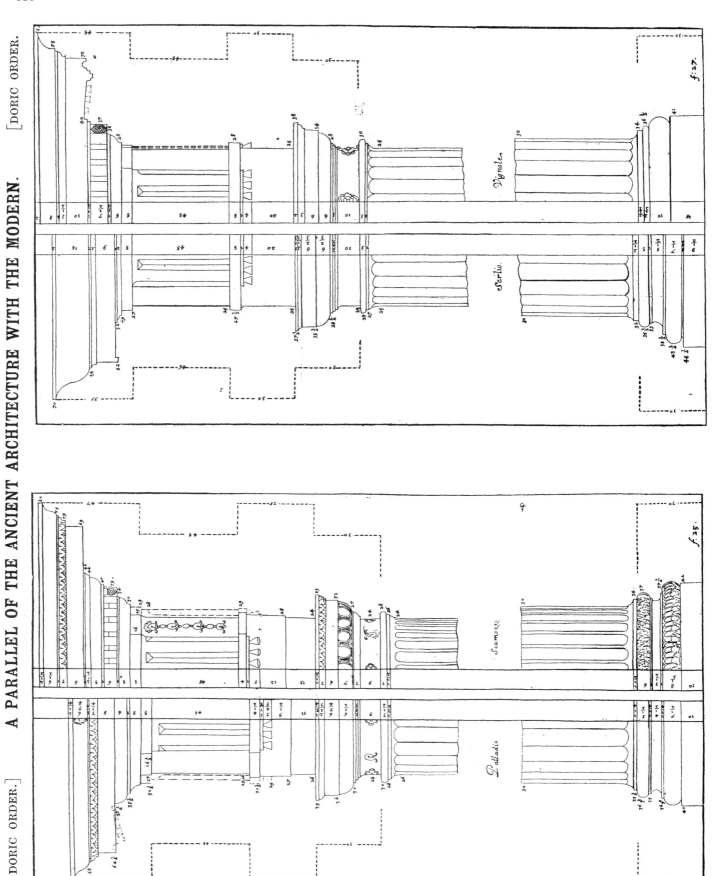

A PARALLEL OF THE ANCIENT ARCHITECTURE WITH THE MODERN.

DORIC ORDER.

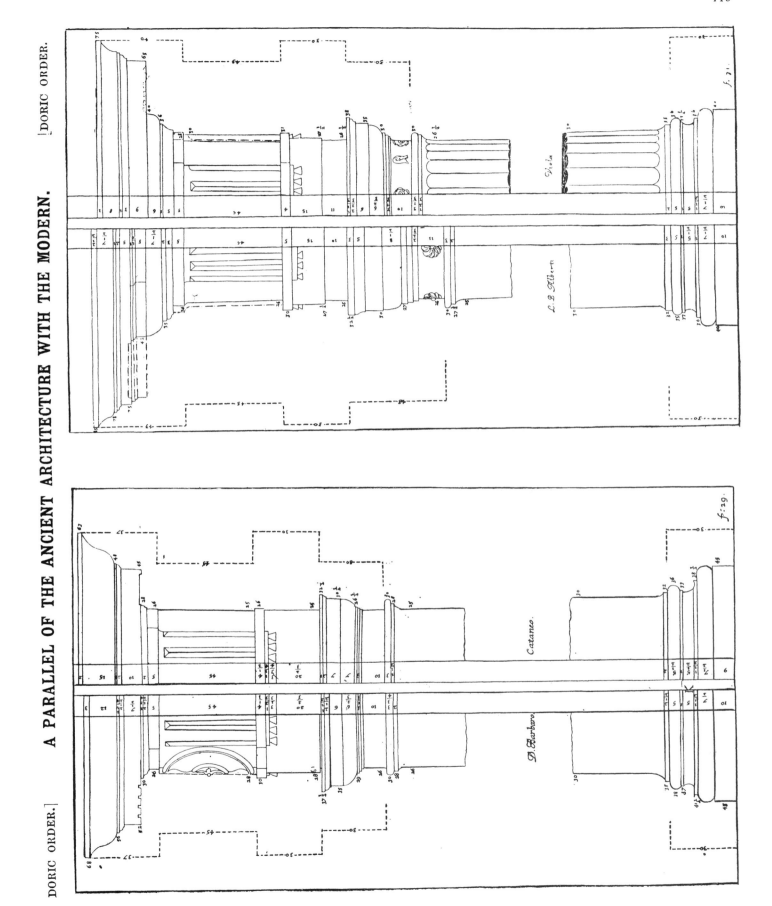

DORIC ORDER.

A PARALLEL OF THE ANCIENT ARCHITECTURE WITH THE MODERN.

A RULE FOR DRAWING THE SPIRAL LINES OF THE VOLUTE OF THE IONIC ORDER.

PLATE VIII.

Take your Compasses, and extend from 1 in the Eye of the Volute, to the greatest Extent, and sweep with them a Quarter of a Circle; then holding still in the Point where the Compasses ended the Quarter Circle, bring the other Point of the Compasses to 2, in the Eye of the Volute; there sweep another Quarter of a Circle, still holding your Compasses in that Point; bring the other Point of your Compasses to 3 in the Eye of the Volute, and sweep another Quarter of a Circle; then hold your Compasses in that Point, and bring the other Point of your Compasses to 4 in the Eye of the Volute, then sweep the other Quarter: so by this Means you will complete one Round of the Volute. Then proceed in the same Manner from 4 to 5, 6, 7, and so on to 12. Take Notice of the Eye of the Volute at large, and observe to divide each Division into three equal Parts, as is done between 2 and 6, and let the Point of your Compasses be placed in the Points c, d, f, &c. to diminish the Fillet of the Volute.

"The Parallel of the Ancient Architecture with the Modern," is from the French of Roland Freart, and translated into English by the famous John Evelyn. The author compares ten of the chief writers who, up to his time, had written upon the Five Orders. These writers all belong to the period of the Renaissance, and they are Palladio, Scamozzi, Serlio, Vignola, D. Barbaro, Cataneo, L. B. Alberti, Viola, Bullant, and De Lorme.

John Evelyn was born at Wotton, Surrey, in 1620, and educated at Lewes Grammar School. Sayes Court, his residence in Kent, was the seat of his wife, Mary, daughter of Sir Richard Browne—King Charles' Minister at the French Court. He died in 1706, and was interred at Wotton in a stone coffin, over which was this inscription: "That living in an age of extraordinary events and revolutions, he had learned from thence this truth, which he desired might thus be communicated to posterity; That all is vanity that is not honest, and that there is no solid wisdom but in real piety." He published about twenty-five works, besides papers on the transactions of the Royal and other societies. He dedicated the above work to Charles II. Like most dedications of the time it is full of flattery and panegyric, for sample: "Your exact judgment and marvellous ability in all that belongs to naval architecture, have brought the Antipodes to meet, and the Poles to kiss each other," etc, etc.

D. Barbaro was at one time Ambassador from Venice to England.

De Lorme was architect of the Tuilleries, the Louvre, etc., etc.

DOORIC ORDER.]

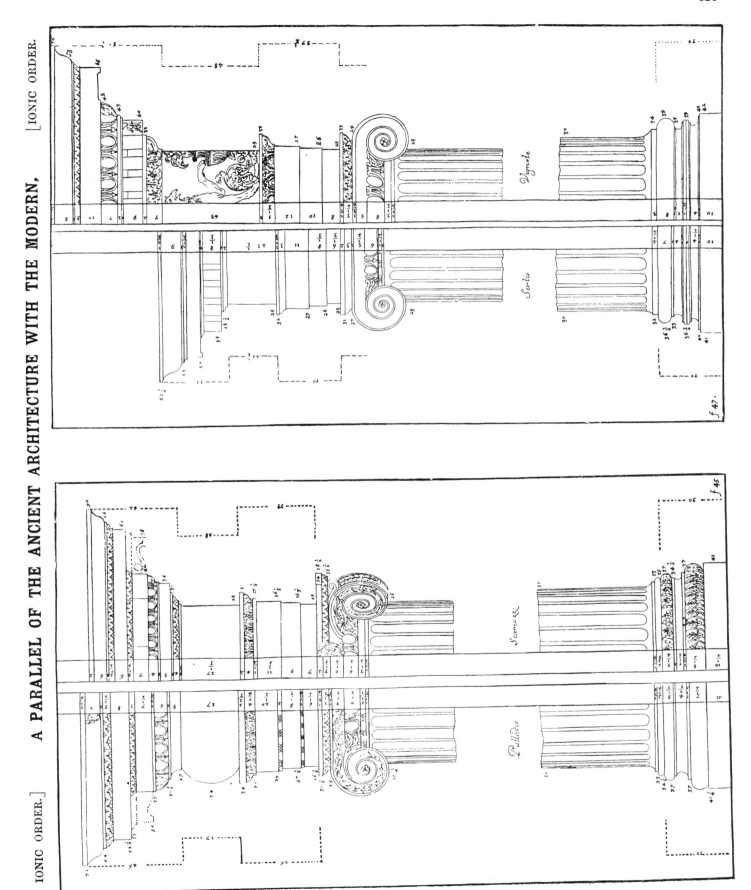

Vignole

Serlio

Scamozzi

Palladio

f 47.

f 45

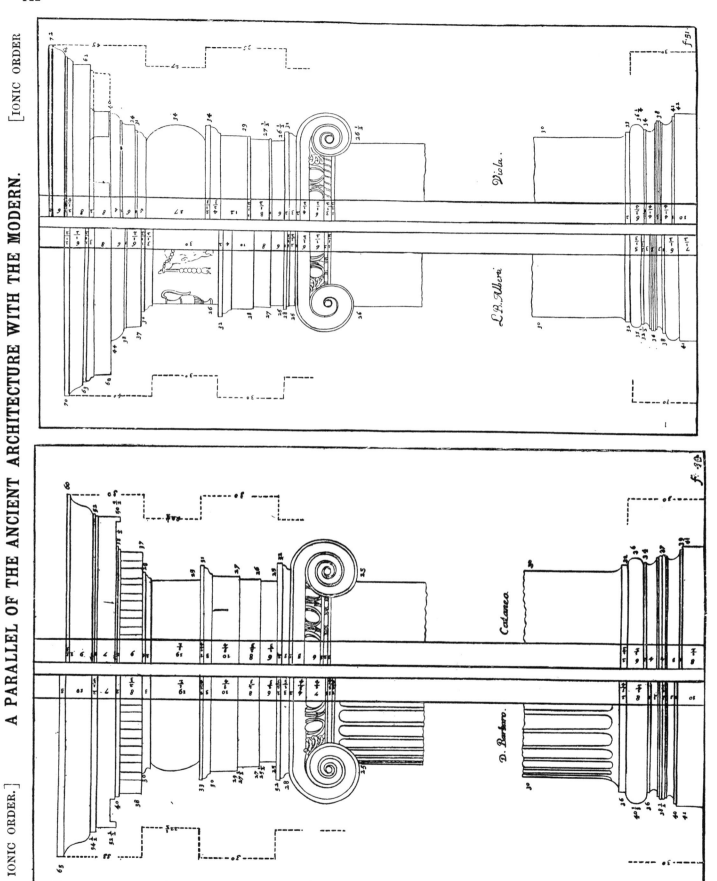

A PARALLEL OF THE ANCIENT ARCHITECTURE WITH THE MODERN.

[IONIC ORDER

IONIC ORDER.]

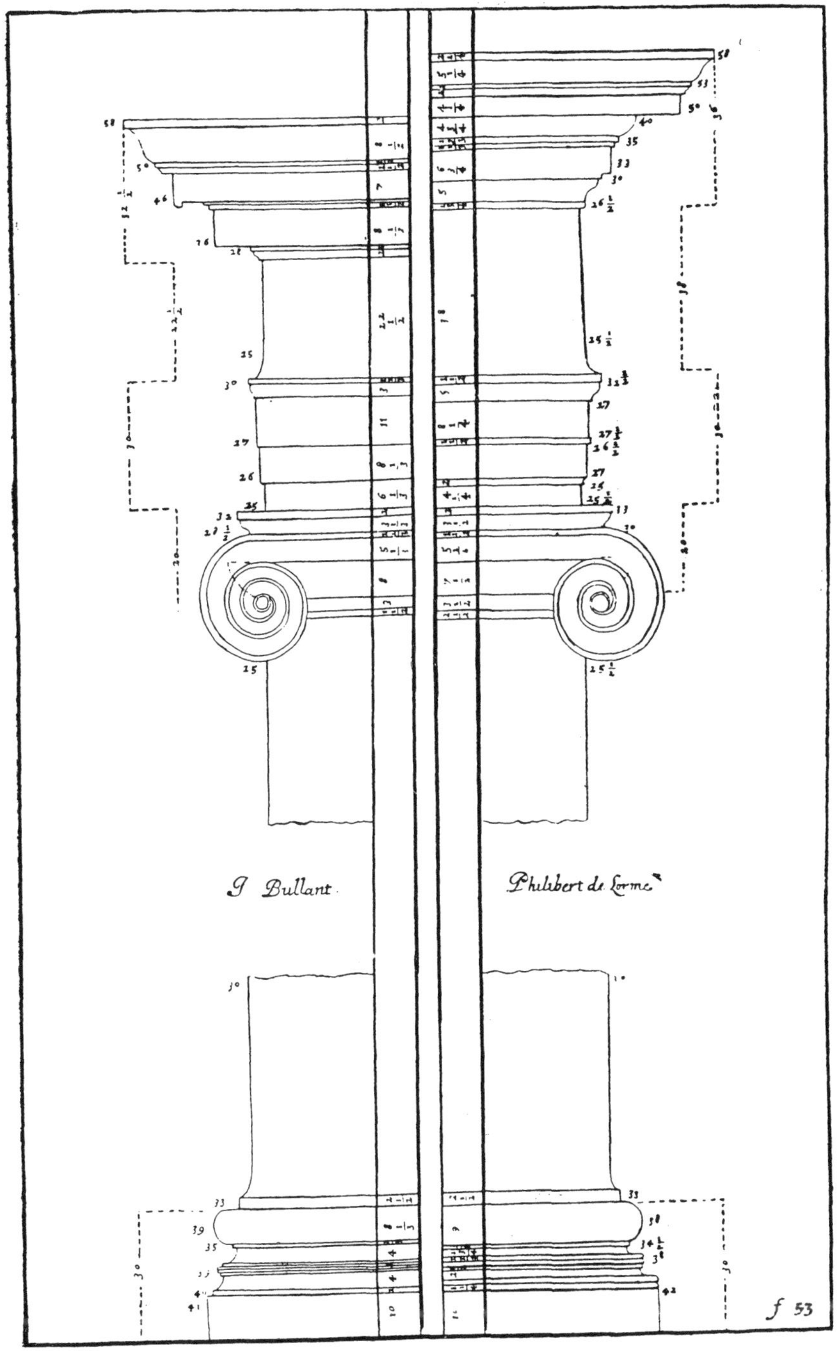

A PARALLEL OF THE ANCIENT ARCHITECTURE WITH THE MODERN. [CORINTHIAN ORDER.]

IONIC ORDER.

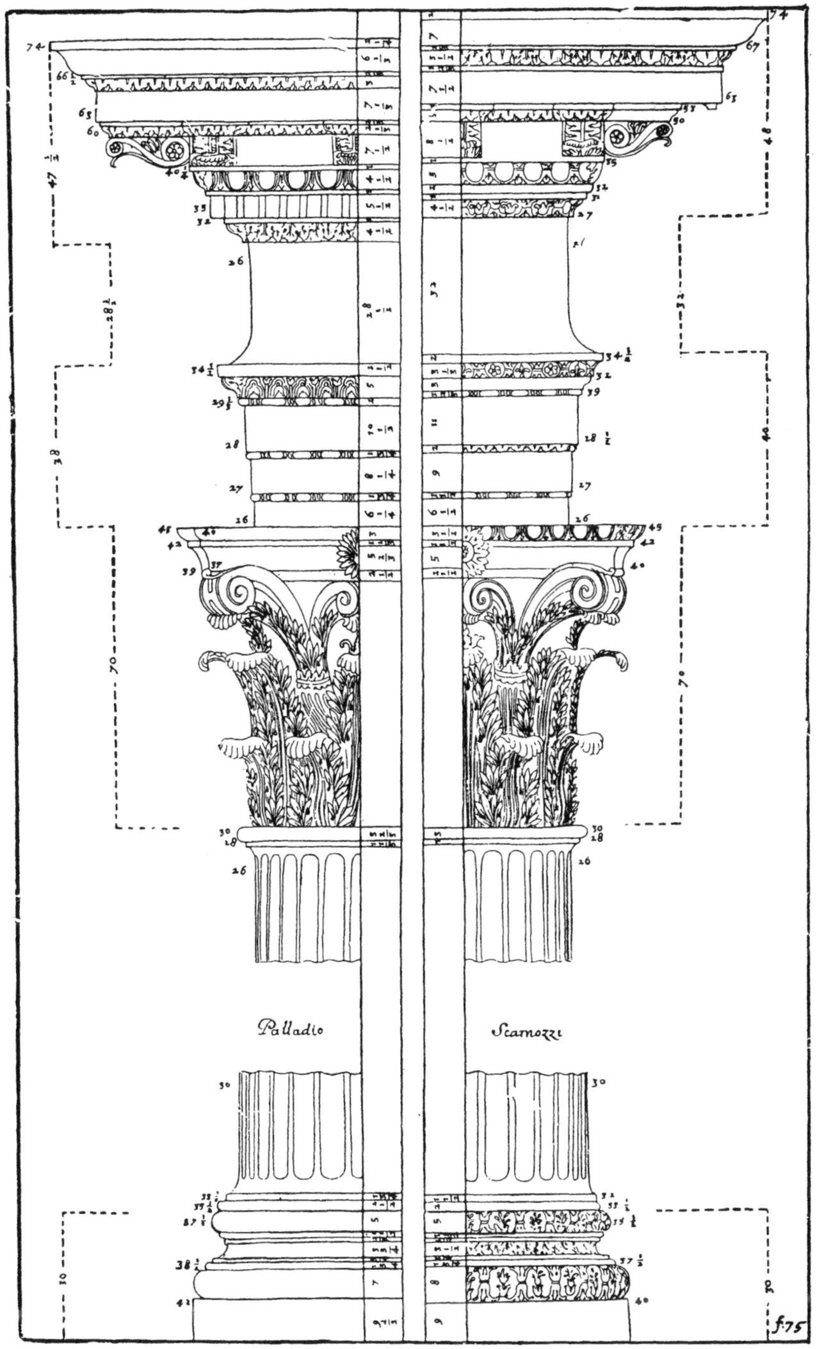

Scamozzi

Palladio

Philibert de l'Orme

J. Bullant

CORINTHIAN ORDER.] A PARALLEL OF THE ANCIENT ARCHITECTURE WITH THE MODERN. [CORINTHIAN ORDER.

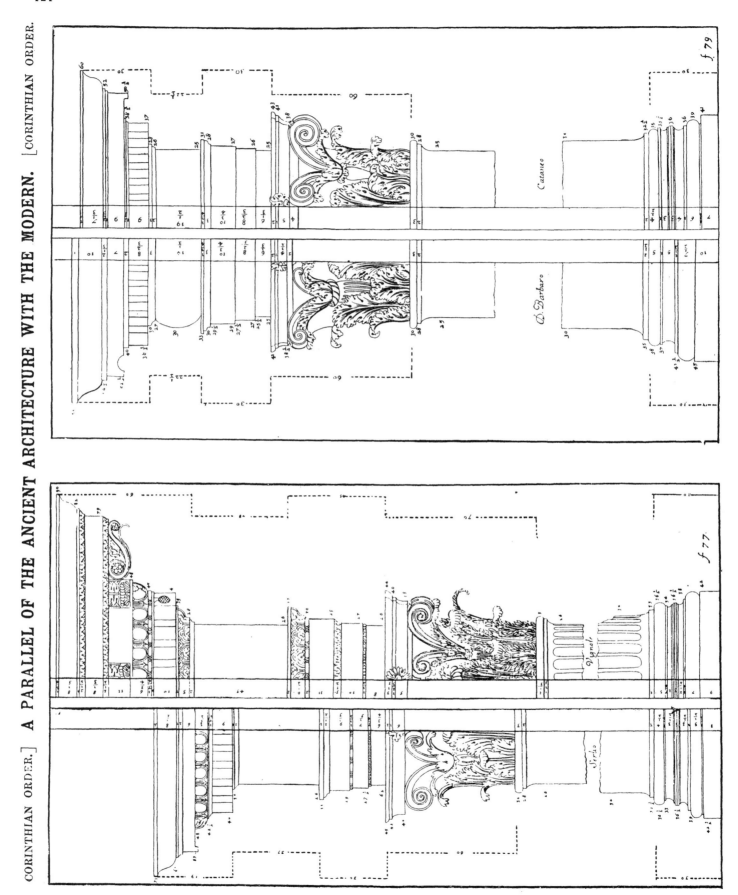

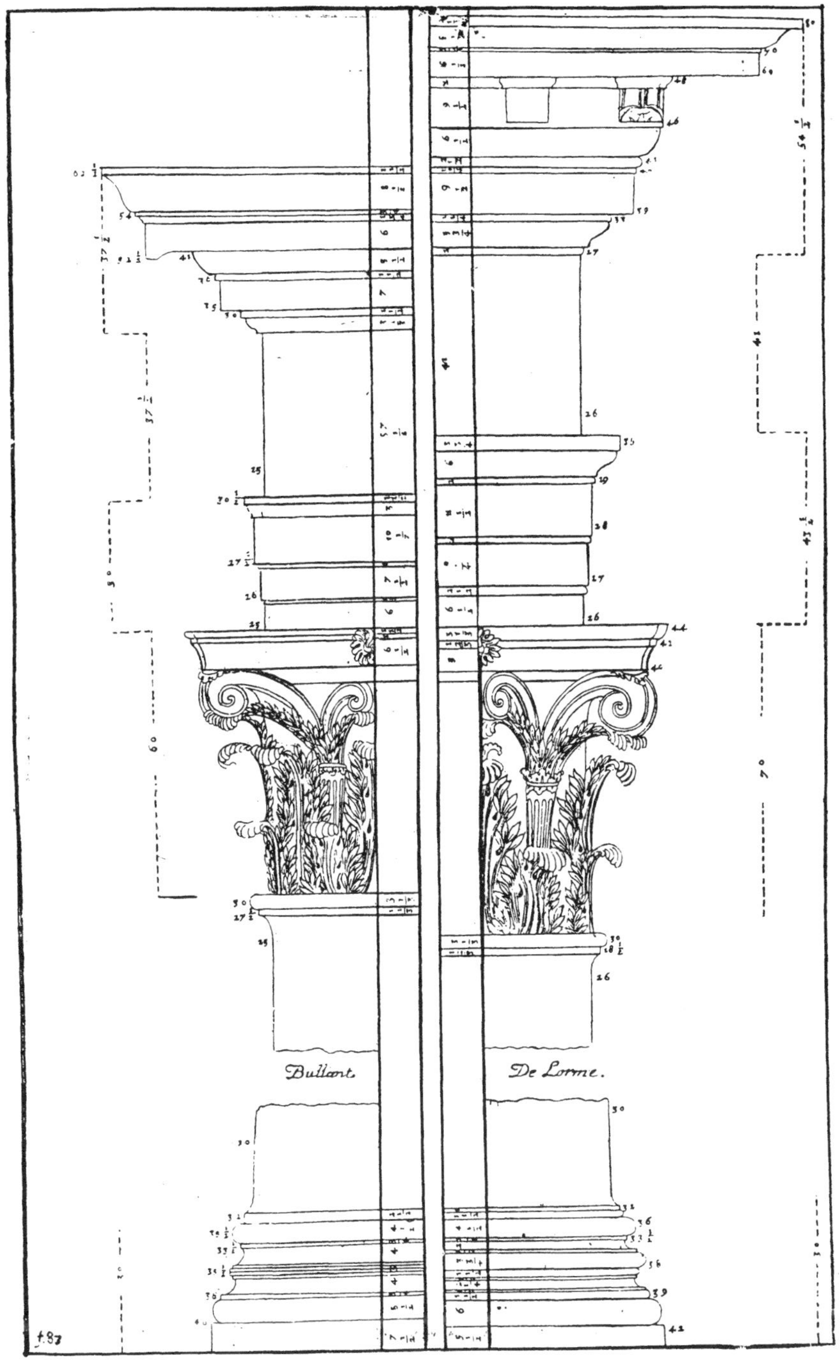
Bullant.
De Lorme.

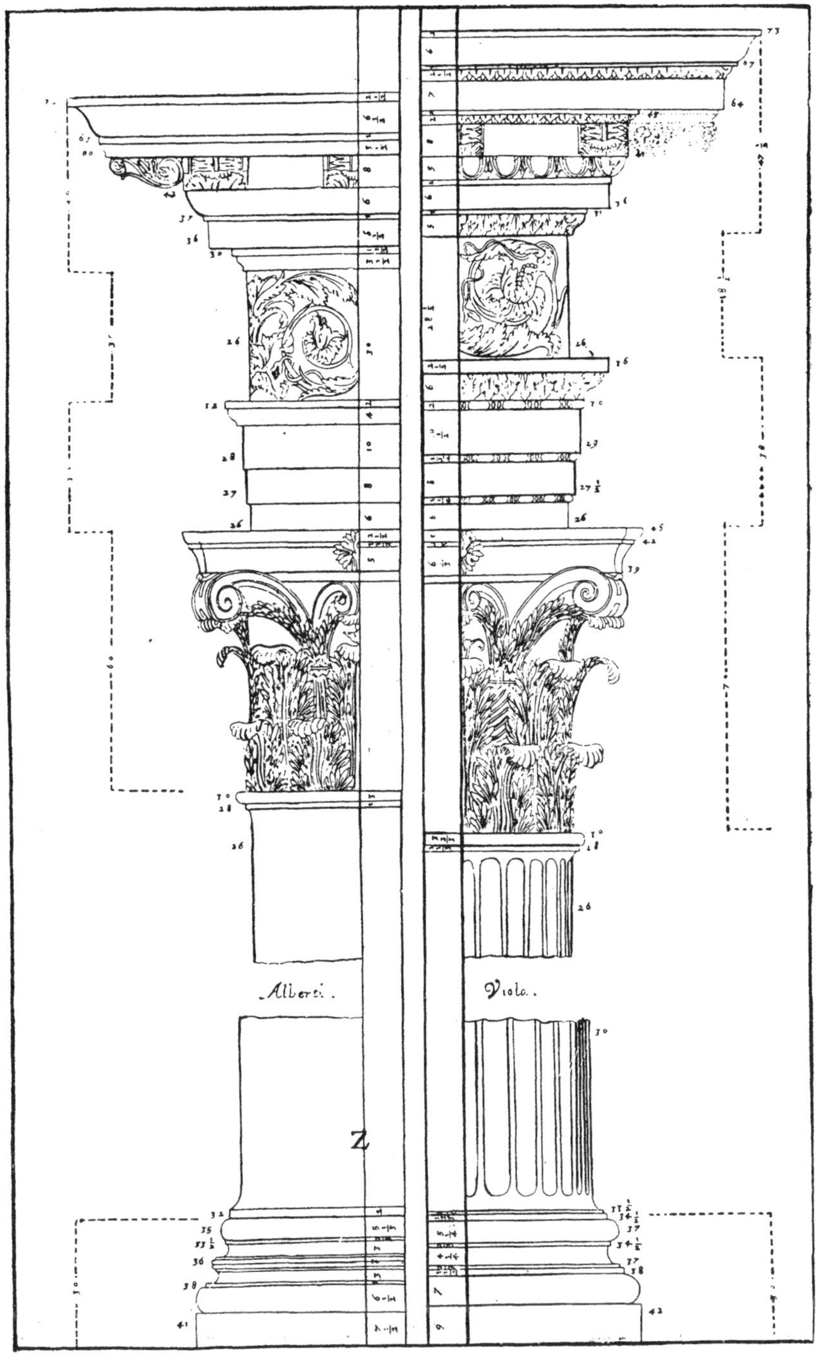
Alberti.
Viola.
Z

A PARALLEL OF THE ANCIENT ARCHITECTURE WITH THE MODERN. [TUSCAN ORDER.

TUSCAN ORDER.]

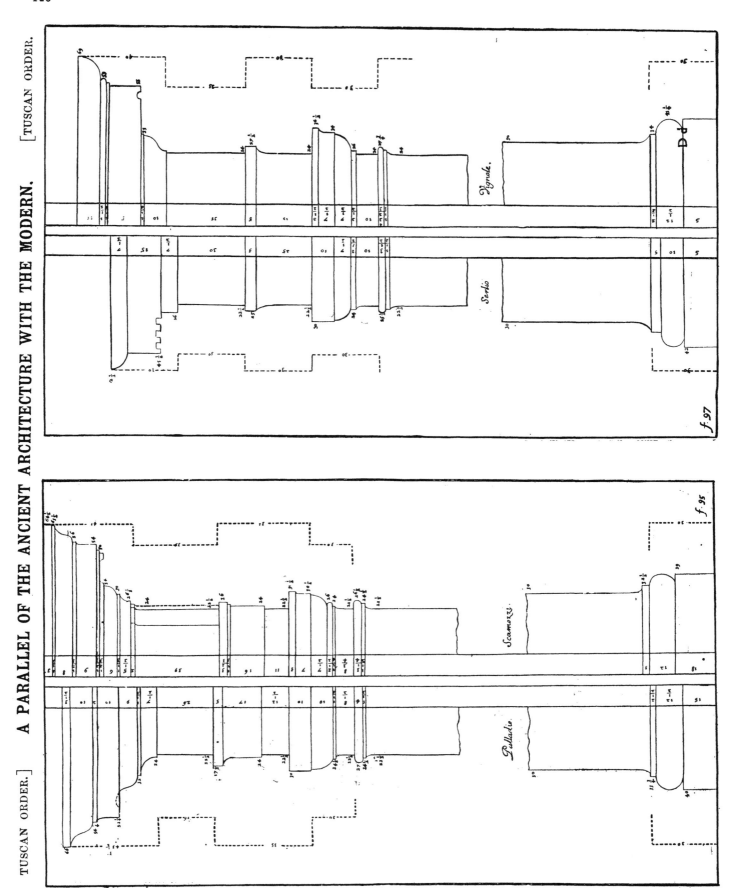

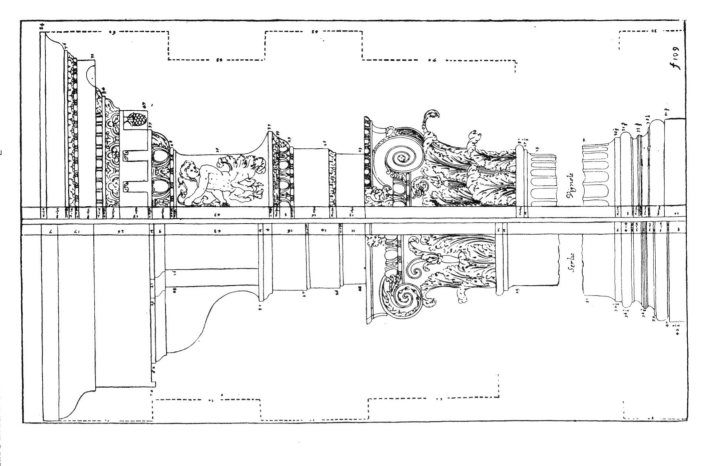

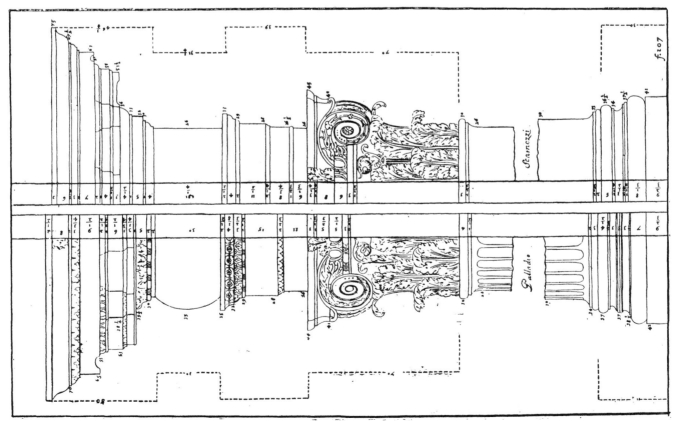

CHIPPENDALE   Middle 18th Century.

Little is known of the personal history of Chippendale or his sons. It is supposed he was descended from a family of carvers. He copied the French fashion extensively, as is shown by the " Rococo" carving on so much of his furniture, etc. He published a work on Furniture in 1762, which he called " The Gentlemen and Cabinet-makers' Director," being a large collection of the most elegant and useful designs of household furniture in the most fashionable taste. He dedicated it to the Right Honourable Hugh Earl of Northumberland.

Mahogany was the wood he mostly used ; also Rosewood, set off either with carving—which was sometimes gilt, or brass and silver mounts richly chased. But a good deal of his work is made of a soft wood and japanned, or painted and partly gilt. He also used copper mounts.

He prefaced his work with the " Five Orders," which I reproduce on Pages 113 to 117 in this work.

It was usual during the 18th Century for authors of works on Architecture, Furniture, etc., to preface their books with a disquisition on the " Five Orders." Anyone not knowing this, and taking up an original copy of say Chippendale, and after mastering the Preface, and then proceeding to the Designs in the books—and, of course, anticipating to benefit by his previous study—would be disappointed by finding the Designs had little or nothing to do with the Preface ; in fact, in many cases were the very opposite to anything classical. This mystery can be partly cleared up when he calls to mind that the architects designed their buildings on a classical model ; although the furniture manufacturers did not follow them very closely—as in the case of Chippendale, who was influenced by the Gothic at one time, by Chinese Ornament at another, and by the Louis XV. " Rococo" style at another time ; it is by the last that he is mostly known. But exception must be made with regard to some of the designs of Book-cases, Wardrobes, etc., where the mouldings are certainly based on a classical model —while the carvings on the panels, etc., are not so.

It has been asserted that there being so great a difference in some of the pieces of furniture, for instance, between the gilt frames and the wardrobes, that there must have been more than one of the family superintending the execution of Chippendale's designs ; but if so, it is somewhat curious he has not mentioned the fact in the preface or elsewhere, but seems rather to infer that an intelligent workman " could always give full scope to his capacity."

COMMODE.

The Bas Relief in the middle may be carved in wood, or cast in brass, or painted on wood. That part in the middle may be a door, with ornament on it, and the end parts in the same manner. On the top of the Commode is a design for a Surtout, to be made in silver. A Candle-stand at each end is very proper. I would advise to model this design before execution, as it will save time, and prevent mistakes.

CHIPPENDALE SEAT and CHAIR. Middle 18th Century.

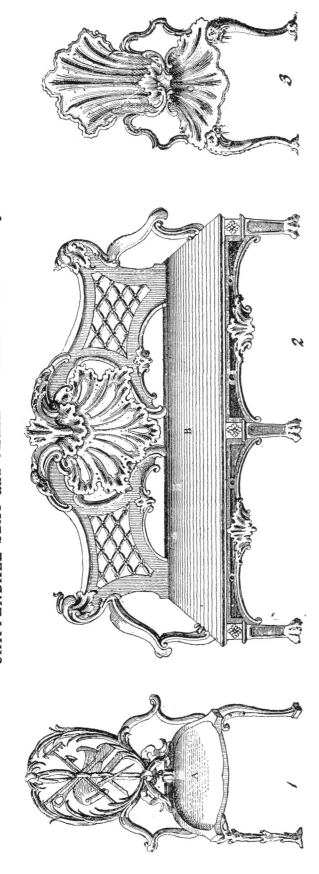

On this page are two designs of Chairs for Gardens, and a long Seat. Those marked 1 and 3 are proper for arbours and summer-houses, and for grottos; the Seat marked 2 may be placed in walks, or at the ends of avenues. The backs may be cut of the solid board, and fixed to the back edges of the seats. The length of Seat 2 is seven feet.

There are eight designs of French Chairs on Page 130 which may be executed to advantage. Some of them are intended to be open below at the back; which make them very light, without having a bad effect. The dimensions are the same as below, only that the highest part of the back is 2-ft. 5-ins.; but sometimes these dimensions vary, according to the bigness of the rooms they are intended for. A skilful workman may also lessen the carving, without any prejudice to the design. Both the backs and seats must be covered with tapestry, or other sort of needlework.

Two designs of French Chairs with Elbows, and for the greater variety the feet and elbows are different. The little moulding round the bottom of the edge of the rails has a good effect. The backs and seats are stuffed, and covered with Spanish leather, or damask; etc., and nailed with brass nails. The seat is 27-ins. wide in front, 22-ins. from the front to the back, and 23-ins. wide behind; the height of the back is 25-ins, and the height of the seat 14½-ins., including castors. These relate to the bottom centre one on Page 130, and Chair on lower right-hand corner on Page 136.

Various designs of Chairs for Patterns. The front feet are mostly different, for the greater choice. Care must be taken in drawing them at large. The seats look best when stuffed over the rails and have a brass border neatly chased; but are most commonly done with brass nails in one or two rows; and sometimes the nails are done to imitate fretwork. They are usually covered with the same stuff as the window-curtains. The height of the back seldom exceeds 22-ins. above the seats. Sometimes the dimensions are less, to suit the chairs to the rooms. These relate to Chairs on Pages 131, 132, 133, 135, and 136, without they are otherwise specified. Nos. 19, 20, 21, 22, 23, 26, and 27 on Page 133 are what Chippendale calls "Gothic Chairs."

Three designs of Chairs with Ribband-Backs. Several sets have been made which have given entire satisfaction. If any of the small ornaments should be thought superfluous they may be left out, without spoiling the design. If the seats are covered with red morocco they will have a fine effect. These relate to Nos. 12, 15, and 16 on Page 132.

CHIPPENDALE CHAIRS.   Middle 18th Century.

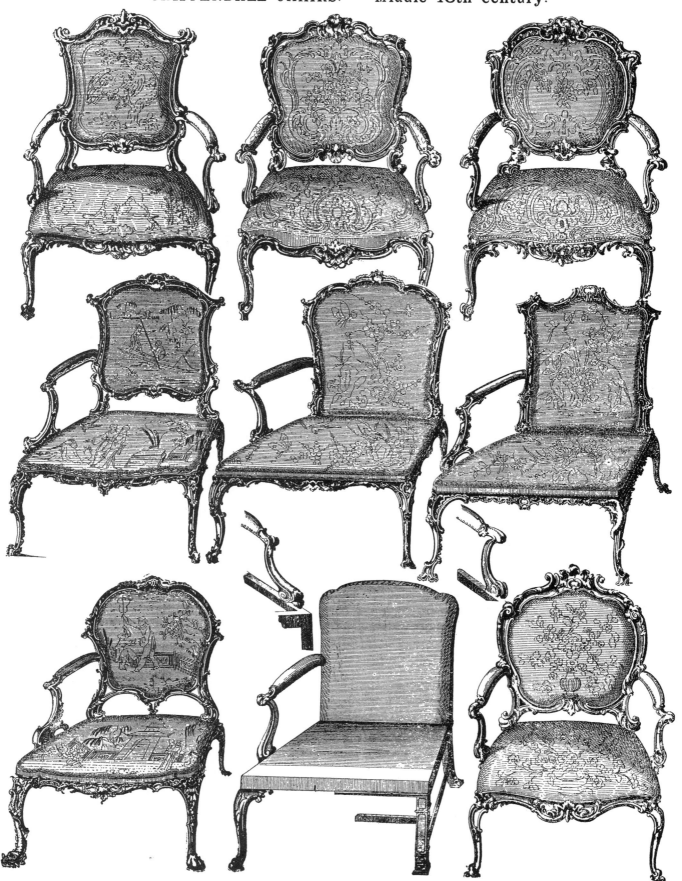

See Page 129

See Page 129

CHIPPENDALE CHAIRS. Middle 18th Century.

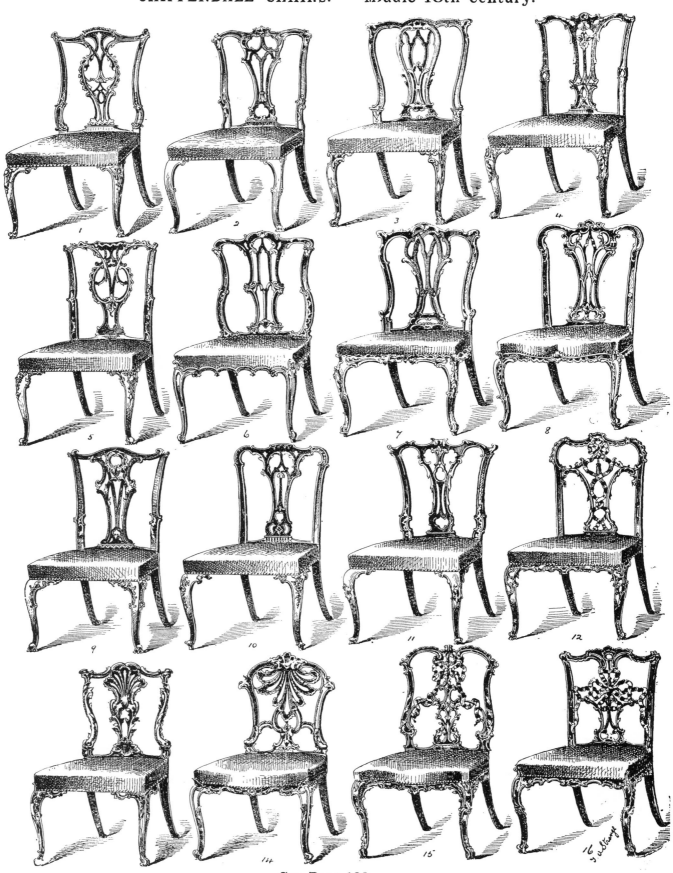

See Page 129.

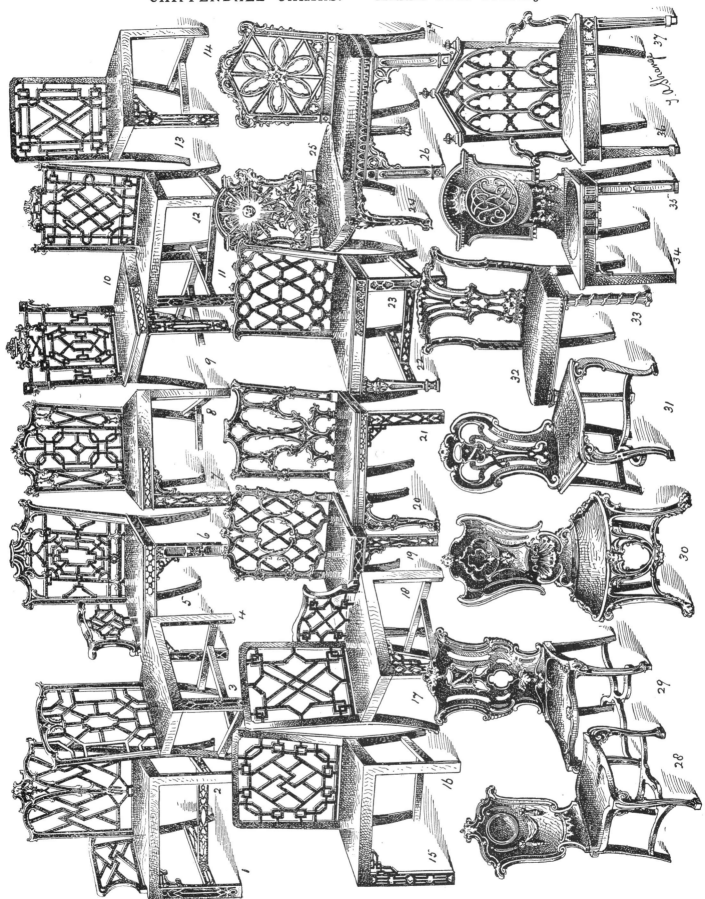

See Page 129.

CHIPPENDALE SOFAS.   Middle 18th Century.

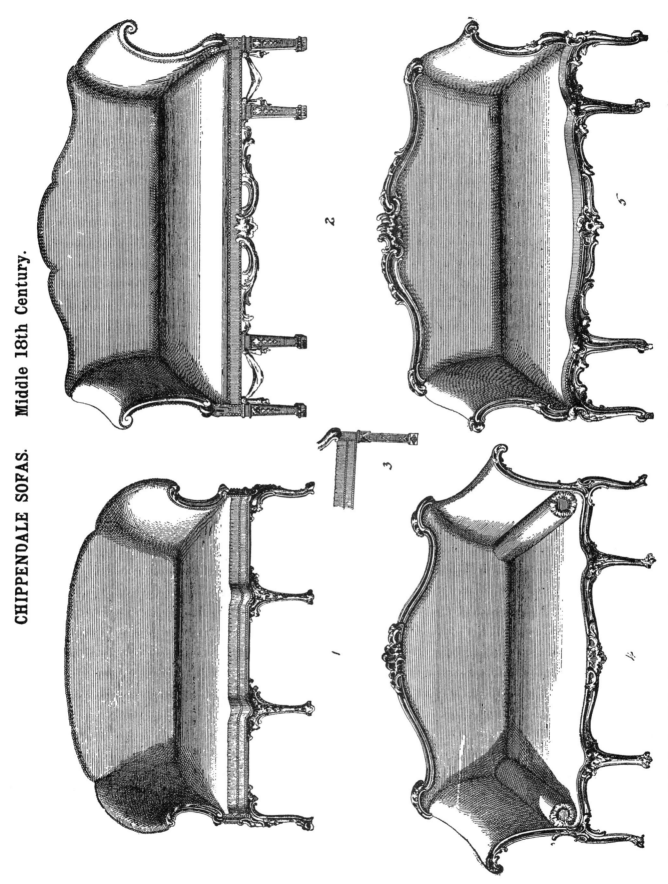

Six designs of Chairs for Halls, Passages, or Summer-houses. They may be made either of mahogany, or any other wood, and painted, and have commonly wooden seats. If the carving of the Chairs was thought superfluous, the outlines may be preserved, and they will look very well. The height of the Gothic back is 2-ft. 4-ins., and the others 1-ft. 11-ins., and the height of the seat 17 or 18-ins. If you divide the height of the backs in the number

CHIPPENADLE CHAIRS and SOFA.   Middle 18th Century.

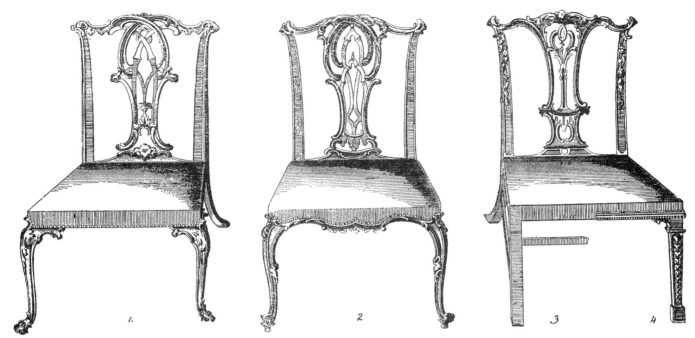

1.   *2.*   *3.*   *4.*

of inches given, you will have a measure to take off of the breadth of the circular parts of each back.   Arms, if required, may be put to those Chairs.   These relate to Nos. 28, 29, 30, 31, 34, 35, 36, 37, on Page 133.

CHIPPENDALE STOOLS, COUCHES and CHAIRS.

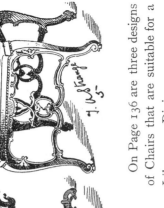

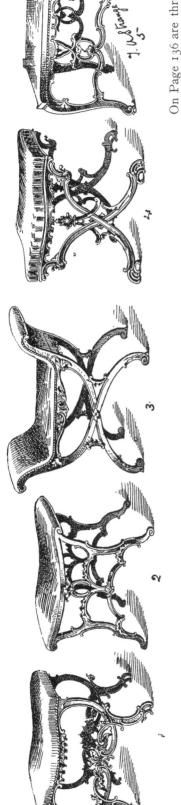

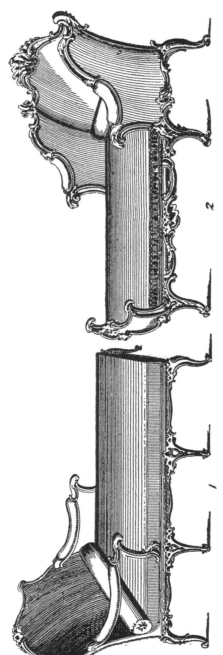

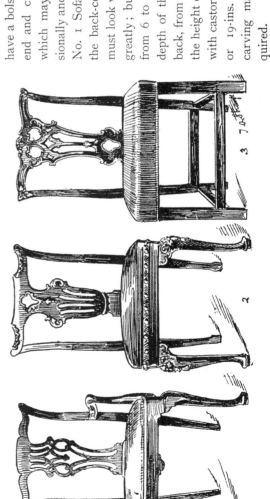

On Page 136 are three designs of Chairs that are suitable for a Library or Dining-room.

Nine designs of Chairs after the Chinese manner, and are very proper for a lady's dressing room; especially if it is hung with India paper. They will likewise suit Chinese Temples. They have commonly cane bottoms, with loose cushions; but, if required, may have stuffed seats and brass nails. These are Nos. 1 to 18, on Page 133.

Four designs of Sofas on Page 134. When made large, they have a bolster and pillow at each end and cushions at the back, which may be laid down occasionally and form a mattress. The No. 1 Sofa is designed to have the back-corners circular, which must look well. The sizes differ greatly; but commonly they are from 6 to 9, or 10-ft. long; the depth of the seat, from front to back, from 2-ft. 3-in. to 3-ft.; and the height of the seat 1-ft. 2-in., with castors. The scrolls are 18 or 19-ins. high. Part of the carving may be left out, if required.

CHIPPENDALE WRITING TABLES.   Middle 18th Century.

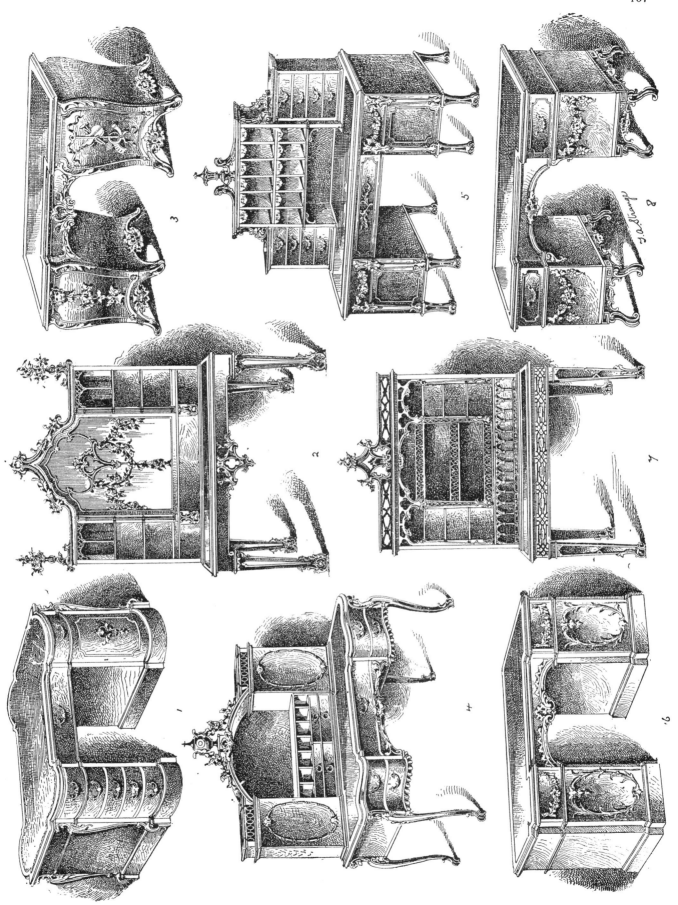

CHIPPENDALE WRITING TABLES.   Middle 18th Century.

On Page 135 is a design of a Sofa for a grand apartment, and will require great care in the execution, to make the several parts come in in such a manner that all the ornaments join without the least fault; and if the embossments all along are rightly managed, and gilt with burnished gold, the whole will have a noble appearance.   The carving at the top is the emblem of Watchfu'ness, Assiduity, and Rest. The pillows and cushions must not be omitted, though they are not in the design. The dimensions are 9-ft. long, without the scrolls; the broadest part of the seat, from front to back, 2-ft. 6-in.; the height of the back from the seat, 3-ft. 6-in.; and the height of the seat 1-ft. 2-ins., without castors.   I would advise the workman to make a model of it at large, before he begins to execute it.

Two designs of Couches on Page 136 are what the French call *Péché Mortel.* They are sometimes made to take asunder in the middle; one part makes a large Easy chair, and the other a stool, and the feet join in the middle; which looks badly.   Therefore, I would recommend their being made, as in these designs, with a pretty thick mattress.   The dimensions are 6-ft. long in the clear, and 2-ft. 6-in. to 3-ft. broad.

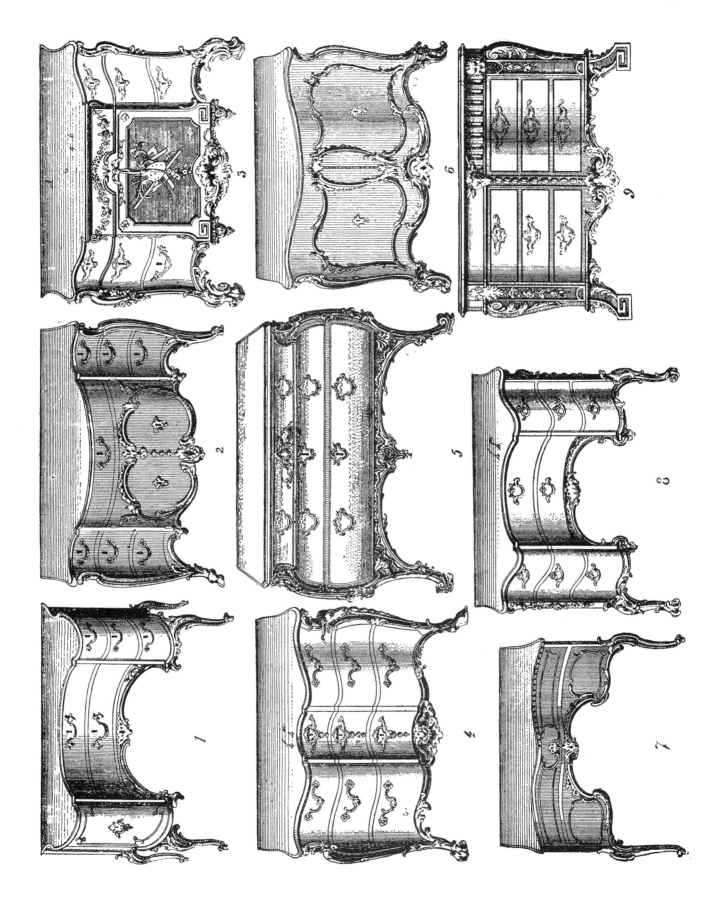

CHIPPENDALE COMMODE STOOLS

CHIPPENDALE WRITING TABLES, BOOK-CASES, etc.

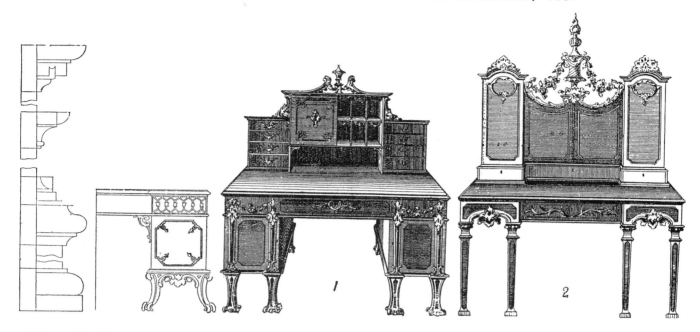

Chippendale shows a great variety of Writing Tables, Bureaux, Commodes, etc. No. 1 has a writing-drawer, which draws out at one end, and has tern feet to support it, details of which are to be found at No. 6, Page 142.

The first Writing Table on Page 138 is in the Gothic style; it has three-quarter pillars fixed on the edges of the doors, and they open with them. For details of this Table see Page 142.

In the plan of the above Table, with its mouldings; a, a, a, are the places where the pillars are fixed. A is the Plan of the pillars, and a scale Figure 2, Page 142.

Figure 2, Page 142, is a method for working and mitreing mouldings of different projection. Suppose B a quarter of a circle, or moulding, divided into nine parts, and the last division into two; then plan the moulding B at D, and divide it into the same number of parts, and draw the diagonal, suppose, L, L; and where the divisions intersect in L, L, draw the

COMMODE BUREAU TABLES.

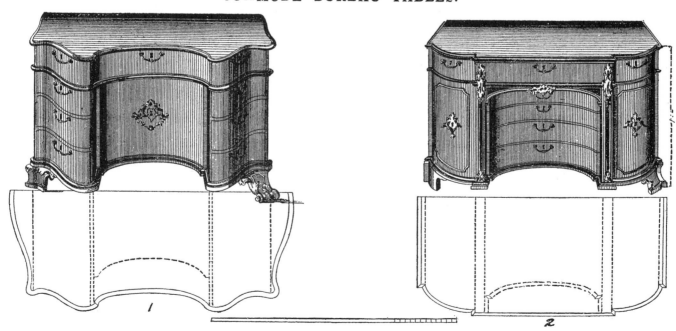

CHIPPENDALE COMMODE TABLES.   Middle 18th Century.

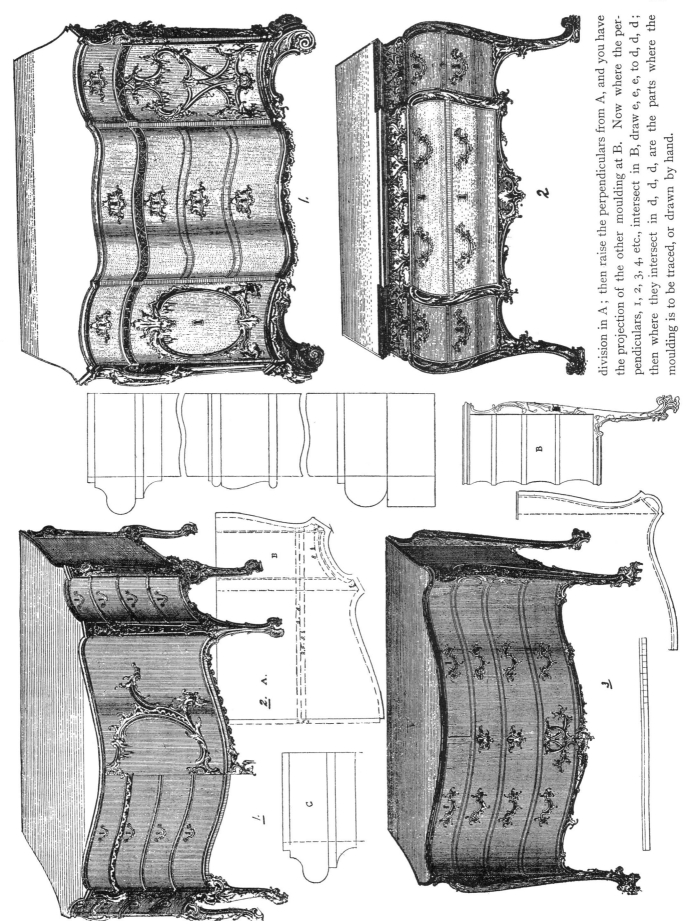

division in A; then raise the perpendiculars from A, and you have the projection of the other moulding at B. Now where the perpendiculars, 1, 2, 3, 4, etc, intersect in B, draw e, e, e, to d, d, d; then where they intersect in d, d, d, are the parts where the moulding is to be traced, or drawn by hand.

Details of CHIPPENDALE WRITING TABLES, etc.

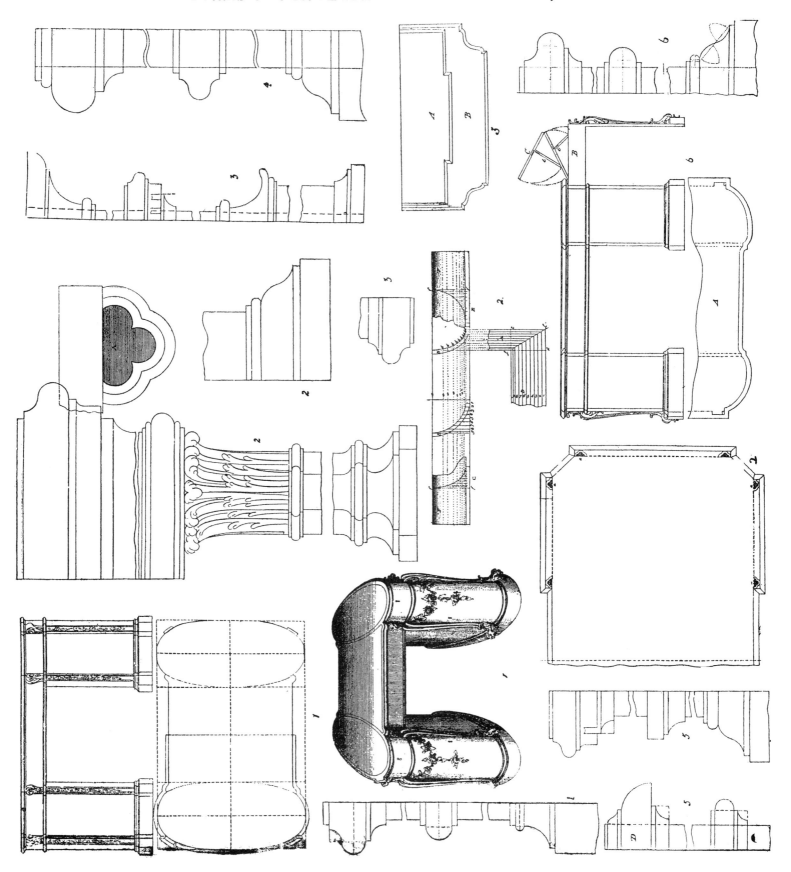

Details of CHIPPENDALE WRITING TABLES, etc.

CHIPPENDALE WRITING TABLES.   Middle 18th Century.

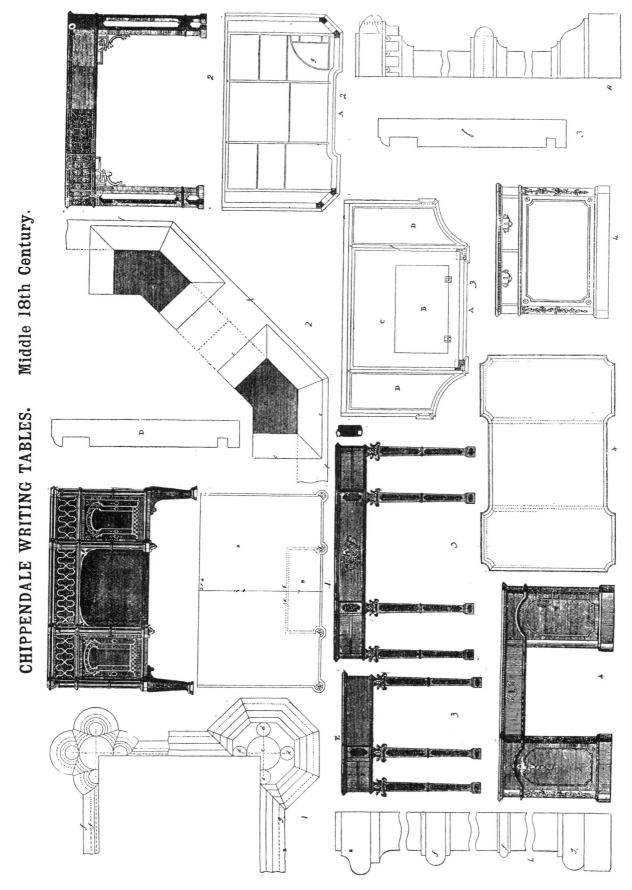

To cut the Mitres.   Suppose the mouldings worked at F, F, and fit for the mitres to be cut, draw a line across the mouldings f, f, f, etc., then take the distance c, L, and set it off at C, f, after the divisions at A; then take the distance e, L, and set it off at E, f, after the divisions at D.   Raise perpendiculars at C and E; then draw the parallels at e, e, e, to the perpendiculars C and E, and where they intersect are the points where you are to cut, directed by the diagonal line L, L.

The centre large Table on Page 138 has circular doors at each corner.   No. 1 on Page 139 may have either doors or drawers at the end.

HANGING MIRRORS, MAHOGANY, and GILT ORNAMENTS. First half of 18th Century.

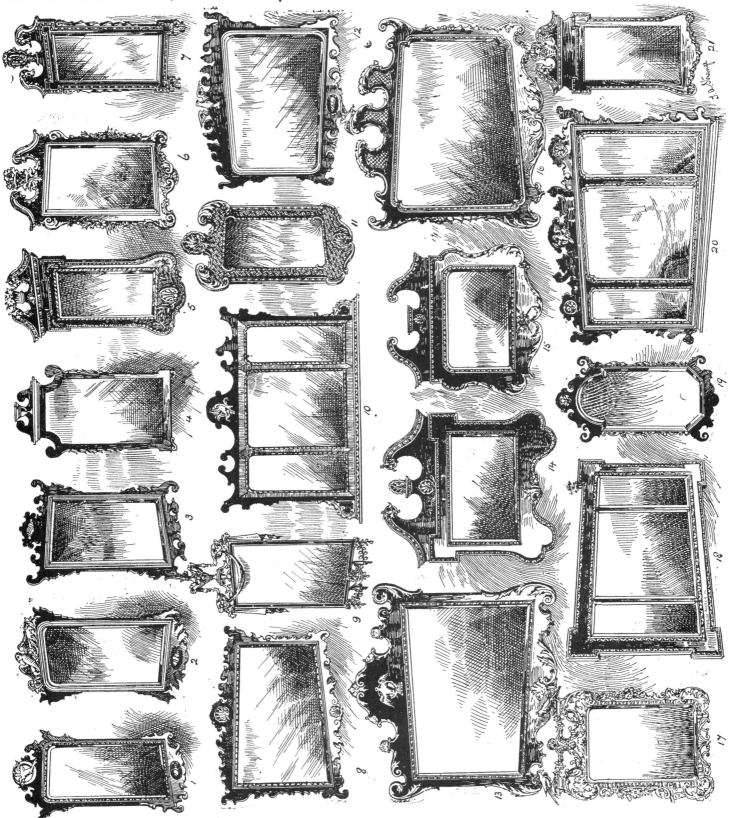

For particulars see Page 157.

ORGANS by T. CHIPPENDALE.

Two small organs suitable for a music room. These organs differ in size according to the number of stops, and to the size of the room.

The centre organ, No. 2, is fit for a small church. The middle part projects; the breaks of the pedestals are in a circular form to the end parts. The end parts go off at the corners, and make an angle in front, which may be perceived by the shaded parts of the pedestal. If the ornaments on the tower in the centre should be disapproved, they may be omitted. The contrasting segmental curves in the pediments tend to show that in these designs Chippendale was largely influenced by the Louis XV. style, and yet there is sufficient in the general effect to remind one of the style of the woodwork in Wren's city churches.

ORGANS by T. CHIPPENDALE.

Two small organs suitable for music-room—one in the Gothic style, and one to match the architecture then in vogue—they have little ornament, and should be easy of execution.

No. 2, an organ in what Chippendale calls the "Gothic Taste"; he further says that "as most of the Cathedral Churches are of the Gothic Architecture, it is a pity that the organs are not better adapted to that style." The out-pipes are returned upon the corners, to complete the spires; and if the ends fall with the same sweep as in the front, it would have a good effect. These designs help to show the wonderful versatility of the last century cabinet-makers, who seem to have been trained to make almost any-thing in the way of cabinet work.

148

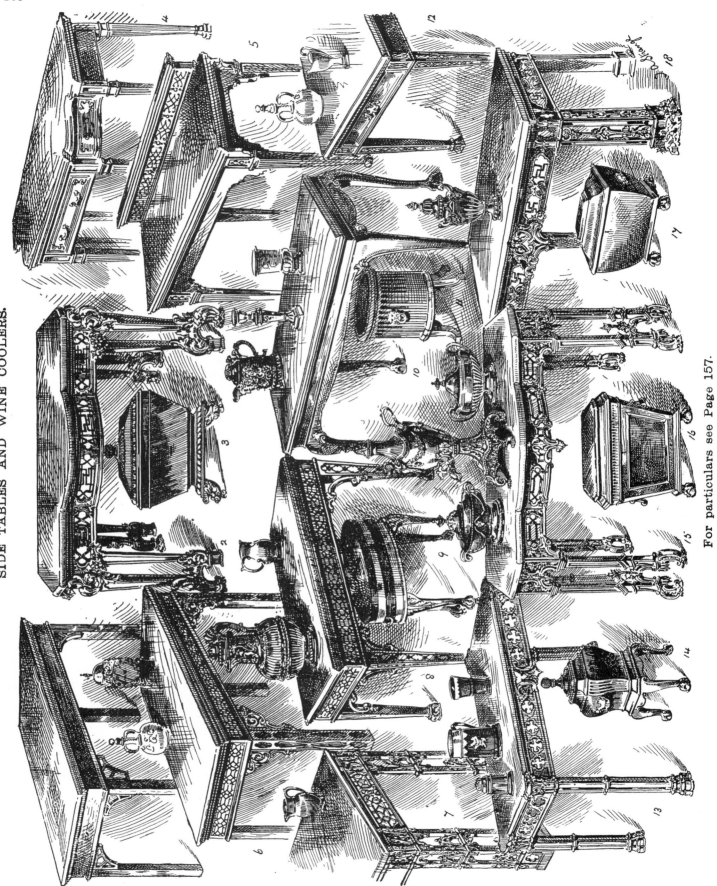

T. CHIPPENDALE, INCE and MAYHEW, MANWARING, and others.
SIDE TABLES AND WINE COOLERS.

For particulars see Page 157.

T. CHIPPENDALE, INCE and MAYHEW, MANWARING, and others.

For particulars see page 157.

CONSOLE TABLE,
VASE STANDS,
AND CHAIRS OF A
LOUIS XV. CHARACTER.

For Particulars see Page 155.

For particulars see Page 155.

T. CHIPPENDALE, SHERATON, HEPPELWHITE and others.

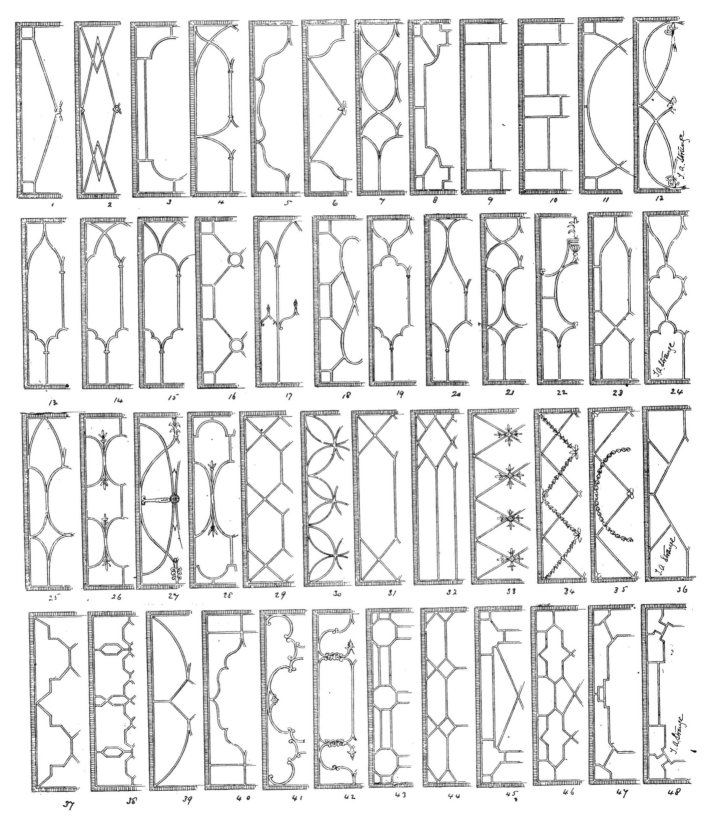

BOOKCASE DOORS, etc.

For particulars see Page 155.

T. CHIPPENDALE, SHERATON, HEPPELWHITE and others.

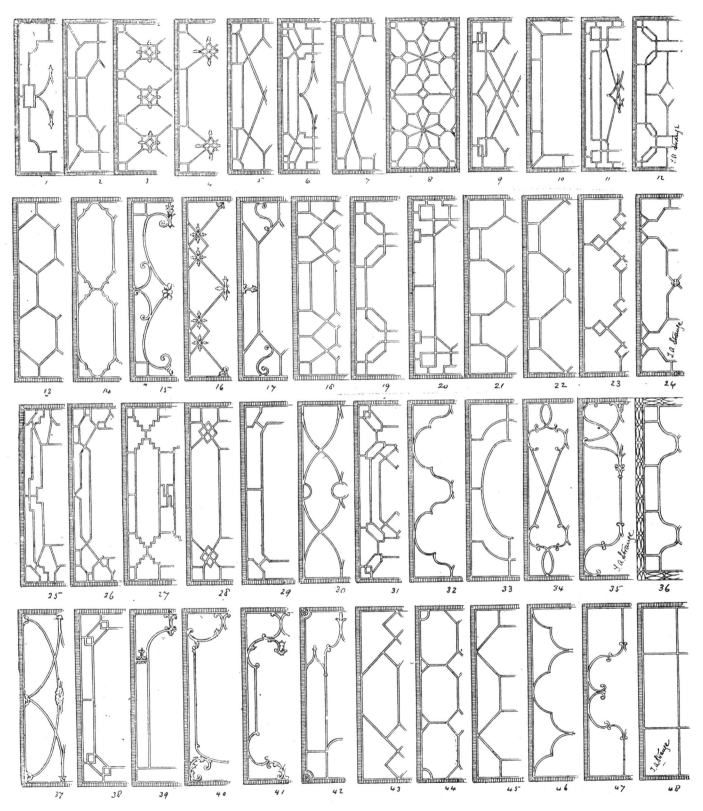

BOOKCASE DOORS, etc.

For particulars see Page 155.

CHIPPENDALE, SHERATON, HEPPELWHITE, and others.

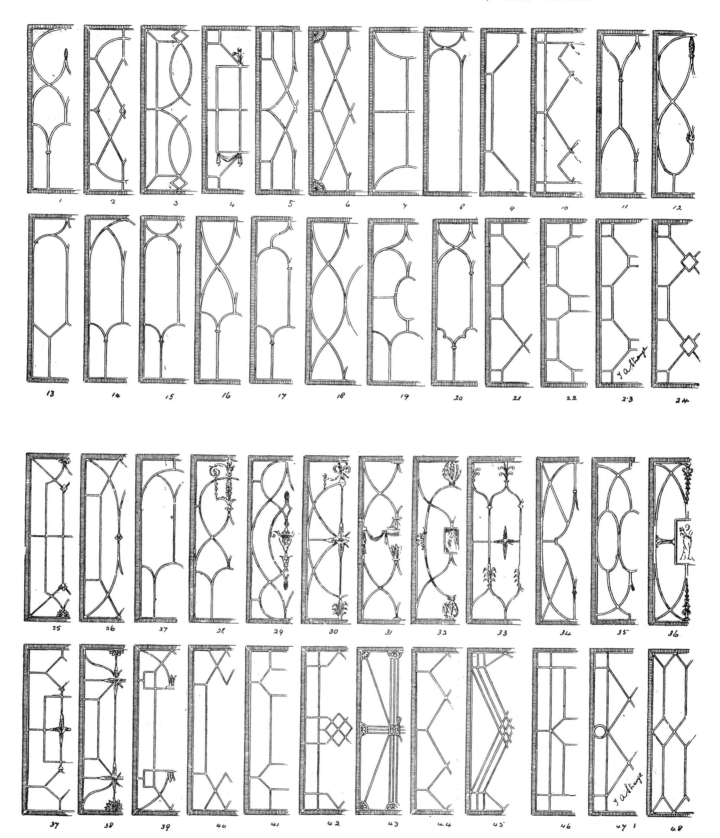

For particulars see Page 155.

CHIPPENDALE, SHERATON, HEPPELWHITE and others.

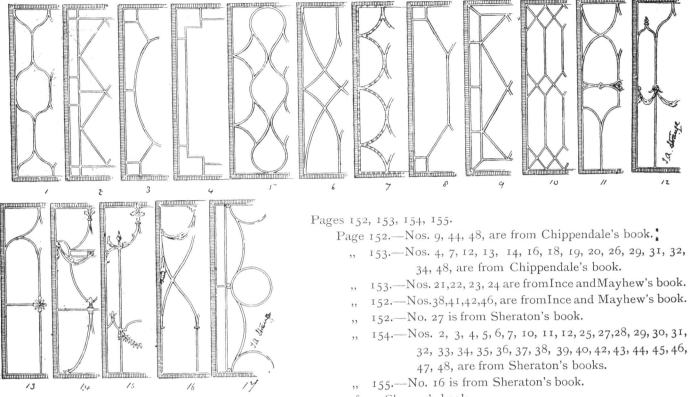

Pages 152, 153, 154, 155.

Page 152.—Nos. 9, 44, 48, are from Chippendale's book.

",, 153.—Nos. 4, 7, 12, 13, 14, 16, 18, 19, 20, 26, 29, 31, 32, 34, 48, are from Chippendale's book.

",, 153.—Nos. 21, 22, 23, 24 are from Ince and Mayhew's book.

",, 152.—Nos. 38, 41, 42, 46, are from Ince and Mayhew's book.

",, 152.—No. 27 is from Sheraton's book.

",, 154.—Nos. 2, 3, 4, 5, 6, 7, 10, 11, 12, 25, 27, 28, 29, 30, 31, 32, 33, 34, 35, 36, 37, 38, 39, 40, 42, 43, 44, 45, 46, 47, 48, are from Sheraton's books.

",, 155.—No. 16 is from Sheraton's book.

Page 152.—Nos. 14, 15, 16, 17, 18, 19, 20, 21, 22, 23, 24, 25 are from Shearer's book.

",, 154.—Nos. 13, 14, 15, 16, 17, 18, 19, 20, 21, 22, 23, 24 are from Shearer's book.

",, 152.—Nos. 28, 29, 30, 33, 34, 35 are from Heppelwhite's book.

",, 155.—Nos. 9, 10, 11, 12, 13, 14, 15, are from Heppelwhite's book.

Pages 150 and 151.—No. 3 (Page 150), is what Chippendale calls a Pier Glass and Table, but what we should call now a Console Table. It is carved and gilt with marble-top, and is of a Louis XV. design.

Page 150.—The two chairs, Nos. 4 and 5, are what Chippendale calls French chairs. The seats are 27 inches wide in front, 22 inches from the front to the back, and 23 inches wide behind. The height of seat is $14\frac{1}{2}$ inches including castors. The height of the back is 2 feet 5 inches. But sometimes these dimensions vary according to the size of the room. A skilful workman can also lessen the carving without any prejudice to the design. Both the backs and seats must be covered with tapestry or other sort of needlework. The patterns on the seats and backs are after the Chinese style, which was fashionable about that time.

Nos. 1 and 2 (Page 150) are Candle-stands 3 feet 6 inches to 4 feet 6 inches high, which, if finely executed with burnished gold, will have a very good effect; they can also be made in mahogany.

No. 2, on Page 151, is a Dressing Table for a lady. The end parts open with doors. In the recess are two drawers. On the top is a large looking-glass, which comes to the front with joint hinges, and over it a compartment; and on each side, end parts, with doors that represent drawers—a very favourite device of Chippendale and his contemporaries. The ornaments should be gilt in burnished gold; or the whole work may be japanned, and the drapery may be silk damask, with gold fringes and tassels.

No. 3 (Page 151) is a Tea-table, or table to hold china.

Pipkins in Copper and Brass.

T. CHIPPENDALE, J. CRUNDEN, and others.

For particulars see Page 157.

T. CHIPPENDALE, J. CRUNDEN, and others
FRETS.

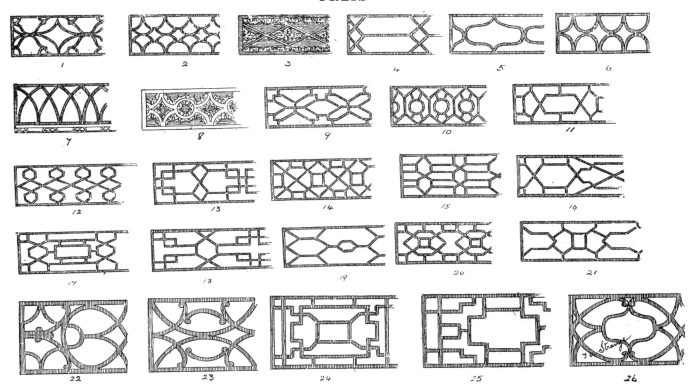

The hanging mirrors on page 145 were common during the earlier part of the 18th Century. They were made in mahogany, sometimes with inlaid shells as Nos. 1, 2, and 3, and sometimes with gilt pediments. The moulding round the mirror was usually a gilt leaf, and the edges of the glass had a bevel, much slighter and smaller than is used now.

Pages 148 and 149.—These were the sideboards of the period (middle 18th Century), often made to go in recesses of walls, and were sometimes of a good length. Nos. 1, 2, 6, 7, 8, 13, 15, and 17, on page 148, and No. 7, on page 149, are Chippendale's.

The side tables, having cut-through rails and legs, should have wood tops, as they are hardly strong enough for the marble tops which they generally had.

Nos. 1, 2, 5, 6, 10, and 15 are Ince and Mayhew's, whose work, published about the same time as Chippendale's, was dedicated to a nobleman—as was usual during this period, and in this case to George Spencer, Duke of Marlborough, Marquis of Blandford.

The wine coolers often had brass bands round them—like No. 9, on page 148, which is at Locock Abbey.

The side tables on page 149, Nos. 3, 11, 12, 13, and 18, are by Manwaring, who published his work in 1766; he calls them slab tables.

Pages 156 and 157.—Nos. 1, 3, 4, 11, 14, 25, 27, 31, 32, 34, 35, 36, and 37, on page 156; and Nos. 1, 3, 4, 5, 6, 7, 8, 22, 23, and 26, on page 157, are from Crunden's book of frets, the rest are Chippendale's.

J. Crunden was born in Sussex, and was the pupil of Henry Holland. He published several works; among others, "Designs for Ceilings," 1765; "Convenient and Ornamental Architecture," 1768; "The Joiner and Cabinet-Maker's Darling," 1770; and "The Carpenter's Compositions for Chinese Railings, Gates, etc.," 1770. From the title of this last work, which was dedicated to His Grace the Duke of Newcastle, readers will learn the source of his inspiration in designing the frets here illustrated. He died in 1828. Among his designs for ceilings are ornamental centres illustrating such subjects as "Fame sounding her Trumpet," "Cupid and his Bow and Arrow," trophies, birds, squirrels; a complete sporting ceiling, including the "Death of the Fox," etc., etc., and fables of the "Fox and the Grapes" and "Stork, Crow and Goose."

CHIPPENDALE BOOKCASES and BUREAU BOOKCASES.

In quoting a number of an article, the number of the page must also be quoted as each page is numbered separately.

CHIPPENDALE BOOKCASES and BUREAU BOOKCASES.

Chippendale Bookcases Etc.

Readers will notice among these bookcases some that are based on the Gothic, which style Chippendale and his contemporaries tried to revive, but their efforts appear to have been very feeble. There is also what is called "Chinese Chippendale," which is, no doubt, based on some of the publications of Sir William Chambers, who had visited China, and who published some Chinese designs, although panels imitating the Chinese and Japanese styles of decorations had been introduced earlier in the century; but "Chippendale" is mainly based on the Louis XV. style. These are made in mahogany, and have the Rococo ornaments (from the words *rocaille coquille*, rock and shell curves) which are peculiar to this style. This Rococo work lends itself well to show off gilding. The bureaux illustrated above were often used in bedrooms, which, in the early part of the century, were sometimes used in boudoirs or studios, so that a piece of furniture which could quickly lock up papers, letters, etc., was a desideratum.

159

CLOTHES PRESSES

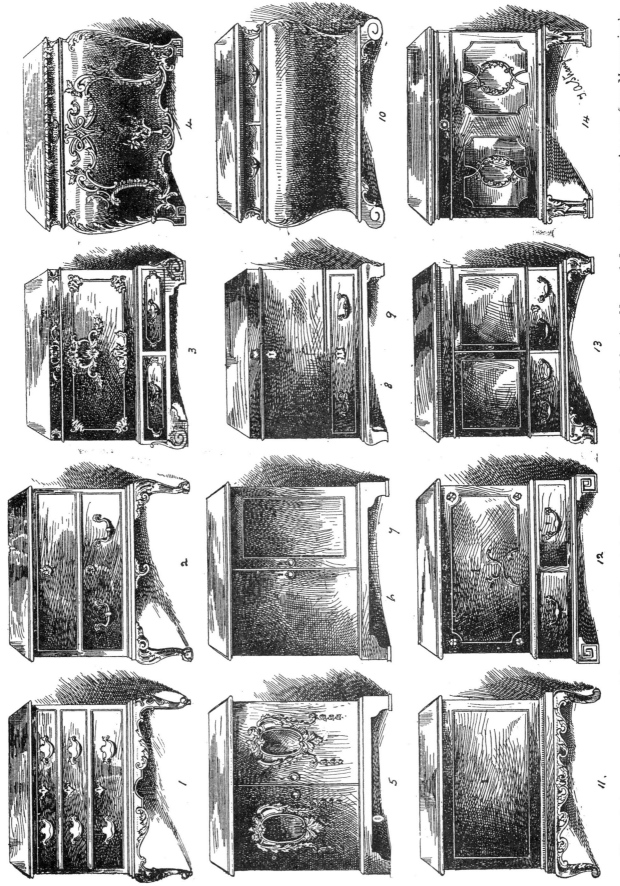

These clothes presses were much in use during this period. Nos. 3 and 4 are Ince and Mayhew's; Nos. 5, 6, 8, 9, 10, 12, 13, and 14 are from Manwaring's book; and the rest are Chippendale's. A few more of these are illustrated elsewhere. (See Index.)

GRANDFATHER CLOCKS.

One-Year Clock at Hampton Court Palace; late 17th Century, by Daniel Quare.

In possession of Baron Rothschild. English make, by H. E. Batterson, London.
See Page 170.

Black and Gold Case, Eight-Day Clock by J. Harrison, of Burrow, 1715 Guildhall Museum, London.

GRANDFATHER CLOCKS.

18th Century.
Louis XV. design.

18th Century, with Panels of Chinese design.

Walnut, inlaid.
See Page 174.

Late 17th and early 18th Century, Walnut, Inlaid Marqueterie, from South Kensington Museum, now called the Victoria and Albert Museum, London.

GRANDFATHER CLOCKS.

Readers who are desirous of studying this branch of art should buy " Old Clocks and Watches, and their Makers," by F. G. Britten ; published by Batsford of High Holborn, London. Of course, it relates especially to the inside works. He gives a list of all the old makers, their qualifications, and the improvements they introduced, etc., etc. The work is extensively illustrated.

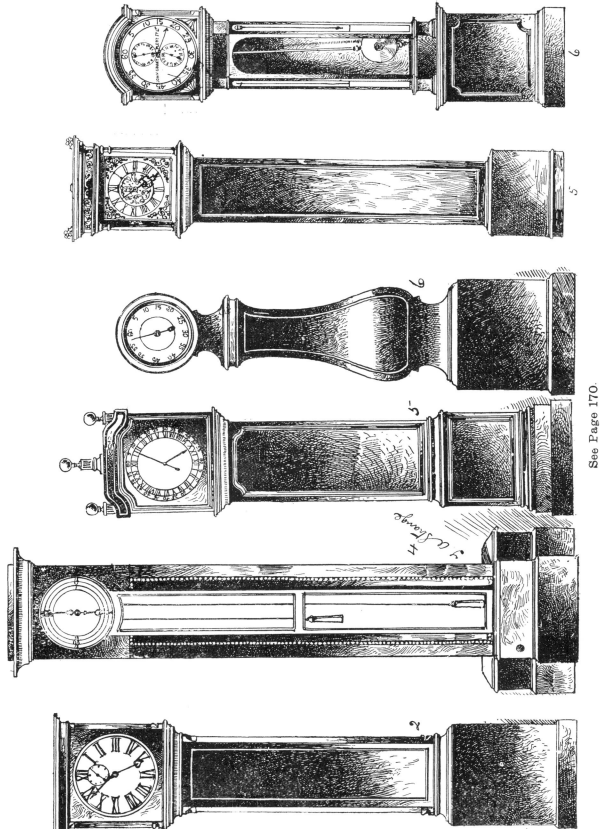

See Page 170.

CHIPPENDALE GRANDFATHER CLOCKS.

See Page 170.

CHIPPENDALE GRANDFATHER CLOCKS.

See Page 170.

CHIPPENDALE BRACKET CLOCKS.

These four Bracket Clocks were made in Mahogany, and, as their name suggests, were carried on brackets.

See Page 170.

CHIPPENDALE GIRANDOLES.

See Page 170.

CHIPPENDALE GIRANDOLES and BRACKETS.

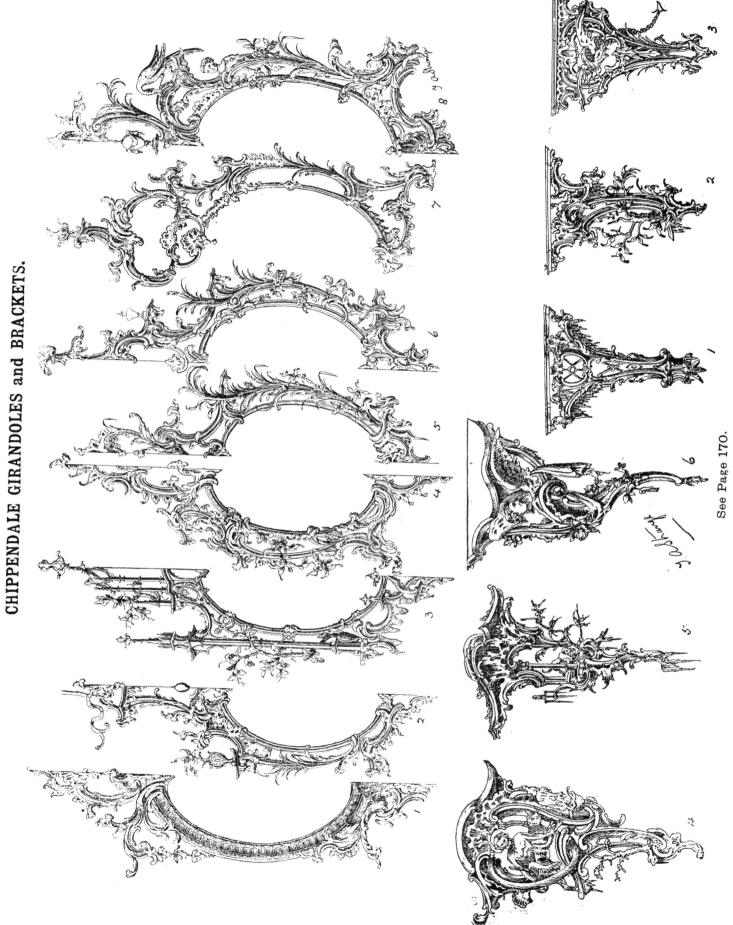

See Page 170.

CHIPPENDALE MIRRORS and BRACKETS.

See Page 170.

Page 161.—No. 1 is at Hampton Court Palace, and was made by the famous Daniel Quare, the contemporary of the equally famous Tompion. It is a one-year clock, in light wood (maple) with elegantly chased brass work on plinth, and figures in brass on top. It has the herring-bone band round panels—an ornament peculiar to this period (late 17th Century).

The large centre one, from the collection of Baron J. Rothschild, is of English make, and of the time of George I. It is in walnut wood, enriched with copper mounts. Some of the smaller figures are allegorical. The dial is surrounded by a carved copper border, and is surmounted by a figure of Abundance. There are several pieces of ornament in the Chinese style, which was fashionable about this period (1720). The maker's name is H. E. Batterson London.

No. 3 is a long eight-day clock in the Guildhall Museum, London, by J. Harrison, of Burrow. It is dated 1715, and has a black and gold case.

Page 162.—No. 1 is in South Kensington Museum, London (now called Victoria and Albert Museum). It is in walnut, the inlay dark on light ground; early 18th Century; marqueterie of various woods.

No. 2, Clock in marqueterie case, by Henry Poissons, London early 18th Century. The ground work of the marqueterie is in light walnut, the marqueterie being both darker and lighter than the ground, but the whole is light in effect. From Victoria and Albert Museum, London.

No. 3 has a marqueterie case, and the twisted column, which is a legacy from the Jacobean period, although the twist was used during the reign of William III. and Mary, and Queen Anne; but it was not this straight twist, but one thin at the top and much thicker at the bottom, as is seen in the altar rails in Sir Christopher Wren's churches. This clock is by Mansell Bennett, of Charing Cross. The marqueterie is of Dutch design (pinks, tulips, quaint birds, etc.) and is on dark ground. In Victoria and Albert Museum London.

No. 4 has a walnut case with geometric bands of inlay; late 17th Century. The Clock with Chinese designs in panels belongs to the early part of 18th Century.

PICTURE FRAMES and MIRRORS.

See Page 175.

CHIPPENDALE CHIMNEY-PIECES and FIRE SCREENS.

For particulars see Pages 175 and 176.

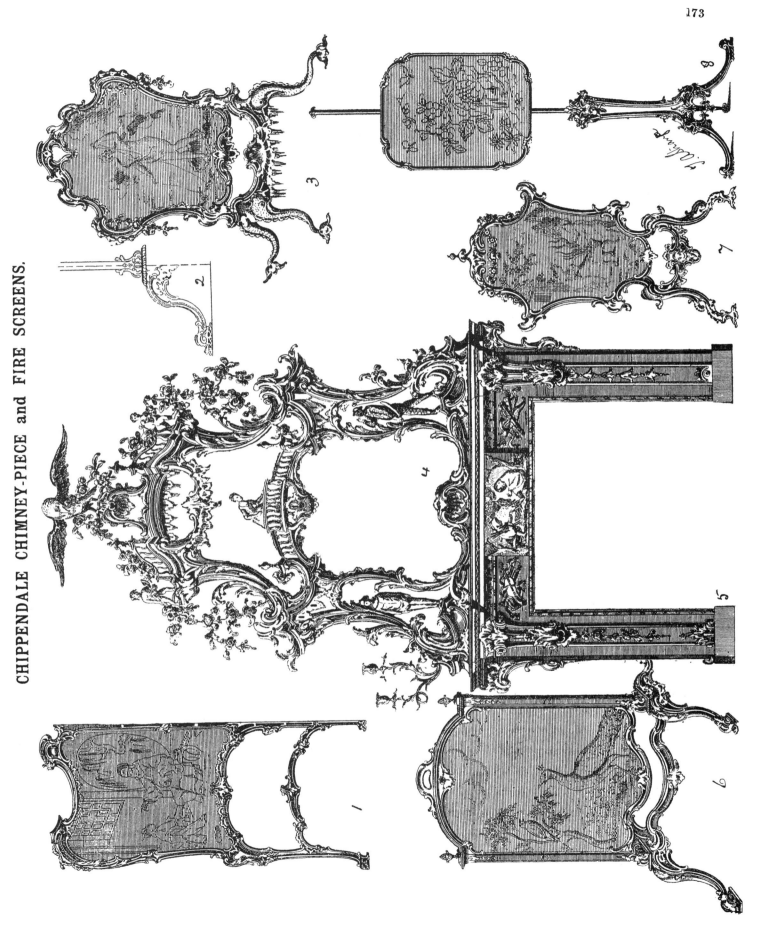

CHIPPENDALE CHIMNEY-PIECE and FIRE SCREENS.

173

CHIPPENDALE CHIMNEY-PIECES.

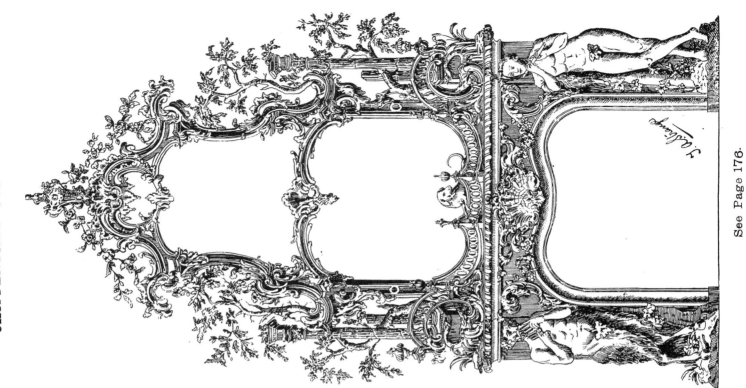

See Page 176.

The four large Girandoles on Page 167 are based on the Louis XV. style, and show groups emblematical of war, paintings, etc.

The oval Girandoles on Page 168 are also of the Louis XV. style, with the exception of No. 3, which is based partly on the "Gothic Taste," as the makers of that day called it. The Brackets on Page 168 are of the same period. No. 6 shows the irregular shaped shelf, one side being different to the other.

The large Girandole, or Mirror, on left of Page 169 has a group in the "Chinese Taste." The long Mirrors on Page 170 were favourites with Chippendale and seem to be elaborate copies suggested by the older Florentine Mirrors.

The Picture frames on Page 171 are very elaborate, with emblems suggestive of the French designs of Le Brun.

The Screens on Pages 172 and 173 are of the usual Louis XV. style, with needlework centres mostly in the "Chinese Taste"; some with flowers, and others with nymphs in the "French Taste." No. 1 on Page 173 is meant to have another wing or wings on straight edge.

Eight Shields, which, as they are often placed very high, should be very bold. They may serve as ornaments to pediments.

CHIPPENDALE PIER GLASSES.

These Pier-Glasses were sometimes placed over tables somewhat similar to our modern Console Tables.

The Chimney-pieces on Pages 172, 173, and 174 were mostly carved in pine and gilt, and have the usual mixture of ornaments in the "Chinese" and "Gothic Tastes." Chippendale, speaking of these, says "a skilful carver may, in the execution of these designs, give full scope to his capacity." The space in Over-mantels were filled with glass.

Chippendale says of No. 5, on Page 173, "Chimney-piece which requires great care in the execution. The embossments must be very bold, and the foliage neatly laid down, and the whole properly relieved. The top may be gilt, as likewise some other ornamental parts. The lower part would be in marble."

Of No. 1, on Page 174, he says "a Chimney-piece of Architecture intermixed with trophies," etc.

Of No. 2, on Page 174, "a Chimney-piece of Architecture, Sculpture, and Ruins. Great care will be necessary in executing the upper part. The ornaments must be carved very bold, so that the Ruins may serve as bas-relief. The under part should likewise be very bold, and the dog entirely free. It would not be amiss if the whole was modelled before it began to be executed."

The Picture-frame on Page 175 is called "A Frame for a Picture of an Engagement at Sea."

Three Brackets for Marble Slabs.

No. 4 may be the front rail to any of them. It must be remembered that marble-tops were extensively used about 1760, and earlier.

CHIPPENDALE
GIRANDOLES.
Middle 18th Century.

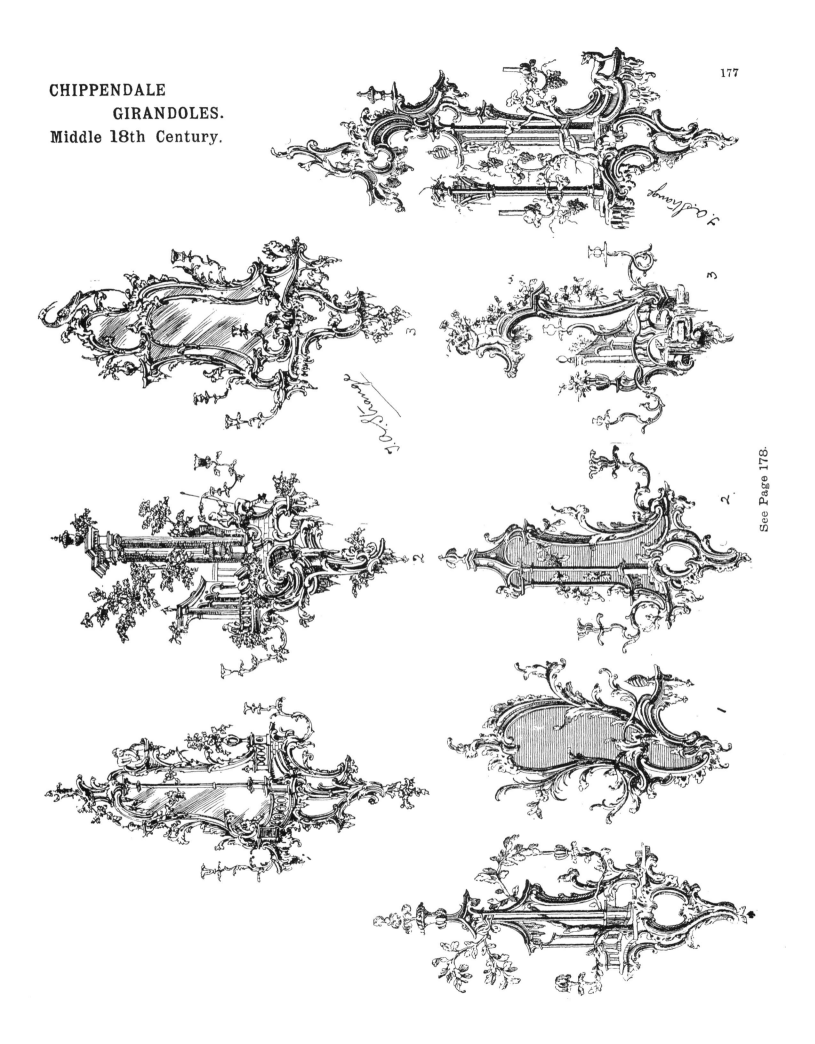

See Page 178.

CHIPPENDALE BUST STANDS. Middle 18th Century.

Eight Girandoles on Page 177.—These can be made in pine and gilt, or could be made in mahogany. They are designed to hold candles. No. 2 is a piece of ruins intermixed with various ornaments. These designs help to show Chippendale's wonderful versatility.

The six Pedestals illustrated on this page are from Chippendale's book   No. 2 is emblematic of Music, and Nos. 3 and 4 of War.

During the early part of the 18th Century there sprang up in France, England, Holland, etc., a taste for " Chinese " ornament, and one of our most noted architects of that time, Sir William Chambers, published a book on it—he having travelled in China. There also came into " fashion " a revival of the " Gothic Taste," as it was then called. Authors of that period seem to have been very particular to describe their designs as being in the " fashion." Chippendale for instance on his title page, describes his designs as being in " the most Fashionable Taste." He thinks it prudent to add—" Upon the whole, I have here given no Design but what may be executed with Advantage by the hands of a Skilful Workman, though some of the Profession have been diligent enough to represent them (especially those after the Gothic and Chinese Manner) as so many Specious Drawings, impossible to be worked off by any Mechanic whatsoever. I will not scruple to attribute this to Malice, Ignorance, and Inability ; and I am confident I can convince all Noblemen, Gentlemen, or others, who will honour me with their Commands, that every Design in the Book can be improved, both as to Beauty and Enrichment, in the execution of it, by Their Most Obedient Servant, THOMAS CHIPPENDALE."

CHIPPENDALE CANDLE-STANDS   Middle 18th Century.

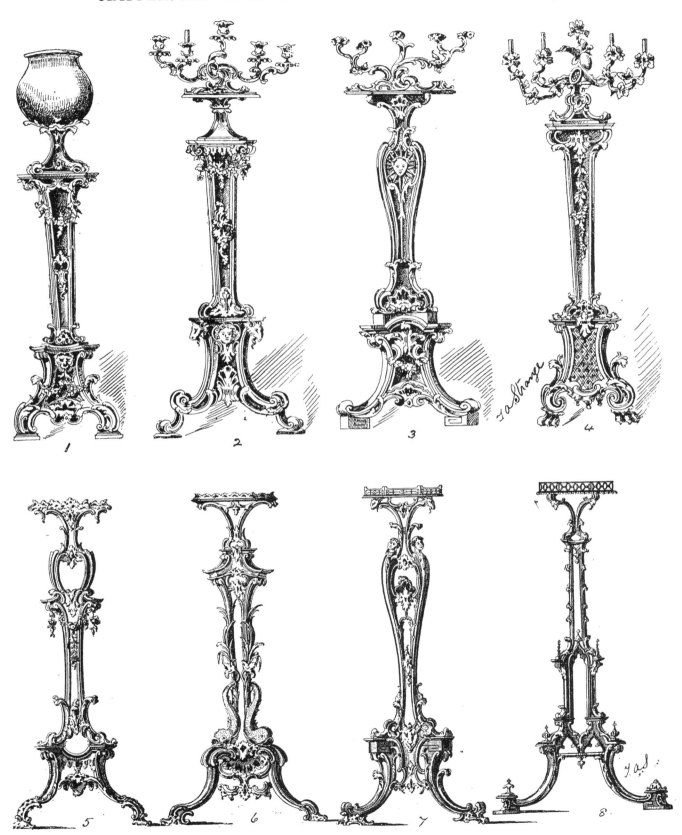

See Pag 180.

CHIPPENDALE CANDLE-STANDS. Middle 18th Century.

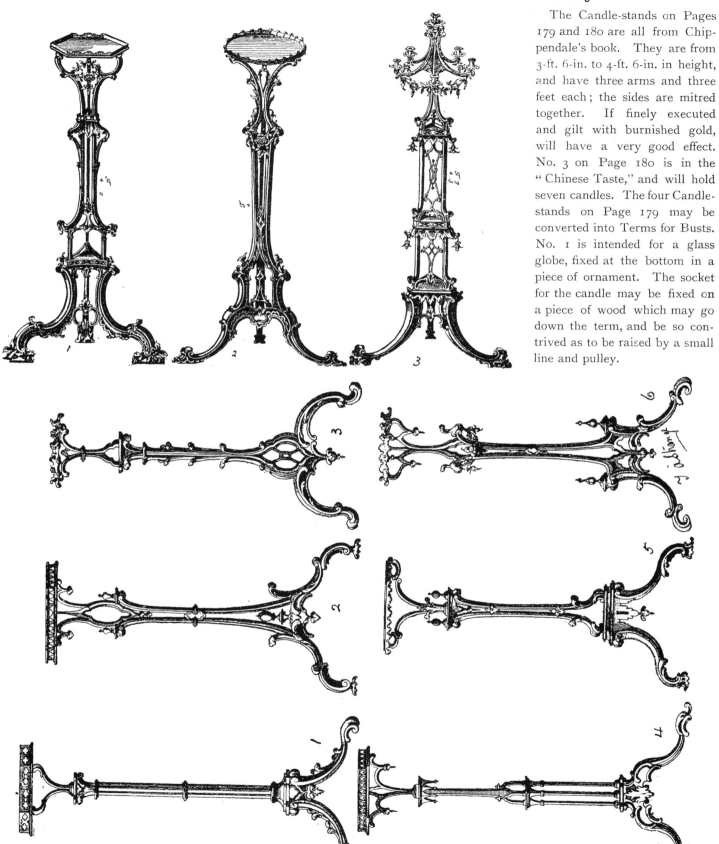

The Candle-stands on Pages 179 and 180 are all from Chippendale's book. They are from 3-ft. 6-in. to 4-ft. 6-in. in height, and have three arms and three feet each; the sides are mitred together. If finely executed and gilt with burnished gold, will have a very good effect. No. 3 on Page 180 is in the "Chinese Taste," and will hold seven candles. The four Candle-stands on Page 179 may be converted into Terms for Busts. No. 1 is intended for a glass globe, fixed at the bottom in a piece of ornament. The socket for the candle may be fixed on a piece of wood which may go down the term, and be so contrived as to be raised by a small line and pulley.

CHIPPENDALE SHELVES FOR BOOKS, etc.　Middle 18th Century.

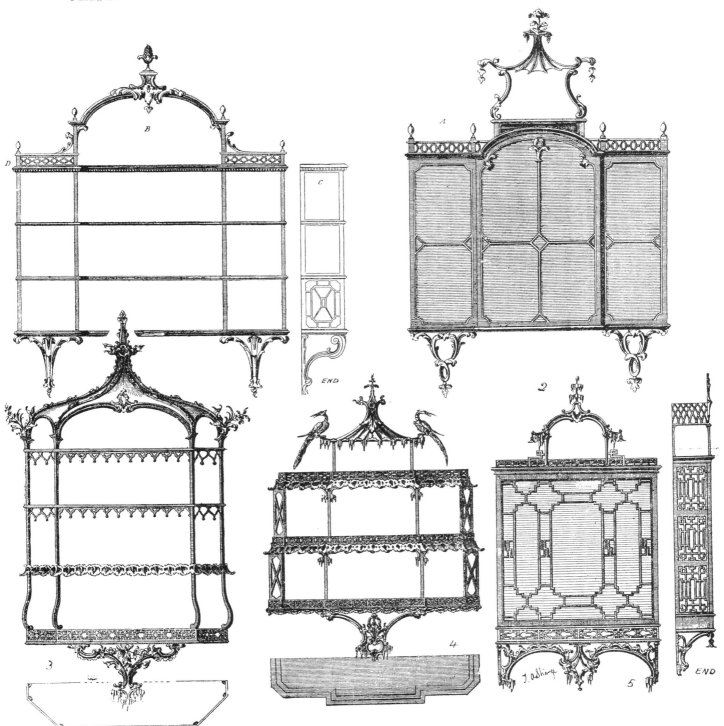

Nos. 1 and 2 on this page are two Shelves for Books or China.　No 2 is intended for glass in the doors and ends.　No. 1 has no doors, nor frets on the edges of the shelves, but may, if desired; under the end parts are brackets which make a good finishing.　Nos. 3 and 4 are Book or China Shelves with Canopies.　No. 5 is a Hanging China Cabinet; the canopy is pierced, and the fret at bottom may be two drawers.

No. 1 on Page 182 is a Shelf intended for japanning; the fretwork on the sides is designed for doors.　The supporters of the canopies of the ends stand at the corners, and are joined in the middle; the feet are pierced through.　No. 2, cupboards at sides.　No. 3, Shelf for China.　The canopy is a kind of dome, pierced through.　The plan, profile, and section are on the right.

CHIPPENDALE CHINA or BOOK SHELVES. Middle 18th Century.

See Page 181.

1

2

3

PLAN of Nº 3

END

J. A. Strange

CHIPPENDALE'S DESIGNS for BRASS HINGES and ESCUTCHEONS.   Middle 18th Century.

The three Stands on Page 185 are for china vases, and may be either gilt or japanned.

The four Terms for Busts would look well in Mahogany.

On Page 151 there is a similar design to the last vase stand with cherubs on Page 185. These are suitable for gilding, and recall the " French " fashion.

Chippendale and his contemporaries designed some very beautiful Tea " Caddys." Tea, no doubt, in those days was a great deal more expensive than it is to-day, and was, for that reason, kept under lock and key by the mistress of the house, and the Caddy was put on the side table as an ornament; but now it appears to have lost its importance with its reduction in price. The above six designs for Tea-chests should have brass or silver ornaments.

CHIPPENDALE STANDS FOR CHINA JARS. Middle 18th Century.

See Page 184

See Page 184

CHIPPENDALE FRAMES FOR MARBLE SLABS.   Middle 18th Century.

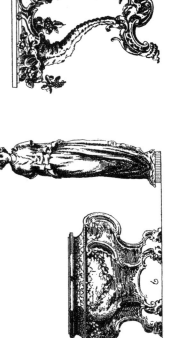

Nos. 1, 3, 4, and 7 on this page are what Chippendale calls "Frames for Tables"; they usually had marble-tops. The two centre ones, Nos. 2 and 5, are also Frames for Tables. Chippendale describes No. 2 as "supported by two piping Fauns, leaning against two vines, intermixed with foliage, etc. It will have a grand appearance if executed with judgment, and neatly gilt." No. 5 he describes as "a Doric Entablature, with its Triglyphs and Metopes, supported by two Cariatides." Readers who are versed in classic lore will, no doubt, admire these designs; but whether they are suitable for Furniture must be a matter open to doubt. It is curious what a lot of knowledge these old cabinet-makers had; the fact that they designed furniture in such different styles as Gothic, Chinese, Louis XV., and Italian Renaissance proves this. Chippendale says: "Of all the Arts which are either improved or ornamented by Architecture, that of Cabinet-Making is not only the most useful and ornamental, but capable of receiving as great assistance from it as any whatever. I have therefore prefixed to the following Designs a short Explanation of the Five Orders. Without an acquaintance with this Science, and some knowledge of the Rules of Perspective, the Cabinet-Maker cannot make the Designs of his work intelligible, nor shew, in a little compass, the whole Conduct and Effect of his Piece. These, thererefore, ought to be carefully studied by every one who would excel in this Branch, since they are the very Soul and Basis of his Art."

CHIPPENDALE CHINA-CASE. Middle 18th Century.

The piece of furniture represented on this page is perhaps, to one who is not a student of "Chippendale," one of the most "startling" of his designs; but to one who is a "student," this is one of the most remarkable, and if it was well carried out by the cabinet-maker, I should think one of the most pleasing; but, of course, one must appreciate these endeavours of Chippendale to produce something *a la Chinois.* It is thus described by him— "A large China-case with glass in the doors and ends. The top part is intended to be open in front. The profile is on the right. The ornaments on the feet may be left out, and a plinth put in their stead. This piece of work may be made of a soft wood and japanned, and pointed or partly gilt."

CHIPPENDALE CHINA-CASES. Middle 18th Century.

No. 1 is a China Case; between the middle fret is a small canopy for a Chinese figure, or any other ornament. The profile is on the right.

No. 2, a China Case—" very proper for a lady's dressing-room. It may be made of any soft wood japanned any colour. The middle part has two doors, and the middle stiles are lapped together. It will be best to make the middle and ends separately, as also the upper work of the canopies, frets, etc. The feet are cut through, but the rail of the frame must not be, as it will be too weak to support so large a piece of work The front and ends are intended for glass. The ends of the canopies in the middle project much more than in the fronts."

CHIPPENDALE CHINA-CASES. Middle 18th Century.

For particulars see Page 190.

No. 1 on page 189, Chippendale calls "A China-case. The canopy projects more at the ends than the front."

No. 2, " A Cabinet with Term-feet. The middle part is a door, with Gothic pillars fixed on, which open with the door, and hath a glass, which may be either silvered or transparent. The ornaments are carved wood. The under drawer at D goes the whole length, is pierced through, but may be solid, and relieved or sunk, with a small moulding wrought round."

Nos. 3 and 4 are China-cases with glass in the front and ends to shew the China. The feet are cut through, but may be solid, and the frets glued on as on the rails. The rail in front is divided into three drawers.

Nos. 5 and 6 is what Chippendale calls an " India Cabinet, with drawer in the centre, and different doors at the ends. The frame is pierced through, but may be solid, and the fret glued on."

No. 7 "are Shelves for China, and is intended for japanning."

No. 8, " A Gothic Cabinet. The Gothic work at bottom is intended for a drawer. The middle part at B is open, and hath shelves with frets on the edges."

For plans and sections of China-cases, etc., see Page 192.

On Page 190 is a China-case.

On Page 192 are three Tea-kettle Stands, also two Cabinets. No 2 " hath folding doors, the ornaments which are on them will conceal the joining. These ornaments may be brass, or silver, finely chased and put on ; or they may be cut in filligree-work in wood, brass or silver. No 1 has one door in the middle and drawers on each side. All the ornaments which are on the middle door, at top, bottom and two sides, must be fixed fast, and to open with it. The feet, as well as all the ornamental parts, must be cast in brass or silver, etc."

The sections are on Page 192. No. 1 section belongs to Cabinet on Page 190.

No.	2	belongs	to	No.	8	on	Page	189.
No.	4	„		No.	2		„	„
No.	6	„		No.	1		„	„
No.	7	„		Nos.	3 & 4	„		„
No.	8	„		Nos.	5 & 6	„		„
No.	9	„		No.	2		„	188

Chippendale says in the preface of his work: " I have been encouraged to begin and carry on this Work not only by Persons of Distinction, but of eminent Taste for performances of this Sort ; who have, upon many Occasions, signified some Surprise and Regret, that an Art capable of so much Perfection and Refinement, should be executed with so little Propriety and Elegance. How far the following Sheets may remove a complaint, which I am afraid is not altogether groundless, the judicious Reader will determine ; I hope, however, the Novelty, as well as the Usefulness of the Performance, will make Atonement for its Faults and Imperfections. I am sensible, there are too many to be found in it ; for I frankly confess, that in executing many of the Drawings, my Pencil has but faintly copied out those Images that my Fancy suggested ; and had they not been published till I could have pronounced them perfect, perhaps they had never seen the Light. Nevertheless, I was not upon that Account afraid to let them go abroad, for I have been told that the greatest Masters of every other Art have laboured under the same Difficulty."

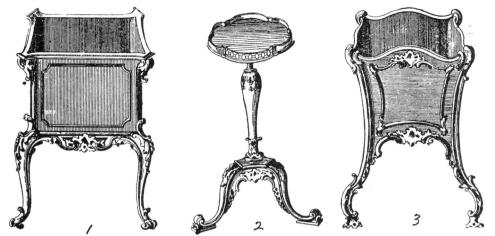

See Page 190.

Chippendale further adds :—

" I am not afraid of the Fate an Author usually meets with on his first Appearance from a Set of Critics who are never wanting to shew their Wit and Malice on the Performances of others ; I shall repay their Censures with Contempt. Let them unmolested deal out their pointless Abuse, and convince the World they have neither Good-nature to commend, Judgment to correct, nor Skill to execute what they find Fault with."

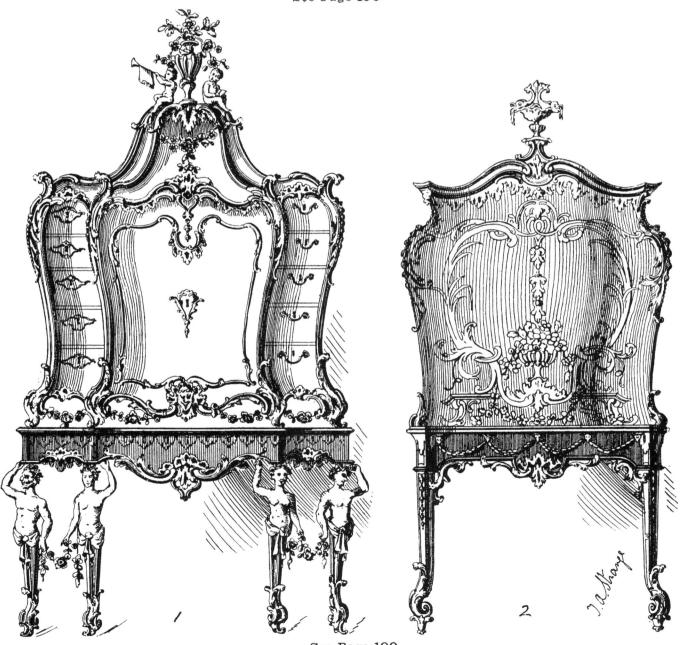

See Page 190.

Details of CHIPPENDALE CHINA CASES, etc.   Middle 18th Century.

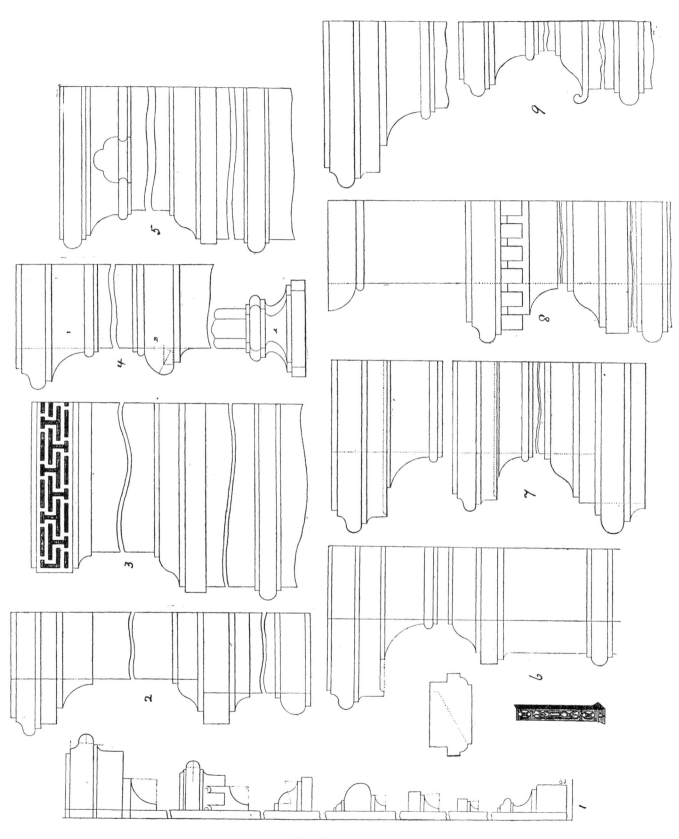

See Page 190.

CHIPPENDALE BOOKCASES.   Middle 18th Century.

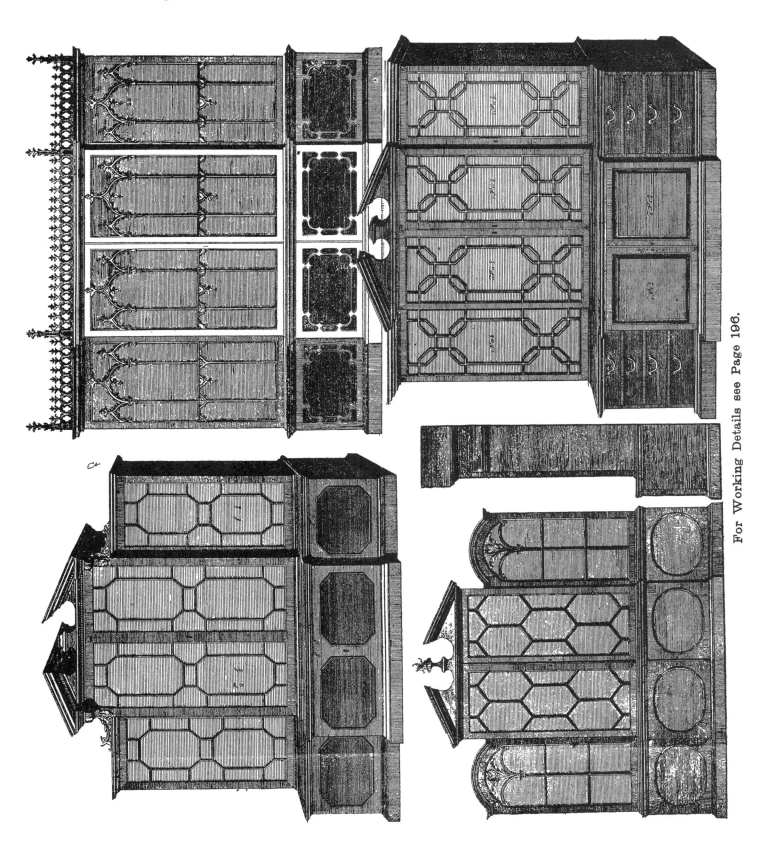

For Working Details see Page 196.

See Page 196.

CHIPPENDALE BOOKCASES.   Middle 18th Century.

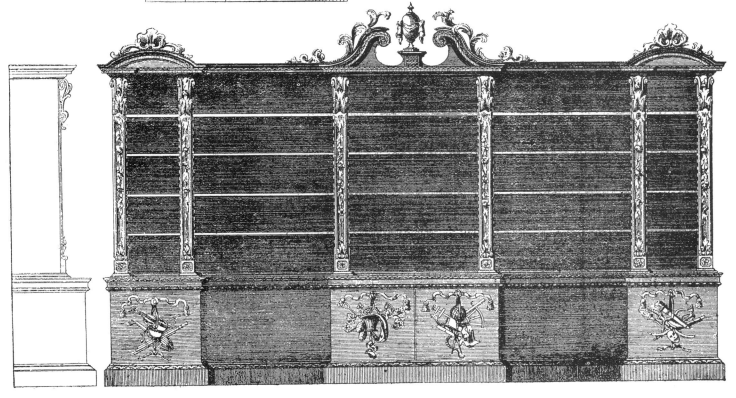

See Page 196.

Details of CHIPPENDALE BOOK-CASES.

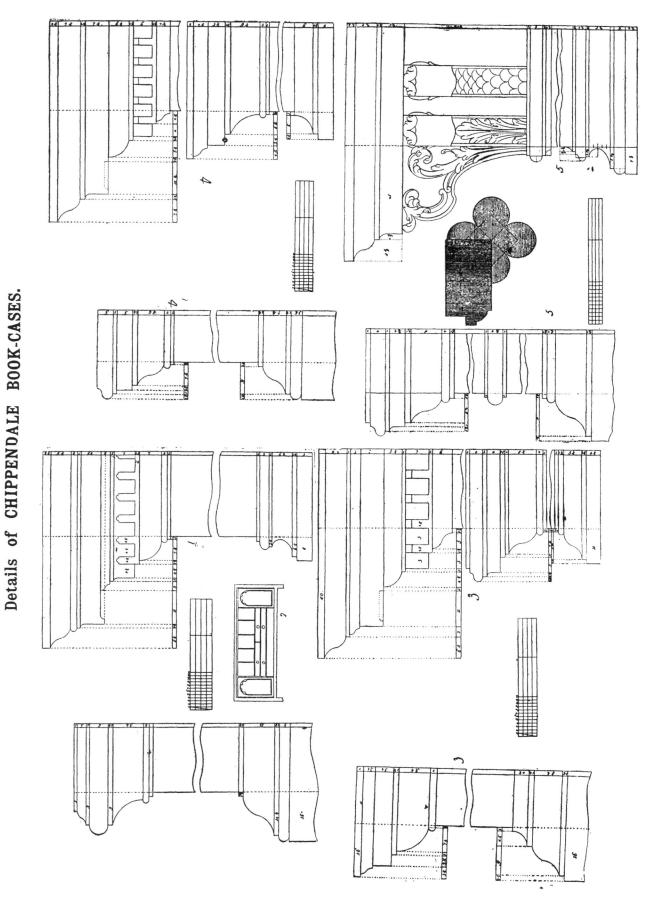

Page 193.—Readers must use their own judgment in interpreting these designs of Bookcases. There are several inaccuracies in some of them ; for instance, in No. 1 on this page (193), the division lines or astragals of both the upper and lower doors in the centre are left out. This is due, no doubt, to the engraver, who would not understand the construction of the Book-case, and being engraved on copper-plates, it would be extremely difficult to alter it when once the mistake was made, so Chippendale had to pass it, or go to the expense of having them re-engraved—no small cost.

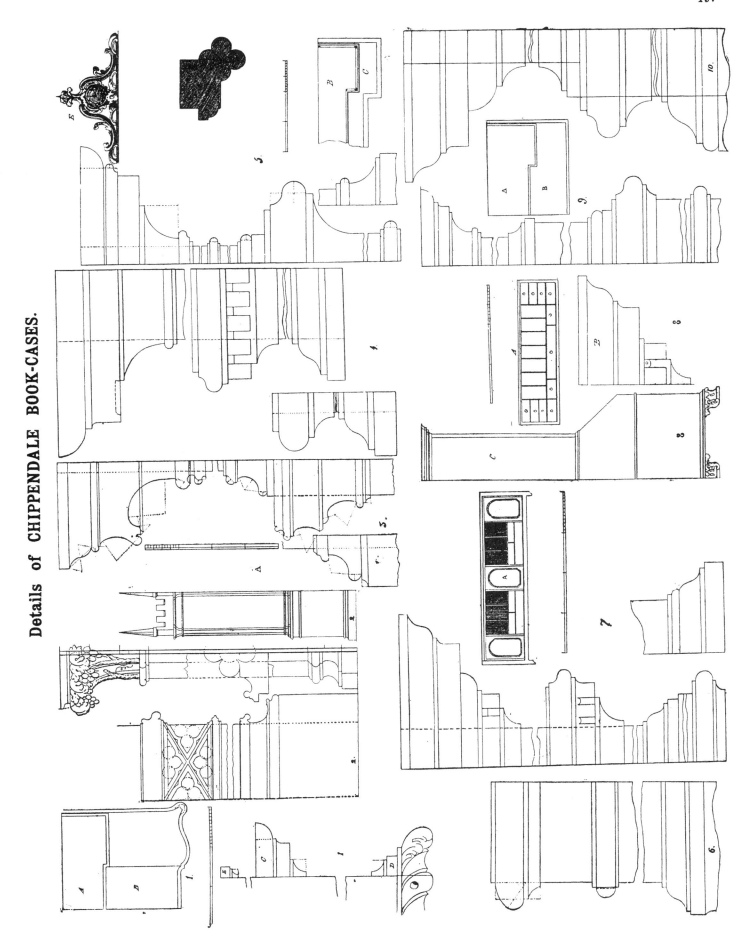

Details of CHIPPENDALE BOOK-CASES.

197

CHIPPENDALE BED-POSTS.   Middle 18th Century.

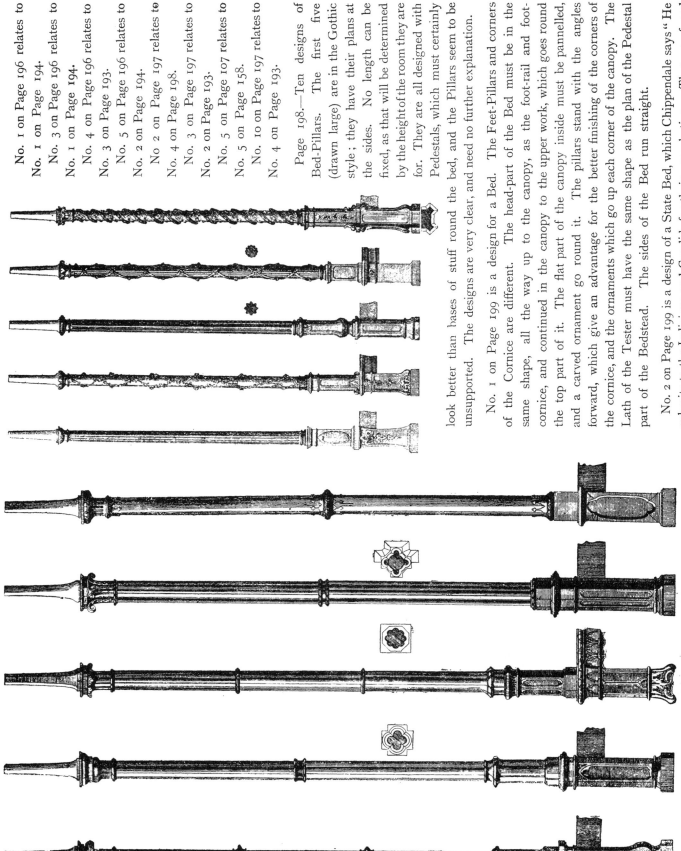

No. 1 on Page 196 relates to No. 1 on Page 194.

No. 3 on Page 196 relates to No. 1 on Page 194.

No. 4 on Page 196 relates to No. 3 on Page 193.

No. 5 on Page 196 relates to No. 2 on Page 194.

No 2 on Page 197 relates to No. 4 on Page 198.

No. 3 on Page 197 relates to No. 2 on Page 193.

No. 5 on Page 107 relates to No. 5 on Page 158.

No. 10 on Page 197 relates to No. 4 on Page 193.

Page 198.—Ten designs of Bed-Pillars. The first five (drawn large) are in the Gothic style; they have their plans at the sides. No length can be fixed, as that will be determined by the height of the room they are for. They are all designed with Pedestals, which must certainly look better than bases of stuff round the bed, and the Pillars seem to be unsupported. The designs are very clear, and need no further explanation.

No. 1 on Page 199 is a design for a Bed. The Feet-Pillars and corners of the Cornice are different. The head-part of the Bed must be in the same shape, all the way up to the canopy, as the foot-rail and foot-cornice, and continued in the canopy to the upper work, which goes round the top part of it. The flat part of the canopy inside must be pannelled, and a carved ornament go round it. The pillars stand with the angles forward, which give an advantage for the better finishing of the corners of the cornice, and the ornaments which go up each corner of the canopy. The Lath of the Tester must have the same shape as the plan of the Pedestal part of the Bedstead. The sides of the Bed run straight.

No. 2 on Page 199 is a design of a State Bed, which Chippendale says "He submits to the Judicious and Candid, for their approbation. There are found

CHIPPENDALE STATE BEDS.   Middle 18th Century.

See Page 198.

CHIPPENDALE CANOPY COUCH and BEDSTEAD.

Magnificence, Proportion, and Harmony.   If the Pedestals of the Bedstead, the Pillars, Cornice, and Top of the Dome, are gilt with burnished Gold, and the Furniture is suitable, the whole will look extremely grand, and be fit for the most stately Apartment.   The ingenious Artist may also, in the Execution, give full scope to his Capacity.   The Bedstead should be six or seven feet broad, seven or eight feet long, and the whole height fourteen or fifteen feet.   A Workman of Genius will easily comprehend the Design.   But I would advise him, in order to prevent mistakes, to make first a Model of the same at large; which will save both Time and Expense."

No. 1 on Page 200 is a Couch with a Canopy.   The curtains must be made to draw up in drapery, and to let down when occasionally converted into a bed.   This sort of couch is very fit for alcoves, or such deep recesses as are often seen in large apartments.   It may also be placed at the end of a long gallery.   If the curtains and valances are adorned with large gold fringes and tassels, and the ornaments gilt with burnished gold, it will look very grand.   The Crane at the top of the canopy is the emblem of Care and Watchfulness, which is not unbecoming a place of rest.   The length of the bed cannot be less than six feet in the clear, but may be more if required; the breadth is three feet, or more, in proportion to the length; the height must be determined by the place it is to stand in.

No. 2 on Page 200.—A Bed which has been made for the Earls of Dumfries and Morton.   One of the pillars is composed of reeds, with a palm branch twisting round.   The tester is covered, and the bottom edge of the cove is cut into the shape nearly that of the cornice, and a thin slight ornament fixed on, and the inside valances fixed to it.   In the middle of the

CHIPPENDALE BEDSTEADS. Middle 18th Century.

CHIPPENDALE FIELD BEDS, and COUCH BED with CANOPY.

tester is a carved oval ornament, 3-ft. 9-in. by 2-ft. 8-in.; and from that to each corner is a piece of foliage and flowerings. The corner-pieces which come down from the cornice are wood, and the valances fixed to them. The pillars are 8-ft. 6-in. high, and the bedstead 6-ft. 7-ins. long, and 6-ft. wide.

No. 1 on Page 201 is a design for a Canopy Bed with its Head-board. Both the curtains and valances are to draw up in drapery.

In Nos. 2 and 3 the curtains may be made either to be tied up in drapery, or to draw on a rod. The pedestal looks better uncovered.

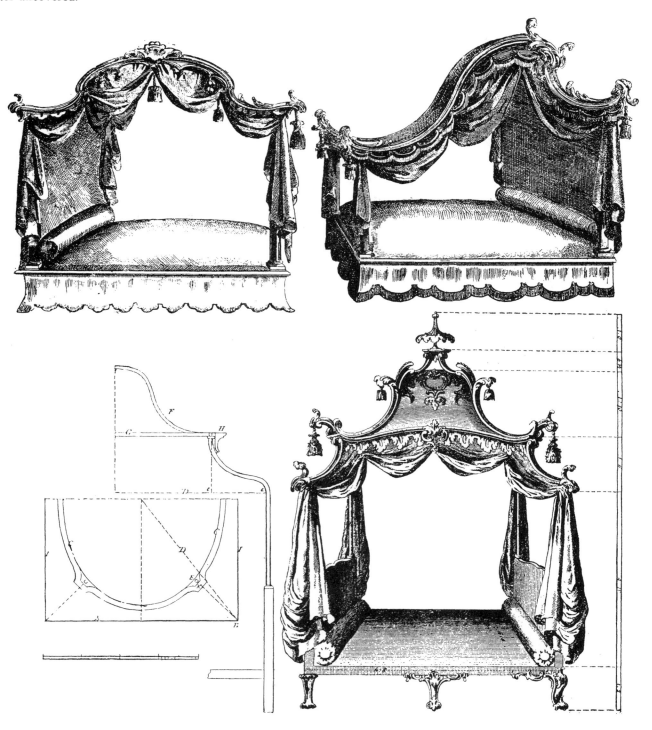

CHIPPENDALE FIELD BEDS and CHINESE SOFA.

Nos. 6 and 7 on Page 201 are what Chippendale calls "Chinese Beds."

No. 9 is a design for a Dome Bed. It is 6-ft. wide, 6-ft. 7-ins. long, and the whole height, without the vase is, 10-ft. 4-ins., and the vase itself 18 or 20-ins.

Nos. 10 and 11 are designs for Gothic Beds, with a flat tester.

Nos. 12 and 13 are designs for Beds, with carved cornices, which may be gilt, or covered with the same stuff as the curtains. The cornice must rise as high as it can, to hide the top of the tester. The bed-pillars have pedestals and the bases are fitted between.

Nos. 1 and 2 on Page 202 are two designs or Field Beds.

No. 3 is a design for a Couch-bed, with a Canopy. The curtains must be made to draw up in festoon, with pulleys properly fixed to the pillars. The dimensions are—6-ft. 8-ins. long, and 5-ft. broad; but there is no necessity for its being so broad. This couch was made for an alcove in Lord Pembroke's House at Whitehall.

Nos. A, B, C, and D on Page 203 are four designs for Tent and Field Beds. The furniture of all these bedsteads is made to take off, and the laths are hung on hinges for convenience of folding up.

On Page 203 is a design for a Sofa with a Chinese canopy, with curtains tied up in drapery, and may be converted into a bed by making the front part of the seat to draw forward, and the sides made to fold and turn in with strong iron hinges, and a proper stretcher to keep out and support the sides when open. The curtains must likewise be made to come forward, and when let down will form a tent.

Details of Bedsteads on Page 204 :—
No. 1 belongs to No. 1 on Page 201.
Nos. 2 and 3 belong to Nos. 2 and 3 on Page 201.
„ 4 and 5   „   „   4 and 5   „   „
„ 6 and 7   „   „   6 and 7   „   „

Details for CHIPPENDALE BEDSTEADS.

Details of Bedsteads on Page 204 continued :—

No. 8 belongs to No. 8 on Page 201.

„ 9 „ „ 9 „ „

Nos. 10 and 11 belong to Nos. 10 and 11 on Page 201.

„ 12 and 13 „ „ 12 and 13 „ „

The twelve designs on Page 205 are Cornices for Beds, or Windows. There is also one on Page 206. The Fenders here shown are not all from Chippendale, but are from Manwaring's and Ince and Mayhew's books, and from other contemporary sources. I have thought it best to keep them together as more easily available for reference.

No. 1 on Page 207 is a Clothes-press. The under part is in shape, with carved ornaments for the feet, which go up the corners.

No. 3 is similar to above but more ornate.

No. 2, a Clothes-press in shape of a commode.

No. 4, similar in shape to No. 2.

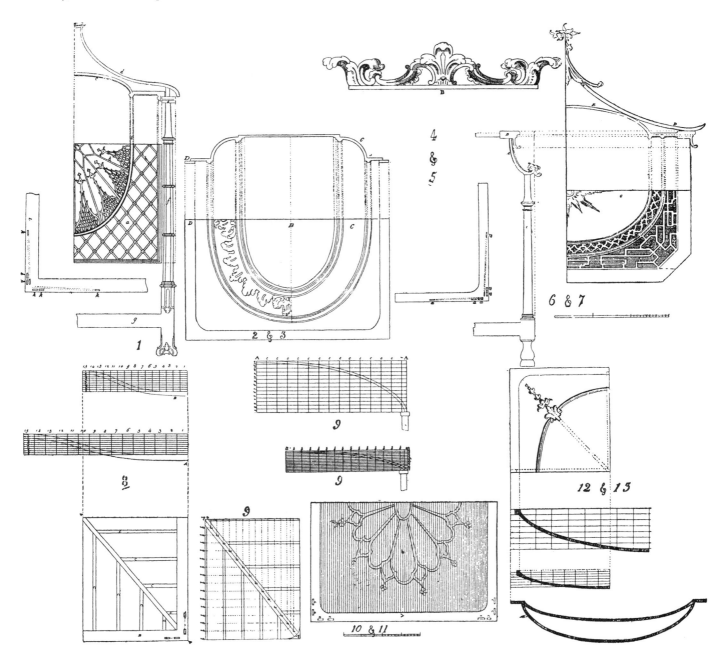

CHIPPENDALE BED CORNICES, or for WINDOWS.

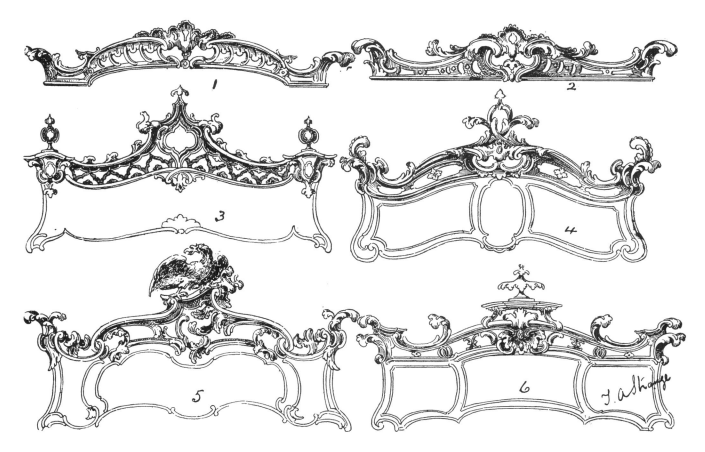

See Page 204.

See Page 204.

On Page 207 are three designs for Basin-stands. No. 1 has four feet and four Gothic pillars, and an arch on every side. The others are so easy to understand that they want no description.

Also on Page 207 is a Basin-stand with a glass to rise, as a shaving-table.

The other one is a design for Shaving-table with a folding top, and a glass to rise out with a spring-catch. A-A are places for holding soap and other necessaries, and behind them are places for razors. B-B are places for bottles. D is a scheme to bring the glass forward when a gentleman is shaving. G is the glass brought

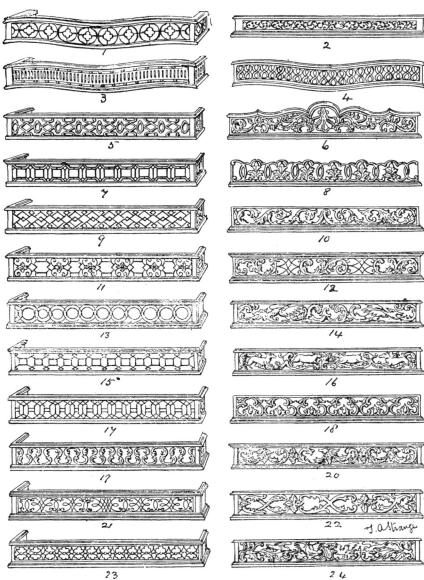

forward, with a brass frame. F-F-F are the joints as it is hung. C is a small piece of brass which slides up and down in a groove, as may be seen by the dotted line.

The dimensions are fixed.

Nos. 1 and 2 on Page 208 is a Chest of Drawers, and a Clothes-press with sliding shelves. The fret in the middle may be two drawers.

Nos. 2 and 3 is a Clothes-chest. It may open in front, and have sliding shelves. The mouldings at large is on the right.

No. 4 is a Clothes-press and a Clothes-chest. The Press has sliding shelves, which should be covered with green baize to cover the clothes.

Nos. 5 and 6 are Clothes-chests upon feet. They may be open in front, and have sliding shelves. Mouldings for this underneath.

No. 7 is a Clothes-press in two parts. The under part has drawers for linen. Mouldings at side.

No. 8 is a Clothes-press with sliding trays.

For particulars of Brass Fenders see Page 204. Some of these designs were elaborately chased, as in Nos. 14, 16 and 24.

CHIPPENDALE WARDROBES and WASHSTANDS.   Middle · 18th Century

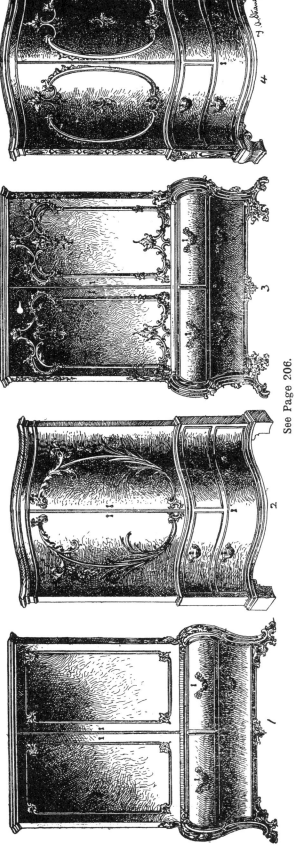

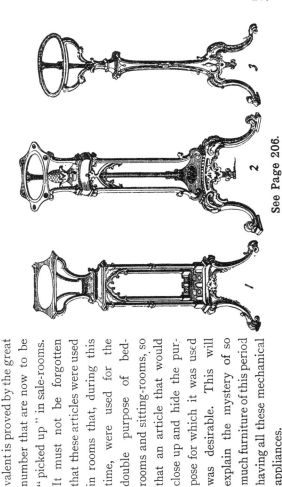

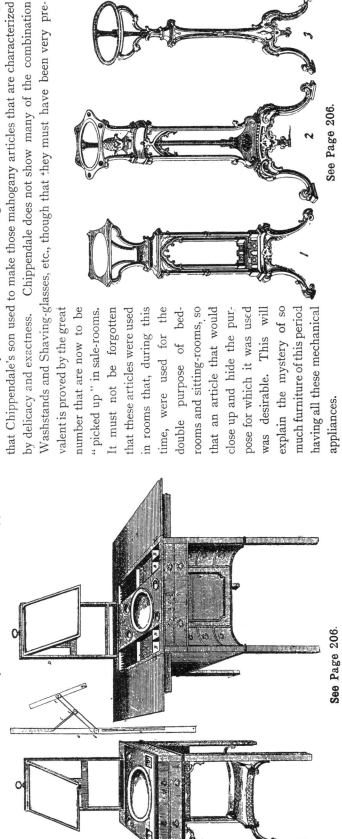

See Page 206.

These Robes, or Presses, are evidently copied from designs fashionable in France, Holland, and Belgium during this period, and which are now often seen in the shops of dealers in antique. The French Presses are set off with chased brass-work, the escutcheons being especially elaborately chased. The Dutch Presses have a coarse sort of inlay on them. These old Chippendale Presses are beautifully made, and it is said, though I do not know on what authority, that Chippendale's son used to make those mahogany articles that are characterized by delicacy and exactness. Chippendale does not show many of the combination Washstands and Shaving-glasses, etc., though that they must have been very prevalent is proved by the great number that are now to be "picked up" in sale-rooms. It must not be forgotten that these articles were used in rooms that, during this time, were used for the double purpose of bed-rooms and sitting-rooms, so that an article that would close up and hide the purpose for which it was used was desirable. This will explain the mystery of so much furniture of this period having all these mechanical appliances.

See Page 206.

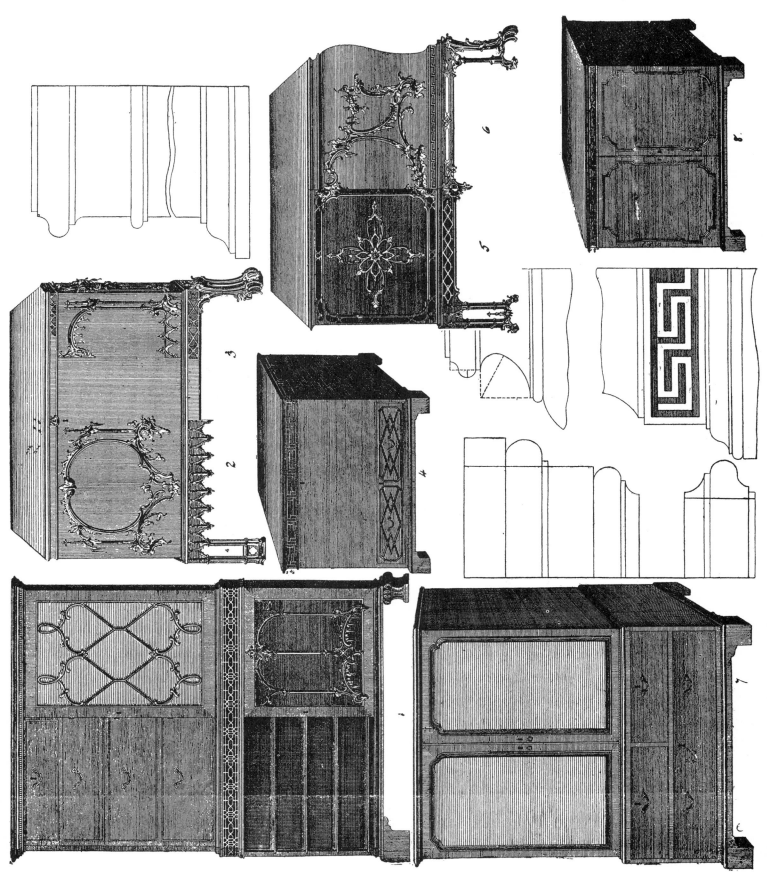

See Page 206.

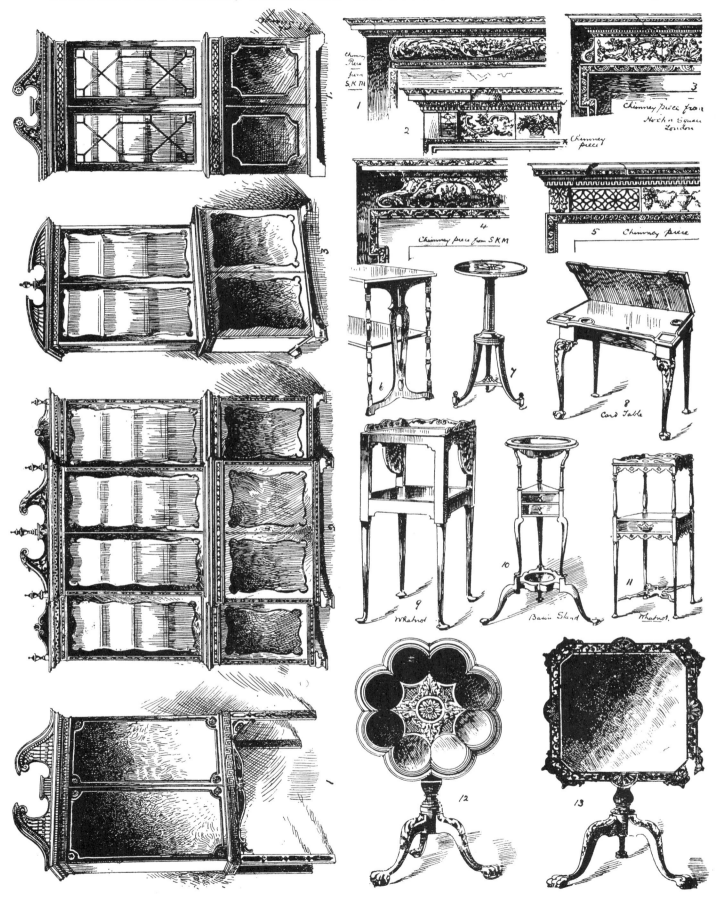

George Richardson published in 1776 "A Book of Ceilings composed in the style of the Antique Grotesque"; in 1781, "A New Collection of Chimney-pieces, ornamented in the style of the Etruscan, Greek, and Roman Architecture"; also in 1795, "A Series of Original Designs for Country Seats or Villas, containing Plans, Elevation Sections of Principal Apartments, Ceilings, Chimney-pieces, Capitals of Columns, Ornaments for Friezes, and other Interior Decorations in the Antique style." Richardson had travelled in Italy.

No. 1 on Page 210 is a Ceiling for a Dressing-room. This design was executed in stucco for Lord Montalt in Dublin. The picture is a representation of Hercules and Omphale. The profiles in the eight small circles may be painted in chiaro oscuro.

No. 2 on Page 210 is a Ceiling for a Bed-chamber. This picture represents the interview between Mars and Venus attended by Cupid. The trophies in the circles on the diagonal lines of the Ceiling should be painted in chiaro oscuro.

No. 3 on Page 210 is a Ceiling for a Dressing-room. The oval picture represents Diana bathing attended by her Nymphs. The small circles contain figures representing hunting pieces and sacrifices, which may be painted in chiaro oscuro, or executed in stucco in the manner of antique bas-reliefs.

No. 4 on page 210. Richardson describes this as a Ceiling suitable for Ante-room. The picture or bas-reliefs in this ceiling represent three Nymphs preparing a sacrifice.

No. 1 on Page 211 is a Chimney - piece suitable to an Ante-chamber or Dressing-room; it is in wood, except the facia of the architrave, which in all chimney-pieces should be done in stucco or marble.

No. 3 on Page 211 is suitable for a Parlour or Dining-room. The ornaments of the frieze may be of white marble, laid on dark grounds If the cornice, with the frieze and back pilasters, be carved in wood, the mouldings of the architraves, in marble, might be quite plain.

No. 4 on Page 211 As the emblems of Neptune are displayed

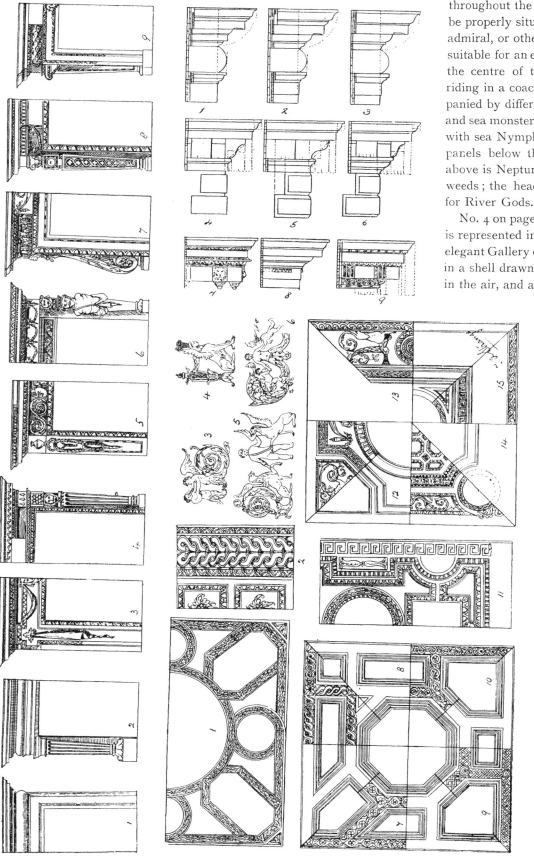

throughout the whole of this design, it might be properly situated in the apartments of an admiral, or other naval officer, and would be suitable for an elegant Hall or Dining-room. In the centre of the tablet Cupid is represented riding in a coach drawn by Dolphins, accompanied by different genii sporting with Tritons and sea monsters. The pilasters are ornamented with sea Nymph's standing on shells; in the panels below them are Dolphins, and in those above is Neptune's trident encircled with sea-weeds; the heads in the circles are intended for River Gods.

No. 4 on page 211.—" A Triumph of Venus " is represented in the tablet of this design for an elegant Gallery or Drawing-room. She is sitting in a shell drawn by Dolphins, guided by Cupid in the air, and accompanied by a Triton blowing his shell trumpet, and holding Neptune's trident. The plain ground round the pilasters, with termes, may be of variegated colours, but all the rest should be of pure white marble.

Richardson, speaking of another Chimney-piece, says: " The plain ground round the pilasters and architrave may be of jasper, or antique green; and the ornaments of the frieze and pilasters might be done of scagliolia, and should be executed in wood; the ornaments will produce a fine effect if painted in the Etruscan manner, in various colours.

Sir William Chambers was born in Stockholm, and educated at Ripon School. At an early age he went to China, where he saw and admired the picturesque buildings and gardens of the Chinese. He made sketches of some of these, and on his return published them. He went to Italy and studied the works of the great architects of the Renaissance.

He also studied in Paris. Soon after his return to England he was appointed tutor to the Prince, afterwards George III. He published "Designs for Chinese Buildings," and a "Treatise on Civil Architecture," illustrations from which are on Page 212. He was made a member of the Royal Academy, which he helped to establish, in 1768. He wrote "A Dissertation on Oriental Gardening," in 1772. Of the many buildings he designed the most important is Somerset House.

Chimney-pieces about this time were made of "Scagliola," a kind of ornamental plaster, or artificial stone, prepared from gypsum and Flanders glue, and made to imitate the colours of marble. This material was extensively used by the Adam Brothers, who are also credited with introducing the very fine plaster work (a composition) which took the place of Plaster of Paris. This being pressed into metal moulds whilst hot, was capable of producing the very thin ornament which we know as the Adam style, and was applied to woodwork as well as ceilings.

The Table given below is from "The Chimney-piece Maker's Daily Assistant, or, A Treasury of New Designs for Chimney-pieces," by Thomas Milton, John Crunden, and Placido Columbani. This work begins with the most plain and simple, and gradually ascends to the most grand and magnificent in the Antique, Modern, Ornamental, and Gothic Tastes, proper to be executed in the following rooms :—

Halls, Saloons,	Vestibules,	Guard Rooms,
State-rooms,	Parlours,	Dining-rooms,
Drawing-rooms,	Ante-rooms,	Music-rooms,
Dressing-rooms,	Bed-rooms,	Cabinets, &c.

A TABLE shewing the true size that Chimney-pieces ought to be, to rooms from 9 feet square to 30 feet square. If the Room be longer one way than the other, add one long side and one short side together, take half that product for the square of the room, and the proportions are as follows :—

If the Square of the room be	The Width of the opening will be	The Height of opening.	The Height of the Cornice.
Feet.	Ft. In.	Ft. In.	Ft. In.
9	2 5	2 11	4
10	2 7	2 11½	4
11	2 8	3 0	4
12	2 9½	3 0½	4
13	2 11	3 1	4
14	3 0½	3 1½	4⅛
15	3 2	3 2	4¼
16	3 4	3 3	4⅜
17	3 5	3 3½	4½
18	3 7	3 5	4⅝
19	3 8	3 5½	4¾
20	3 9½	3 6½	4⅞
21	3 11	3 7	5
22	4 1	3 7½	5⅛
23	4 2	3 8	5¼
24	4 3½	3 8½	5⅜
25	4 5	3 9	5½
26	4 6½	3 9½	5⅝
27	4 8	3 10	5¾
28	4 9½	3 10½	5⅞
29	4 11	3 11	6
30	5 1	4 0	6¼

Architraves to Chimney-pieces should be about one-sixth or one-seventh of the width of the opening. The height of friezes are various, according to the several ornaments with which they are to be decorated; if a swelling frieze, it may be about three-fifths of the width of the architrave: flat friezes should not be less than four-fifths of the width of the architrave.

Placido Columbani published in 1775, "A New Book of Ornaments, containing designs for modern panels, commonly executed in stucco, wood or painting, and used in decorating principal rooms. In 1776 he also published "A variety of Capitals, Friezes, Cornices, and Chimney-

PLACIDO COLUMBANI, CHIMNEY-PIECES. Period 1766.

pieces." I have not illustrated any of the friezes as they are after the style of Pergolesi (see pages 227, 231, and 245 to 256), and do not appear so good.

For particulars of John Crunden, see Page 157.

In 1771, N. Wallis published "A Book of Ornaments in the Palmyrene Taste," containing upwards of sixty new designs for ceilings, panels, pateras, and mouldings, with the Raffle leaves at large; also "The Carpenter's Treasure," a collection of designs for temples, with their plans, gates, doors, rails, and bridges, with centres at large for striking Gothic curves and moulding, and some specimens of rails in the Chinese taste, forming a complete system for rural decoration. He also published "The Complete Modern Joiner," in 1772, reprinted in 1792— a collection of original designs in the taste of that period, for chimney-pieces and door-cases, with their mouldings and enrichments at large. Friezes, tablets, ornaments for pilasters, bases and sub-bases, and cornices of rooms. Tablets are the centre pieces in chimney-pieces and door-cases; these, about this time, were mostly of groups, of figures—such as Cupids, allegorical subjects of the gods, etc.

The words "Raffle leaves" above were leaves used in ornamental foliage in Italian work, the edge of which have small indentations such as the Acanthus leaf.

It is curious to note that the Chimney-pieces, more than any other articles, were mostly of a classical design throughout the century, but of course this was not always the case, for instance, in Johnson's or Chippendale's designs, etc. This is no doubt partly attributed to those articles being designed by architects of the buildings which were mostly based on classical lines.

N. WALLIS, CHIMNEY PIECES, MOULDINGS, etc. Period 1772.

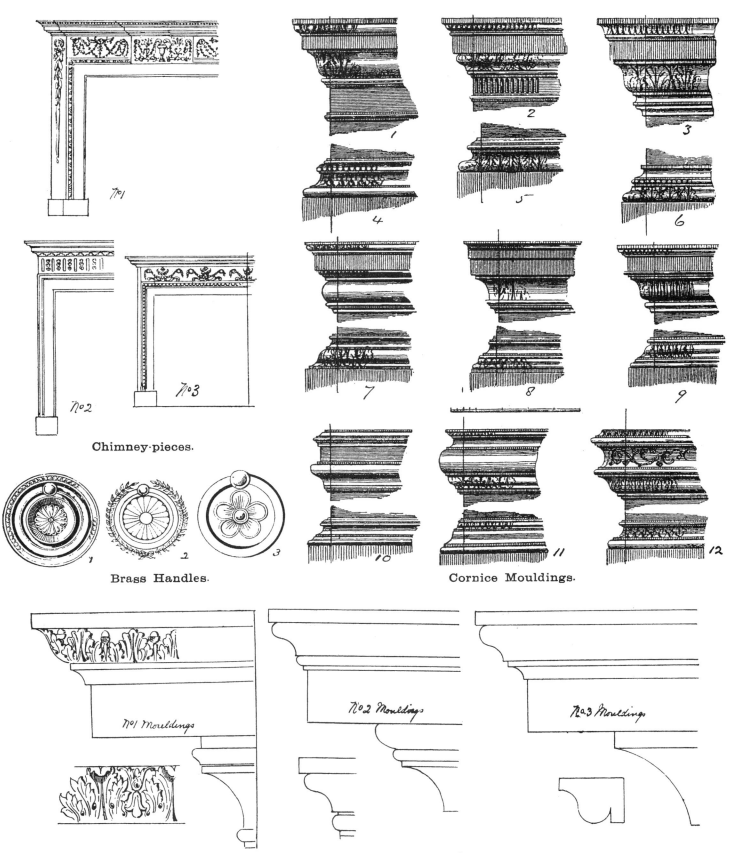

Chimney-pieces.

Brass Handles.

Cornice Mouldings.

Mouldings for above Chimney-pieces

J. CARTER SUNDRIES   Period 1774.

J. CARTER, SIDES OF ROOMS.   Period 1774.

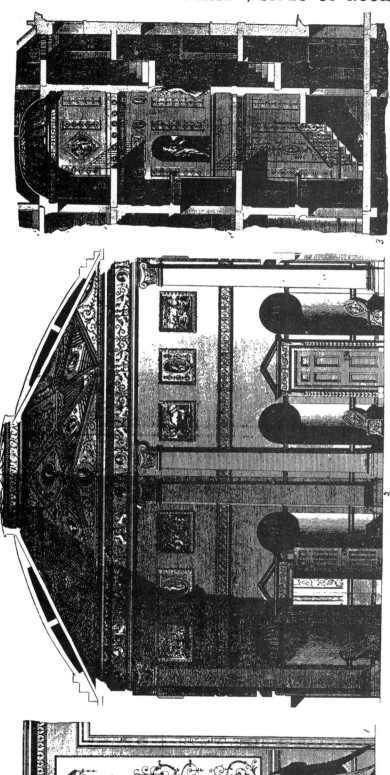

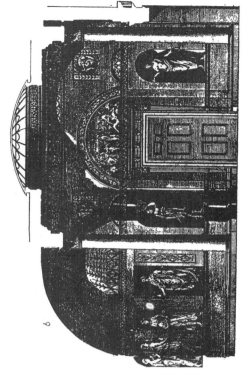

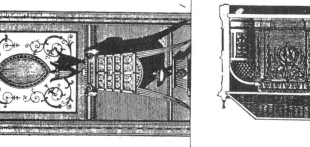

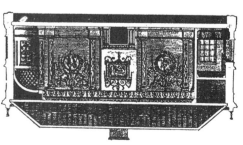

The designs of J. Carter are of great variety, but seem to be based on the Adam lines. In the case of ceilings there is a similarity to Richardson's designs. They are taken from a book published in 1774 by a society of architects called "The Builders' Magazine, or Monthly Companion for Architects, Carpenters, Masons, Bricklayers, etc."

J. CARTER, GATES, GRATES, etc.   Period 1774.

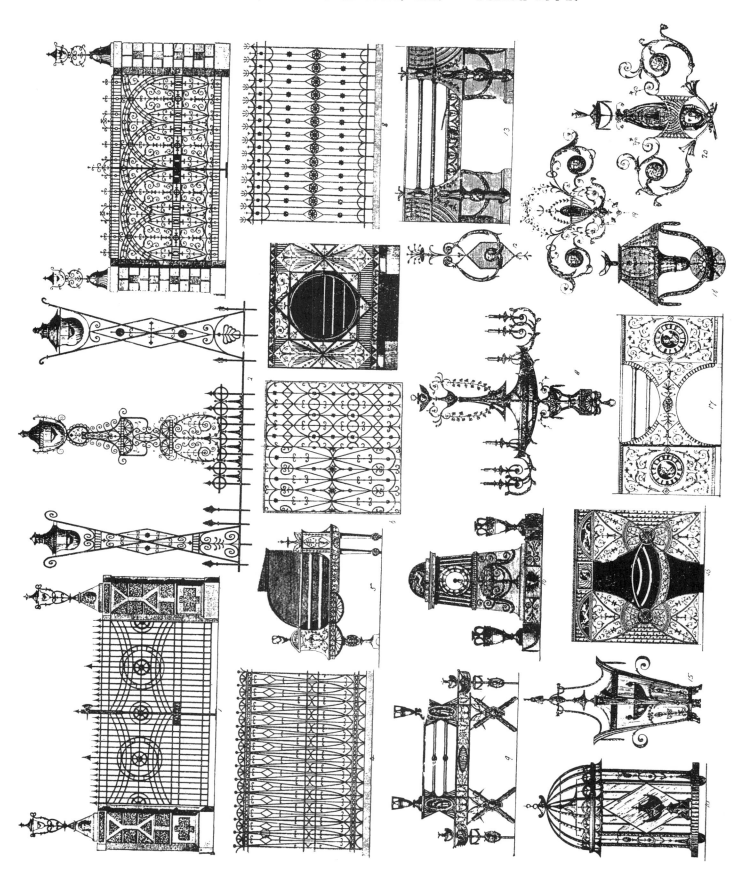

J. CARTER, SHOP FRONTS, DOORWAYS and OVERDOORS.   Period 1774.

Design for Ceiling.   See Page 229.

Robert and James Adam, who established the style known as "The Adam Style," came of a family of architects, their united influence being felt right through the 18th Century. Their father, William Adam of Maryburgh, near Kinross and Kirkcaldie, designed, renovated, and rebuilt a vast number of Scottish mansions. He was appointed Master Mason in Scotland. He had four sons who followed his profession; his eldest son, John, inherited his business, and most probably had a large share in the carrying out of the various buildings attributed to his father. There was another son, William Adam, who died in 1822, and who probably managed the winding up of the various enterprises entered into by his more famous brothers Robert and James Adam. Robert Adam, F.R.S., F.S.A., was the second son of William Adam (the father), and though associated with his brother James in partnership, undoubtedly took a leading part, which is proved by anyone reading the text of their "Works on Architecture" wherein he continually speaks in the "First person, Singular." He was born at Kirkcaldie in Fifeshire, in 1728, and died after the bursting of a blood vessel in 1792, and was buried in Westminster Abbey, where a slab in the south transept records the above dates. He visited Rome in 1756, and made many drawings of antique buildings. After his return in 1751, he made designs among other things

Decoration at Goodwood, the seat of the Duke of Richmond.

Commode in the Countess of Derby's Dressing-room.

of temples, garden seats, etc., which at that time seemed quite the "rage," most architects at that time being similarly engaged. Below will be found a chronological list of some of his and his brother's principal buildings; but, it must be kept in mind, they designed a prolific number of buildings, as independent of their commissions from the nobility and gentry, they were "speculative builders" on a large scale.

Screen in front of Admiralty, about 1760.
Landesdowne House, on the south side of Berkeley Square, London, about 1767.
Kenwood House, Lord Mansfield's, 1764-67.
Adelphi, begun 1768.
Mansfield Place, Portland Place, about 1770. This street contains good specimens of the skill of the interior decoration of the Adam Bros. (R. and J.)
Sir Watkin William Wynn's House in St. James's Square, London, 1770.
Portland Place, begun about 1778.
Harewood House, at the south-east corner of Harewood Place, Hanover Square, about 1776.
White's Club in St. James's Street, London, 1787.
In 1790 they began the east and south sides of Fitzroy Square.
They are the builders of Stratford Place, Oxford Street, and Grafton Street (Bond Street), London.
John, Robert, James, and William Streets, in the Adelphi, London, are named after the four brothers.

Friezes for rooms, probably designed by Pergolesi for the Adam Bros.

Commodes.

James Adams died of an apoplectic fit at his residence, 13, Albermarle Street, London, in 1794.

Design for Panels.

Ceiling of the Library in Sir Watkin William Wynn's House
in St. James's Square, London.

Ceiling in Lady Wynn's Dressing-room in her house in St. James's Square, London.

Design for Girandole.

Speaking of the Ceiling of the Great Room at Kenwood, Robert Adam says : "It is in the form and style of those of the ancients. It is an imitation of a flat arch, which is extremely beautiful, and much more perfect than that which is commonly called the coved ceiling, when there is height sufficient to admit of it, as in the present case. The coved ceiling, which is a portion or quadrant of a circle around the room, and rising to a flat in the centre, seems to be altogether of modern invention, and admits of some elegance in the decoration. It is a sort of middle way, between the flat and horizontal ceiling, and the various forms of arched ones practised by the ancients. As it does not require so much height as the latter mode, it has been found of great use in the finishing of modern apartments, but neither is its form so grand, nor does it admit of so much beauty of decoration as the ancient arched ceilings, which consist of three kinds—the dome, the groin, and the plain trunk arch, such as that now before us,

Designs for Brass Door-handles, Candelabra, etc.

with their various combinations. All the ceilings of the ancients, which continue still to be the objects of admiration, not only on account of their beauty, but also for their duration, were executed in one or other of these modes. Stucco work of these ceilings, and other decoration, is finely executed by Mr Joseph Rolfe. The paintings are elegantly performed by Mr. Antonio Zucchi, a Venetian painter of great eminence ; and the grounds of the panels and friezes are coloured with light tints of pink and green so as to take off the glare of the white, so common in every ceiling till of late. This always appeared to me so cold and unfinished, that I ventured to introduce this variety of grounds at once to relieve the ornaments, remove the crudeness of the white, and create a harmony between the ceiling and the side walls with their hanging decorations."

R. and J. ADAM.   Second half 18th Century.

No. 1.–Chimney-piece from St. James's Palace, London. No. 3.–Design of a Chimney-piece executed in the Great Saloon of the Queen's House.   Various Ornaments, probably designed by Pergolesi for the Adam Brothers.

Robert Adam speaking of Ceilings says : "The term 'Ponderous' is applied to distinguish those (ceilings) that were in use in this country during the last century, from those of the present time; the style of the former being of a most enormous weight and depth.   These absurd compositions took their rise in Italy, under the first of their modern masters, who were no doubt led into that idea from the observation of the soffits used by the ancients in the porticos of their temples and other public works.   These the ancients, with their usual skill and judgment, kept of a bold and massive style, suiting them to the strength, magnitude, and height of the building, and making an allowance for their being on the exterior part, and adjoining to other

R. and J. ADAM, CHIMNEY-PIECES. Last half 18th Century.

Chimney-piece of statuary Marble, with glass frame over it in the Second Drawing-room at the Earl of Derby's House, Grosvenor Square, London.

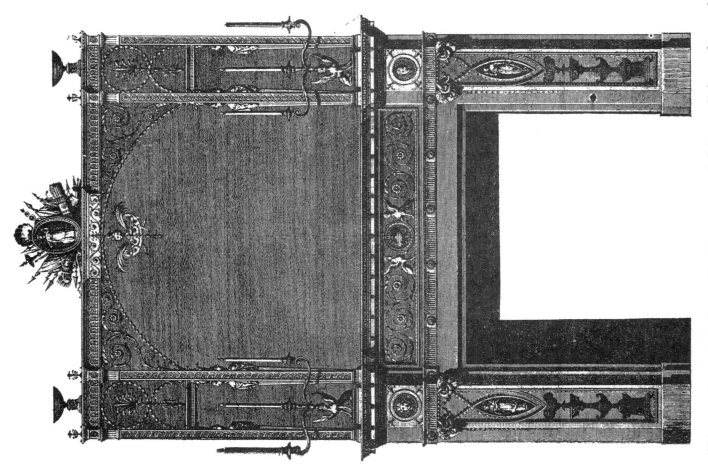

Chimney-piece of statuary Marble, ornamented in scagliola and ormolu, with the glass frame over it, in the Third Dressing-room at "Kenwood," residence of Lord Mansfield.

R. and J. ADAM, CHIMNEY-PIECES,   Last half 18th Century.

Chimney-piece of White Marble, inlaid with ornaments of scagliola and ormolu, with the glass frame over it, for the Countess of Derby's Etruscan Dressing-room, Grosvenor Square, London.

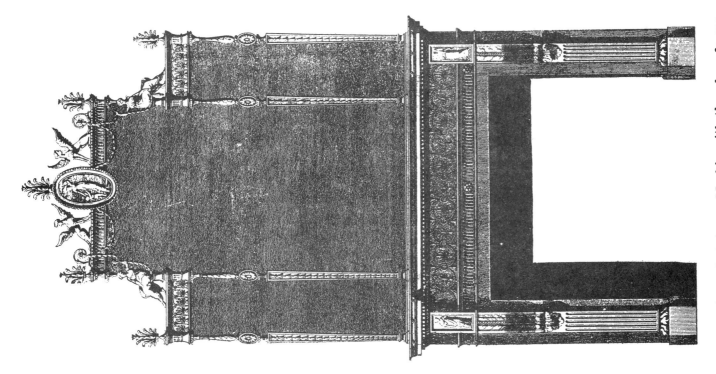

Chimney-piece of statuary Marble with the glass frame over it, in the First Drawing-room at the Earl of Derby's House, Grosvenor Square, London.

R. and J. ADAM (or period about 1780).

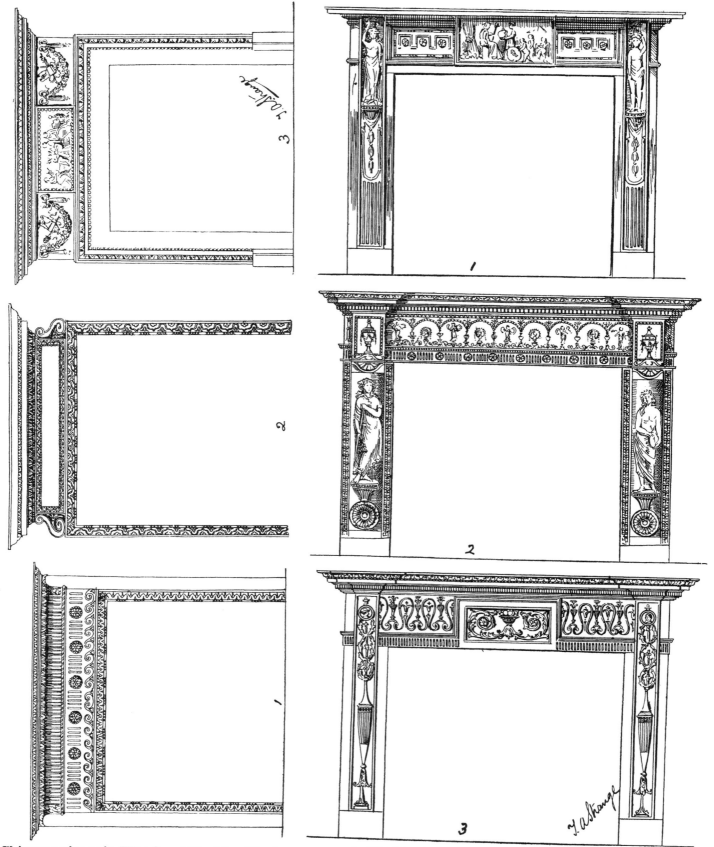

Chimney-pieces in Wood and Marble. The larger ones, in Marble, from mansions built by the Adam Brothers.
Nos. 1 and 2 on left-hand side, in pine wood, are from the Bethnal Green Museum, London.   Nos. 2 and 3 on right-hand side are from Lady Maria Ponsonby's, Stratford Place, London.   No. 1 on right-hand side is from Mrs. James' Boudoir at West Dean.

Chimney-piece from Finsbury Square, London.

Girandole in the Etruscan Room at the Countess of Derby's.

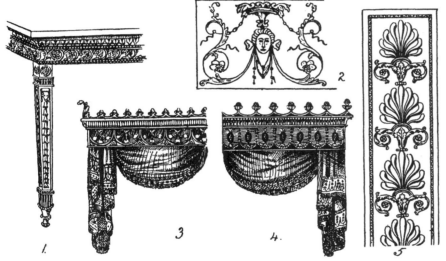

Table from Sir Watkins William Wynn's Hall, Designs for Cornices and Draperies.

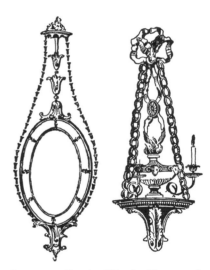

Girandoles at Lady Maria Ponsonby's, Stratford Place, London.

great objects; all which served to diminish and lighten the effect of these compartments.   But on the inside of their edifices the ancients were extremely careful to proportion both the size and depth of their compartments and panels to the distance from the eye, and the objects with which they were to be compared; and with regard to the decoration of their private and bathing apartments, they were all delicacy, gaiety, grace, and beauty.   Michael Angelo, Raphael, and other Italian architects of the Renaissance boldly aimed at restoring the antique.   But in their time the rage of painting became so prevalent in Italy, that instead of following these great examples, they covered every ceiling with large fresco compositions, which, though extremely fine and well painted, were very much misplaced, and must necessarily, from the attitude in which they are beheld, tire the patience of every spectator.   Great compositions should be placed so as to be viewed with ease.   Grotesque ornaments and figures, in any situation, are perceived with the glance of an eye and require little examination.   Inigo Jones introduced them into England (see Page 11) with as much weight, but with less fancy and embellishment.   Vanburgh, Campbell, and Gibbs followed too implicitly the authority of this great name.   Kent's genius for the picturesque, and the vast reputation he deservedly acquired, made him in some measure withstand this prevalent abuse; he has much merit in being the first who began to lighten the compartments,

R. and J. ADAM, COMMODE and CHANDELIER.   Last half 18th Century.

Drawing-room Glass and Table; designed for the Earl of Bute.

Design for Girandole.

Design for Candelabra.

R. and J. ADAM, COMMODES and CHANDELIERS.   Last half 18th Century.

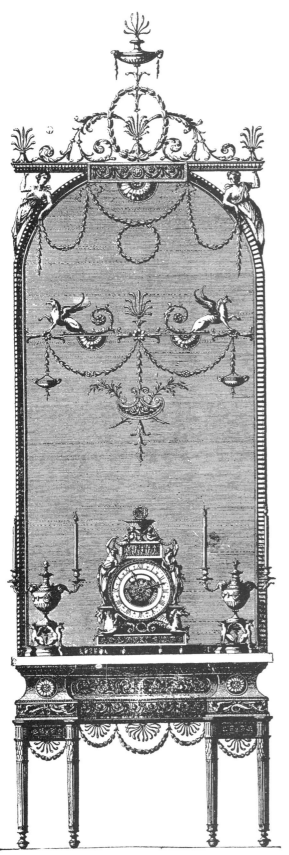

Design of Glass and Commode Table upon which is placed a Clock and Vases with branches for Candles.

Two designs for Brackets and Vases with branches for Candles.

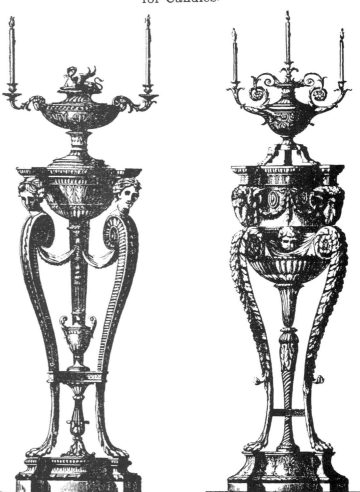

Two designs for Tripods and Vases with branches for Candles.

R, and J. ADAM.   CHAIRS, Period about 1780.

and to introduce grotesque paintings with his ornament in stucco; his works, however, are evidently those of a beginner. Mr. Stuart, with his usual elegance and taste, has contributed greatly towards introducing the true style of the antique decoration; and it seems to have been reserved for the present times to see compartment ceilings, and those of every kind, carried to a degree of perfection in Great Britain, that far surpasses any of the former attempts of other modern nations."

The Brothers Adam decorated the dining-room in large houses with stucco, and adorned them with statues in niches, and with paintings, that they might not retain the smell of the victuals, etc.   The ornaments of the ceilings, side-walls, etc., were of stucco, and were picked out with different tints, sometimes different tints of green, which they claim to have a simple and elegant effect.   The chimney-pieces in a best room was of statuary marble, and the overmantel carved in wood and gilt, sometimes painted; where there were medallions in the centre of pediment they were painted.   The drawing-room they varied from other rooms by having a coved ceiling and painted it in compartments.   The rooms were sometimes divided into compartments by pilasters, and the ornaments of these, with the arches and panels of the doors were painted.   The ornament of the friezes of the room were of stucco, and the ornaments on the door carved.   Sometimes the ornaments in the niches were gilt, as were also the girandoles and stucco ornaments of the ceilings and sides of rooms.   Drawing-rooms were hung with damask, tapestry, etc., but not the eating rooms.   Of the different things I have illustrated in this book of the Adam Brothers, the Folding-Doors on Page 242 have the ornaments painted on *papier maché*, and so highly japanned as to appear like glass.   The Ceilings and Pilasters on Pages 225, 241, 242, and 243 have what Robert Adam calls " Grotesque Ornament," by which is meant that beautiful light style of ornament used by the ancient Romans; and has what artists call the " Rainceau Ornament," by which they mean to express the windings and twistings of the stalk or stem of the acanthus plant, which, flowing round in graceful turnings, spreads its foliage with great beauty and variety, and is often intermixed with human figures, animals and birds—imaginary and real, also with flowers and fruit executed in stucco or painting.   Stoves were executed in brass and steel combined.   Ormolu ornaments were extensively employed by the Adam Brothers.   The Escutcheon and Knocker in centre of Page 230, for the outer door of Sir Watkins William Wynn's house in St. James's Square, London, was executed in brass water gilt.

R. and J. ADAM, SIDES OF LIBRARY.   Last half 18th Century.

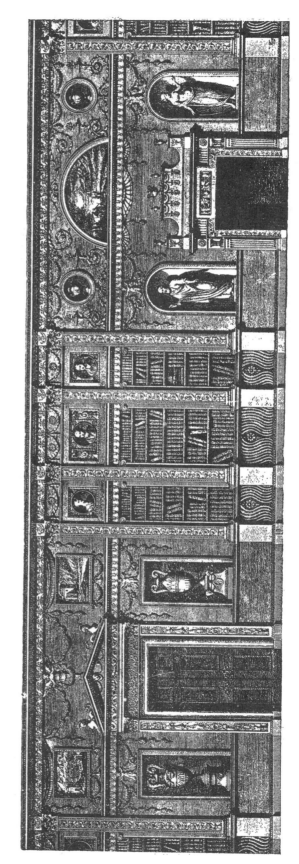

Geometrical Section of the Library in Sion House, seat of the Duke of Northumberland.

Robert Adam says, " We have introduced a great diversity of Ceilings, friezes, and decorated pilasters, and have added grace and beauty to the whole, by a mixture of grotesque Stucco, and painted ornaments, together with the flowing rainceau, with its fanciful figures and winding foliage. If we have any claim to approbation, we found it on this alone : That we flatter ourselves we have been able to seize, with some degree of success, the beautiful spirit of antiquity, and to transfuse it, with novelty and variety, through all our numerous works."

Design for Pilaster.

Sideboard by R. Adam.

Sideboard, Plate, and Wine Cooler by R. Adam.

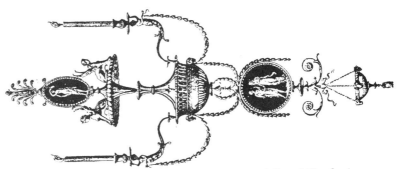

Girandole in the Etruscan Room at Lord Derby's.

Half Design for Ceiling.

Folding Doors in the Countess of Derby's Third Drawing-room.

Among the various ornaments used by the brothers Adam were octagons, hexagons, ovals, rounds, lozenge shaped panels, husks, fans, sphinx, Greek and Roman vases, wreaths, honeysuckle, medallions with figures—the medallions sometimes draped, festoons, fauns, cupids, goats, eagle-headed grotesques, drapery, ribbons, caryatides, mythological subjects, rams' heads, lions' and eagles' claws for feet, griffins, sea-horses, winged sphinx, pateræs, Greek and Roman ornaments, etc., and draped figures.

Design for Pilaster.   Half Design for Ceiling.

CHIMNEY-PIECES by W. THOMAS.   Second half 18th Century.

SIDE OF ROOM by PERGOLESI.   Late 18th Century.

Michael Angelo Pergolesi produced his work on Decoration in parts, extending over a considerable period. He dedicated it "To the Memory of the Late Most High and Puissant Prince, Hugh Percy, Duke of Northumberland, who was A Patron of the Arts, and to Whose Virtues this Work is Dedicated by His Most Grateful and Humble Servant."   This is how he prefaces his work : "Mr. Pergolesi most respectfully begs leave to acquaint his subscribers, as well as the public in general, that the next number, being the XIII., as well as all succeeding numbers to No. XXIV., the whole numbers of the first volume, will have one plate each additional ; the price, 7s. 6d. each number, including a Dedication (by permission), and a portrait of the nobleman or gentleman to whom the number is dedicated. Mr. Pergolesi trusts, at the same time, it will not be thought an overcharge, if he is compelled by new duties being laid upon the principal articles of his work since the year 1777, when he began his publication, to raise the price of the above numbers, which will just indemnify him, for the new duties he must now pay."   The original price was 6s. per part. His designs are for low relief plaster work for walls, ceilings, architraves, chimney-pieces, furniture, etc.   The centre Panel on above wall is painted, and to design and paint this class of subject he employed such decorative artists as Angelica Kaufman, Cipriani, Antonio Zucchi, etc.   He was employed by the Adam Brothers.   The above work extends to seventy large pages full of the most beautiful and delicate designs, and should be studied by those in search of this class of "dainty" ornament.   I have only been able to show a few of his designs in consequence of being limited to space.

"Cupid Bound," by Angelica Kaufman. Engraved by Bartolozzi.

Panel by Pergolesi.

"Beauty Governed by Reason, Rewarded by Merit," by Angelica Kaufman.

Panel by Pergolesi.

ANGELICA KAUFMAN, BARTOLOZZI, and PERGOLESI.   Late 18th Century.

"Judgment of Paris," by Angelica Kaufman.

Panel by Pergolesi.

ANGELICA KAUFMAN and PERGOLESI.   Late 18th Century.

Maria Anna Angelica Kaufman was born in 1741, she painted ceilings for Adam Brothers. The ceiling of the Council Chamber at Burlington House, London (Royal Academy), also the Reading Room at the Arts Club were painted by her. She came to London in 1766. The chief attribute of her compositions is

"The Shepherdess," by Angelica Kaufman.

Panel or Ceiling by Pergolesi.

Decorative Panel by Cipriani.

Decorative Panel by **Cipriani.**

Panels by Pergolesi.

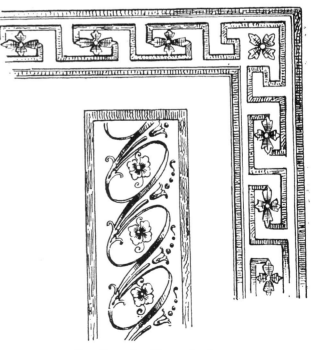

Borders by Pergolesi.

PERGOLESI. Late 18th Century.

Ceiling by Pergolesi.

"Grace." A few only of her compositions are shewn in this work. She was a prolific painter; besides painting ceilings, she painted furniture, table-tops, etc.

Panels by Pergolesi.

Cipriani published a work on the "Rudiments of Drawing," engraved by Bartolozzi, on January 1st, 1786 to 1792. It has some most charming drawings for eyes, noses, ears, hands, feet; also for head groups, cupids, etc.

Francesco Bartolozzi, the engraver, was born in 1727 in Florence, where he was a fellow pupil of Cipriani at the Florentine Academy. He came to England in 1764. Any reader wishing to study "Bartolozzi and his work," should buy Andrew W. Teur's work thereon. Teur mentions that "his name is generally remembered as that of the engraver of the fanciful, and stippled prints now so keenly sought after, in which

Panels by Pergolesi.

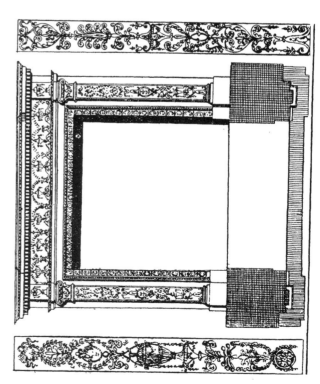

Chimney-piece with Details by Pergolesi.

PERGOLESI. Late 18th Century.

graceful maidens, cherubs, cupids, and sportive children play prominent parts; whereas he achieved his lasting reputation as a line engraver." Bartolozzi engraved a great number of Angelica Kaufman's and Cipriani's productions.

These old engravings go very well with Adam, Sheraton, and Heppelwhite, etc., furniture.

Antonio Zucchi was employed in conjunction with Angelica Kaufman on the painted decorations of the buildings of the Adam Brothers. He married Angelica Kaufman, and returned with her to Italy. He designed the frontispiece to Adam Brothers' work on architecture, and the subject is "A Student conducted to Minerva who points to Greece and Italy, as the countries from whence he must derive the most perfect knowledge and taste in elegant architecture." It was engraved by Bartolozzi. Robert Adam mentions Zucchi in his work in rather flattering terms. In many of the houses in Soho and neighbourhood are to be seen specimens of Pergolesi's interior work, and the reader will find a side of a room in this style a few pages before this; it has a low dado rail, plain plaster walls, panelled round with a moulding,

PERGOLESI.   Late 18th Century.

a pine mantel-piece, mounted with compo ornament, and a compo subject over the mantel-piece, a narrow ornamental compo frieze, and plain ceiling.   Of course this is only a small room, a better class room can be seen on Page 245.

 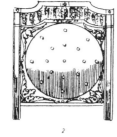 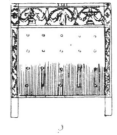  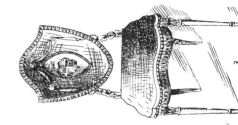

    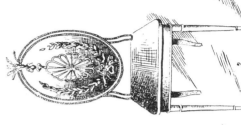

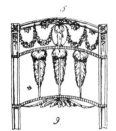 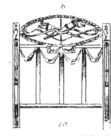   

Chair Backs.   **Hall Chairs.**

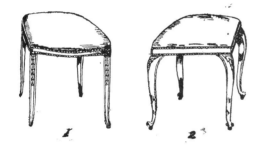  

Drawing-room Stools.   **Gouty Stool.**

Grandfather Chair.

Heppelwhite is probably best known by his designs for Chairs, and I have added on Page 260 a sheet of Chairs, the designs of which have been taken from existing examples; the similarity of design may claim for them that they were probably made about his time. Several of them, as Nos. 5, 9, 10, 19 and 20, are painted. On Page 274 will be found some of his designs for Window Seats, Settees, etc. The Settees were made a great length about this time, and the tops of the backs and fronts of the seats take a gentle curve. The Grandfather's Chair is from Heppelwhite's book.

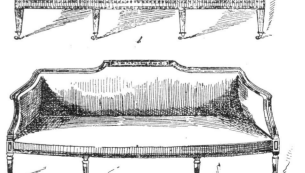

Settees (See Page 274.)

HEPPELWHITE CHAIRS.   Period about 1788.

HEPPELWHITE CHAIRS.   Period about 1788.

HEPPELWHITE CHAIRS.　　Period 1788.

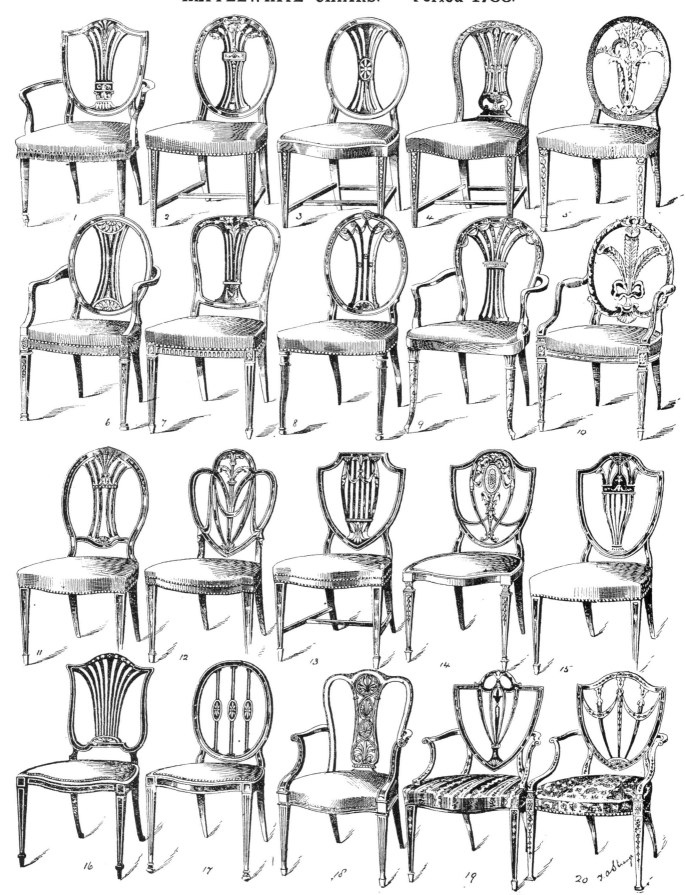

HEPPELWHITE MOULDINGS, KNIFE BOXES, and CELLARETS. Period 1788.

Mouldings.

Knife Boxes.—Inlaid and Banded Edges.

Cellarets. (The Bands were sometimes of Brass.)

HEPPELWHITE SIDEBOARDS and URN-STANDS.   Period about 1788.

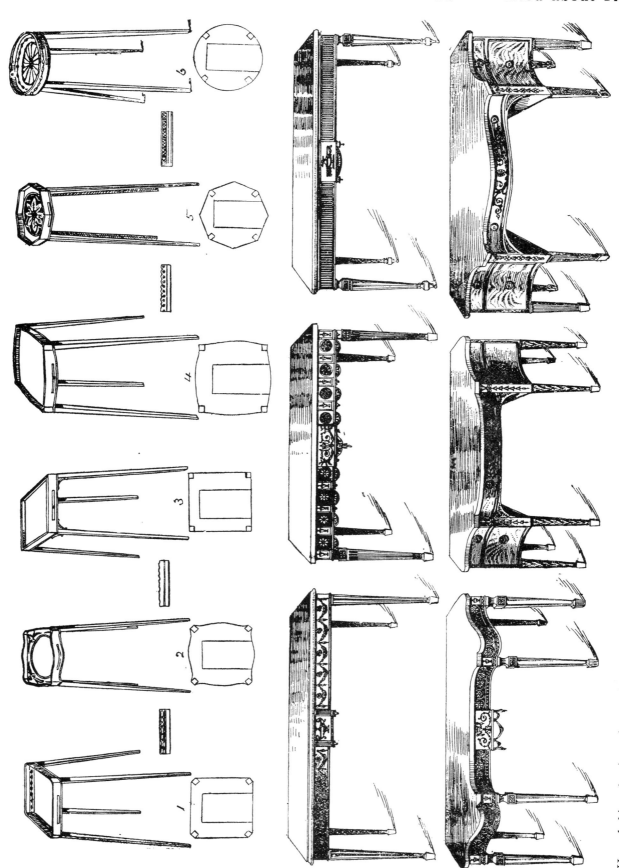

Heppelwhite furniture is mostly inlaid, and the panels are veneered with beautifully figured woods, and the edges are usually banded. There is an absence of moulding on the fronts of doors, drawers, etc. A good deal of the furniture of this period is partly painted (japanned) and partly inlaid. Heppelwhite's Chairs are often distinguished from Sheraton's by their having oval and shield-shaped backs. The square tapering legs were used by him a great deal; the stuffing has the close brass nails—a legacy from earlier times. Round handles seem to have been mostly used. His designs are usually of a light and tasty description.

HEPPELWHITE TEA-CADDIES, PEDESTALS, VASES, & KNIFE-CASES. Period about 1788.

1 *2*

4.

Card and Pier Tables.

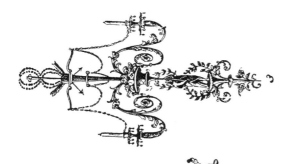

3

The Girandoles shewn on this page are, like all the compo work of this period of a beautiful design and workmanship. This was brought about by such designers as Pergolesi, and such architects as the Adam Brothers, but the workmen seem to have been Italians.

Reading Stands.

Girandoles.

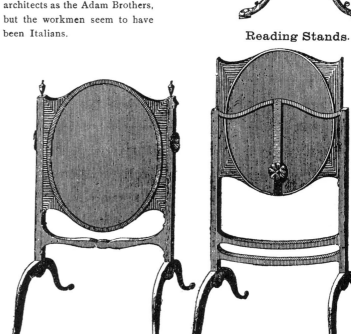

1 *2*

Fire Screens.

HEPPELWHITE BEDSTEADS, DOUBLE CHEST, etc.   Period 1788.

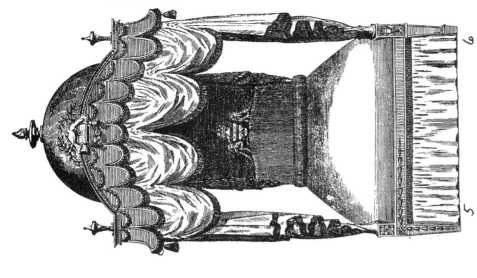

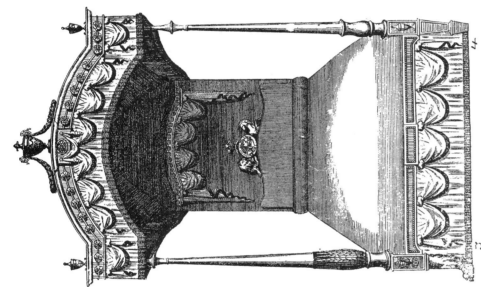

Draped Bedstead.

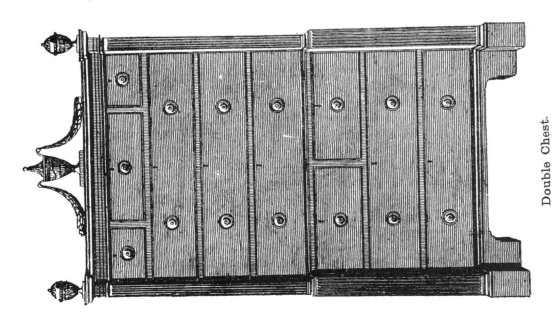

Double Chest.

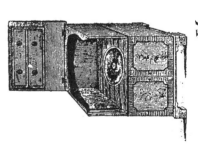

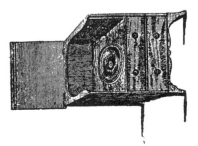

Night Commodes.

HEPPELWHITE ROBES, DOUBLE CHESTS, etc.　　Period about 1788.

HEPPELWHITE COMMODES and CHESTS OF DRAWERS.   Period about 1788.

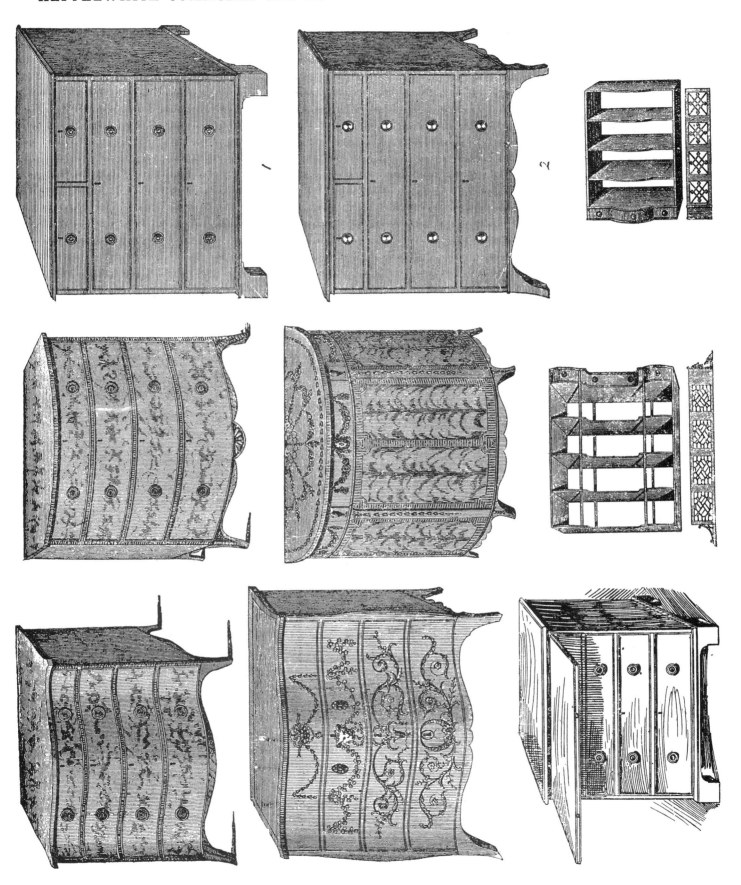

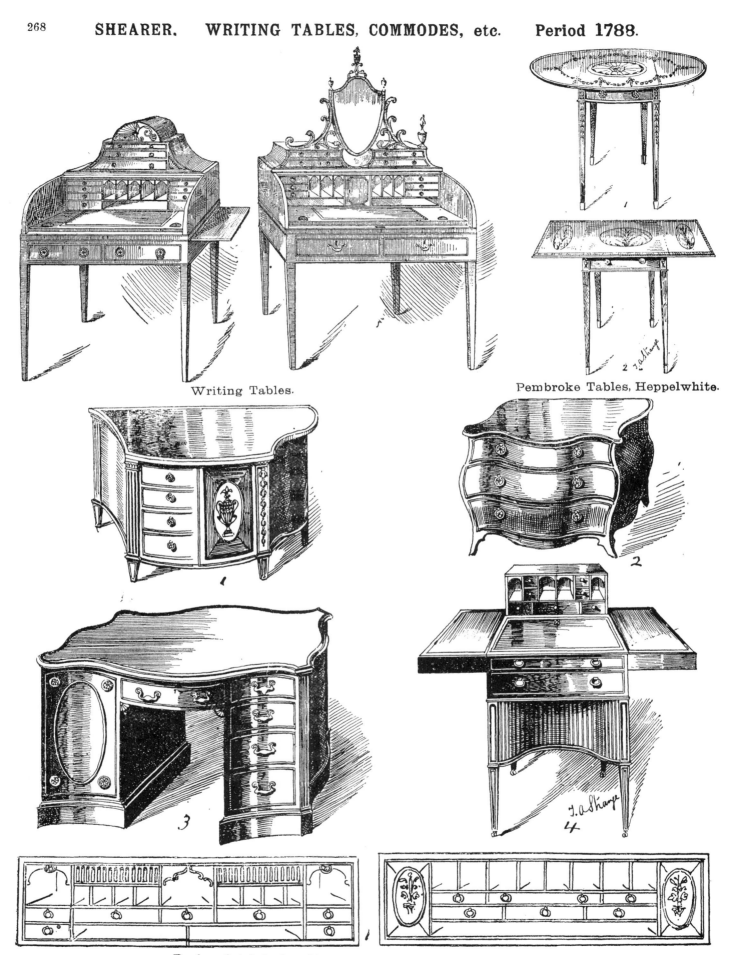

Writing Tables.

Pembroke Tables, Heppelwhite.

Design for interior fitments of Secretaire Writing Table.

SHEARER. DRESSING TABLES and WASHSTANDS. Period 1788.

Designs for Washstands, Dressing Tables, and Combination Dressing Table and Washstand.

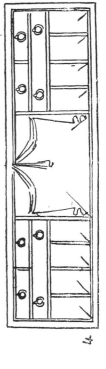

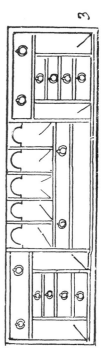

Design for interior fitments of Secretaire Writing Table.

HEPPELWHITE PEDESTAL CUPBOARDS, BIDETS, BASIN STANDS, DRESSING TABLES, etc

Period about 1788.

HEPPELWHITE LIBRARY & TAMBOUR TABLES, TERMS for BUSTS & READING STANDS

It will be noted that Heppelwhite, like Sheraton, designed a good deal of combination furniture like designs on Page 270, which, in some cases, might be taken for designs by Chippendale.

SHEARER. SIDEBOARDS. Period 1788.

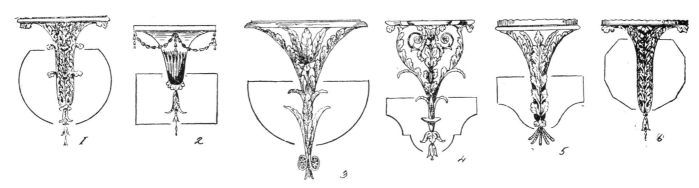

Heppelwhite Brackets, with their Plans.

Shearer published a work about 1788, and was therefore a contemporary of Heppelwhite and Sheraton. His furniture was plain, carved, inlaid, and painted. In the Sideboard shewn below there is a small bead round the edges of the doors and drawers. Some more of his designs will be found on Pages 268 and 269. The panels with figures on Sideboard No. 6, and the basket of flowers on back of the same, were probably painted. Shearer's designs for Dressing Tables, etc., on Page 269, have the combination arrangements so common in designs of this period. Shearer's designs seem to be between the style of Chippendale and Sheraton, but nearer to the latter.

Sideboards by Shearer

HEPPELWHITE and SHERATON (Period) TOILET GLASSES.   Last half 18th Century.

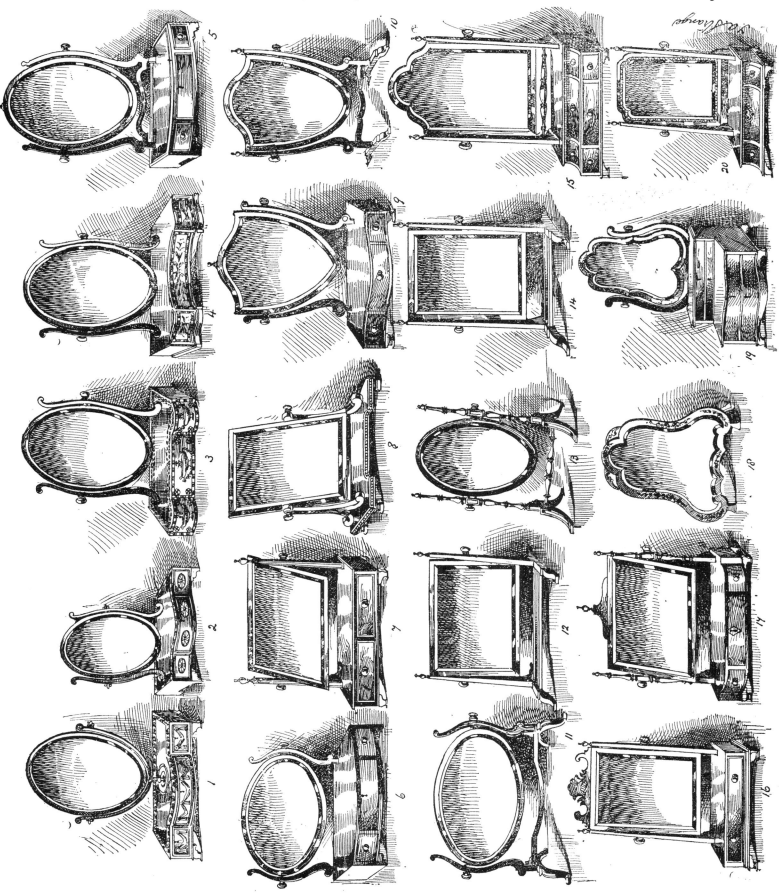

See Page 275.

HEPPELWHITE WINDOW-SEATS, CENTRE OTTOMANS and SETTEES.   Last half 18th Century.

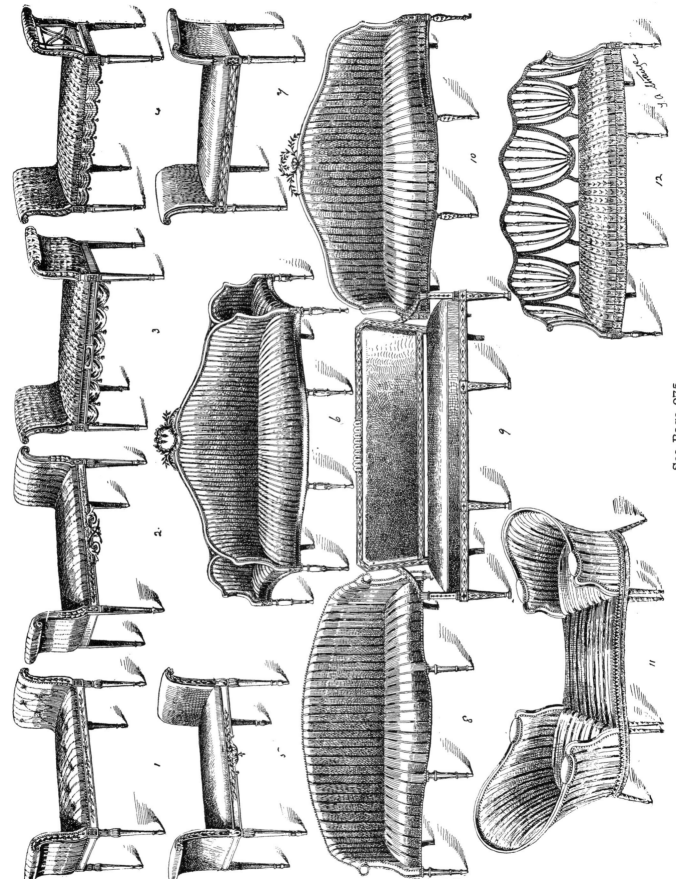

See Page 275.

HEPPELWHITE and SHERATON (Period) TABLE-TOPS. Last half 18th Century.

The Toilet-Glasses on Page 273 are thoroughly representative of this class of article—which was in vogue during the greater part of the century. There are shown the ovals and shield-shape glasses so much patronised by Heppelwhite, Sheraton and contemporary makers, and in such examples as No. 19 one gets the Dutch feeling of the early part of the Century, while the squarer ones are more suggestive of the Chippendale style.

On Page 274 are Window Seats of a very tasteful design. These seem to have been very fashionable about this time; they were sometimes carved, but more often painted and "picked out" with leaves, ivy, rosettes, husks, ribbons, etc., etc. In No. 6 we have a Centre Ottoman, which takes to pieces and makes separately two Settees and two Easy-chairs—the Settee is No. 10. In No. 11 we have an arrangement of two Easy-chairs and a Stool in the centre — which makes a sort of lounge. In No. 12 we have a design of a Settee, a class of pattern which is very often seen in Heppelwhite and Sheraton's work.

The Table-Tops on Pages 275 and 276 were either inlaid with marqueterie or decorated; these Table-Tops were in mahogany or satinwood, which last had just come into fashion. The designs were of a most dainty description, some of the finest artists of the day being employed to paint them—among others, Angelica Kaufman (the friend of Sir Joshua Reynolds) and Cipriani. The effects of the grain in some of the satinwood veneers are extremely beautiful, in some instances like a glorious sunset.

Nos. 1, 2, 3 and 4 on this page were designs for the tops of Butler's Trays.

The Girandoles on Page 277 were gilt, and the influence of the classic taste is here distinctly discernible. Some of these

HEPPELWHITE & SHERATON (Period) CARD, OCCASIONAL & COMMODE TABLE-TOPS.

See Page 275.

HEPPELWHITE GIRANDOLES. Last half of 18th Century.

See Page 275.

designs might be taken to be by the Brothers Adam, so light and tasty are they. The Pediments on Page 278 belong to the Heppelwhite and Sheraton period; Nos. 1 to 8 are Sheraton's the rest being taken from Heppelwhite's book. The Pediments on Page 279 are Heppelwhite's. See also Page 281.

The Panels and Drawer Fronts on Page 279 should prove extremely useful, as showing the manner of veneering: readers will notice that these Fronts are all " flush "—no mouldings on them. These are taken from other contemporary cabinet makers besides Sheraton and Heppelwhite. The Feet at the bottom of this page (279) are likewise taken from contemporary sources.

T. Sheraton published a work on Furniture, etc., late in the century; he called it " The Cabinet-maker and Upholsterer's Drawing Book." In it he gives instructions relative to the art of making perspective drawings and treats of such geometrical lines as ought to be known by both Cabinet-makers and Upholsterers. He also gives the " Five Orders "— as was usually done by authors of this period—but he complains in his preface that Chippendale only gave a few details relative to the Orders, while he (Sheraton) has given a great many. He further on speaks of Chippendale's furniture " as now wholly antiquated and laid aside, though possessed of great merit, according to the times in which they were executed." He lays great stress on the merit of his own work, though the lessons on " Perspective " which it has in it—

HEPPELWHITE & SHERATON (Period) PEDIMENTS. Last half 18th Century.

See Page 277

and which other contemporaries works had not. Sheraton divided his work into four parts. The first part provides the workman with geometrical lines, applied to various purposes in the cabinet branch; the second part applies to perspective; the third part contains designs for furniture; while the fourth part contains mouldings and various ornaments. The work runs into over 440 pages.

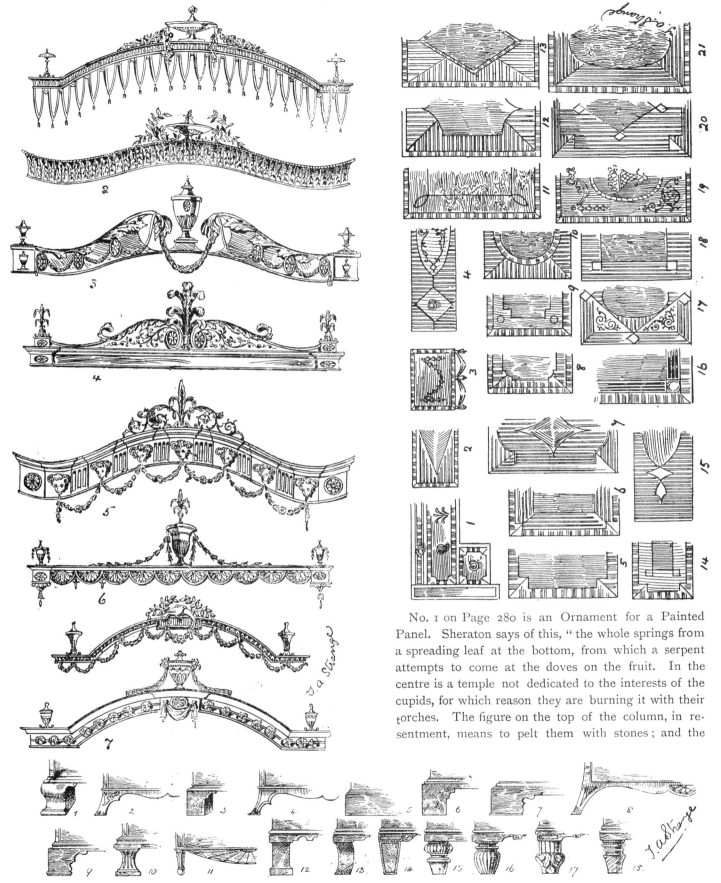

No. 1 on Page 280 is an Ornament for a Painted Panel. Sheraton says of this, " the whole springs from a spreading leaf at the bottom, from which a serpent attempts to come at the doves on the fruit. In the centre is a temple not dedicated to the interests of the cupids, for which reason they are burning it with their torches. The figure on the top of the column, in resentment, means to pelt them with stones; and the geniuses above are pouring down water to quench the flames. The owls are emblematic of Night, at which season these mischiefs are generally carried on." I have inserted this as a sample of Sheraton's interpretation of "classic" taste. Another sample as below—Ornament for a Tablet. "The subject is a faint moonlight scene, representing Diana on a visit to Endymion, who, as the story goes, having offended Juno, was condemned by Jupiter to a thirty years' sleep."

On Page 282 are eight Bed-pillars by Heppelwhite; the three Pilasters underneath are for commodes. "These may be painted, inlaid, or gilt in gold behind glass, and the glass being then beaded in the pilaster, it is secure and has a good effect." Nos. 4, 5, 6 and 7 on lower part of Page 281 are Bed-pillars by Sheraton; they may be painted or carved in mahogany. Nos. 4 and 5 are intended for rich State Beds, carved in white and gold. The pateras which cover the screw-heads are on loose panels let into pillars, and which settle down into a groove at the bottom, by which means they are kept in their place and easily taken out.

On Page 282 is an "English State Bed," with dome top, and crown supported by Justice, Clemency, and Mercy; the cornice, pillars, etc., are adorned with various symbolical figures expressive of the different branches of the British Government. There are various figures supposed to represent, or be symbolical of Democracy, Aristocracy, and Monarchy; the crown is supported by Justice, Clemency and Liberty; and other figures are Law Obedience, Authority, Counsel, etc., etc.

On Page 283 is a Sofa-Bed, with Dome top and French drapery. The frames of these beds are sometimes painted in ornaments to suit the furniture, but when the furniture is of rich silk, they are done in white and gold, and the ornaments carved. The drapery under the cornice is of the French kind; it is fringed all round, and laps on to each other like unto waves. The roses which tuck up the curtains are formed by silk cord, etc., on the wall, to suit the hangings; and observe, that the centre rose contains a brass hook and socket, which will unhook, so that the curtains will come forward and entirely enclose the whole bed. The sofa part is sometimes made without any back, in the manner of a couch. It must also be observed that the best kinds of these beds have behind what the upholsterers call a fluting, which is done by a slight frame of wood fastened to the wall, on which is strained, in straight puckers, some of the same stuff of which the curtains are made.

Ornament for a Painted Panel.

Ornament for a Tablet.

No. 2, an Alcove Bed, is represented on ascending steps covered with carpet, and with drapery round the arch of the alcove.

No. 3 is an Elliptic Bed, dome top, with drapery, ornamented cornice, medallion-valence, and couch ends. The circular part at the top is intended to be panelled out in gilt mouldings, which cannot fail in producing a fine effect—particularly so if the furniture and the covering be light blue.

HEPPELWHITE BED PILLARS. Last half 18th Century.

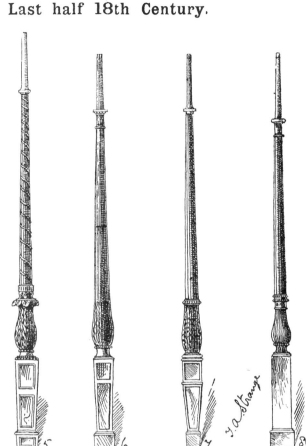

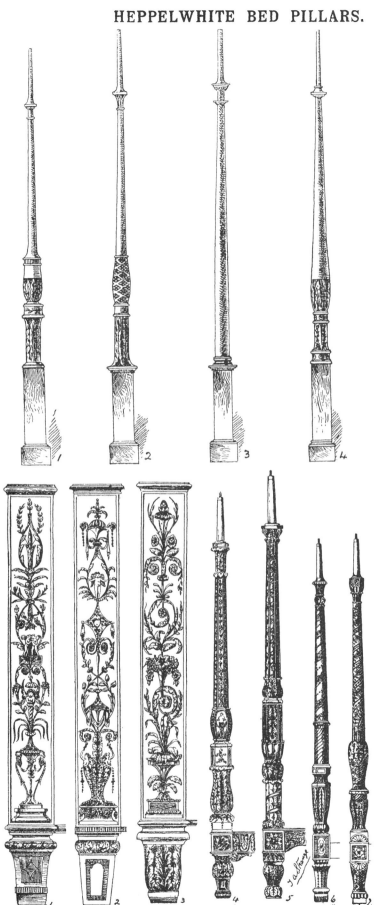

The foliage ornament which runs round the under-cornice may be either of composition metal or cut in wood, and fixed on wire, in the same manner as the tops of ornamented glasses are managed.

With respect to the Pediments on Page 278, No. 1 is from Sheraton's book; it should have the facia, or ground board, glued up in three thicknesses, having the middle piece with the grain right up and down. The foliage ornaments are cut out along with the astragal, and planted on; and the whole may easily be made to take off with the cornice, by having a tenon at each end and one in the centre.

No. 2.—The Tablet is intended to have a cross band round it, and the drapery may be japanned. The astragal on the top of it is meant to return over the ogel. The square of the ogel may come forward level with the Tablet, to prevent too great a projection.

Of the Cornices on Page 284, No. 1 is intended for carving and gilding, No. 2 for japanning, and Nos. 3 and 4 may be either carved or japanned. The circular ends of this cornice are sometimes formed of a faintish curve, and sometimes of a quick one. When they are of a faint sweep, they ought to be made somewhat longer at each end than the outside of the architraves,

State Bedstead.

to give place to the curtain rods, so that they may be brought sufficiently forward on the lath, and not leave too great a vacancy between the rod and the cornice leaves, otherwise the lath will be seen when there is no drapery. In making these cornices it is best to plough and tongue in the leaves to the under-side of the facia of the cornice. The ends may be formed by gluing blocks of deal one on another till they come nearly to the sweep; and after having formed the outside curve, I would advise to gauge on for the plough groove for the leaves, before the wood in the inside is brought to its form, that the pieces for the leaves may be put in without splitting off the groove. After these are well dried, then the superfluous wood on the inside can be taken away. When the cornices are made at each end with a quick curve, the whole is first worked in straight mouldings, and mitred together at each end, the same as if intended to be square, according to the old fashion. When they are glued in the mitres, get out blocks of deal about $2\frac{1}{2}$-ins. square, and cut them down angle-wise, and let their length be equal to the width of the cornice and length of the leaves. After these blockings are dry, cut off as much of the old mitre as is sufficient to form the curve, and work the mouldings again by hand; and observe, that as the block was left long enough, the curved leaf is intended to rest against it, by which it will be much strengthened. The cornices made thus, with a quick, curve need not be made longer than usual, because the quick curve admits the rod to come forward more easily than the other.

As regards the sheets of Bookcases, the first sheet, No. 286, belongs to about this period (Sheraton), and has been gleaned from various sources. No. 2 on page 287 is from Sheraton's book. He says " the use of this piece is to hold books in the upper part, and in the lower it contains a writing-drawer and clothes-press shelves. The design is intended to be executed in satinwood and the ornaments japanned. It may, however, be done in mahogany; and in place of the

SHERATON BEDSTEADS with DRAPERY.   Last half 18th Century

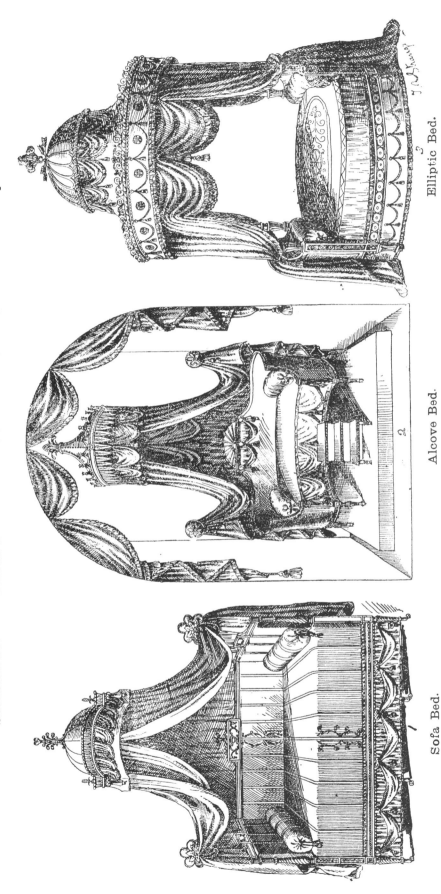

Elliptic Bed.

Alcove Bed.

Sofa Bed.

ornaments in the friezes, flutes may be substituted. The pediment is simply a segment of a circle, and it may be cut in the form of a fan, with eaves in the centre. The vases may be omitted to reduce the work; but if they are introduced, the pedestal on which the centre vase rests is merely a piece of thin wood, with a necking and base moulding mitres round, and planted on the pediment. The pilasters on the Bookcase doors are planted on the frame, and the door hinged as usual. The tops of the pilasters are made to imitate the Ionic Capital.

No. 8, Page 287, is also from Sheraton's book. A Bookcase with writing drawer. The writing drawer represented out, has only the appearance of a frieze when in, it being but 1¾ or 2-ins. deep. The drawer is thrown out by a spring fixed on the back framing, and when in, is retained by a spring thumb catch, which strikes into a plate fixed on the side of the drawer. The place where the thumb presses is the centre of the patera at each end of the drawer, as shewn in the design, which relieves the spring behind, and consequently the drawer comes forward, so much as to afford hold for the hands to draw it entirely out. The drawer is locked by the door-lock below, which is so contrived as to send the bolt upwards under the edge of it. In the lower part are clothes-press shelves, and the glass doors above are intended to have looking-glass in the centre-squares—or they could be painted as shewn; lastly, the drapery is of green silk, fixed first to the curtain, and then both are pinned on to the inside of the door-framing together.

Nos. 4, 9, 10, and 11 on Page 287 are from Heppelwhite's book.

No. 2 on Page 288 is what Sheraton calls a "Library Bookcase." The middle lower part of this bookcase may have wardrobe shelves, the rest is

SHERATON WINDOW CORNICES. Last half 18th Century.

furnished with plain sliding shelves for books only. The circular wings of the upper part may be glazed, or finished without glass, by a green silk drapery only, with its drapery at the top. The diamond part is intended to have looking-glass inserted, which has a pretty effect. The panels of the lower doors do not come flush with their framing by a strong eighth of an inch, which looks both better, and is more calculated to hide the defects if the panel should shrink. The workman must observe that the plinth, surbase, and cornice frames are made and finished entirely separate from the carcasses, and are screwed to them to keep the whole together.

On page 285, No. 1, 2, and 5 are intended for Splats of Parlour Chairs, carved in mahogany. Nos. 3 and 4 are for Painted Chairs.

Bookcase No. 3 on Page 286 shows the brass fret-work on the upper doors that they used to put in front of curtains about this time.

Nos. 4 and 6 on Page 286 are from Shearer's book, which was published about 1787, and whose class of cabinet-work is somewhat similar to Heppelwhite's.

No 5 on Page 286, is rather of a Chippendale character; it is in mahogany. It was exhibited in the Bethnal Green Museum some time since, and was lent by the Under-Secretary of State for India.

No. 1 on Page 287 was formerly in the Honorable East India Company's House in Leadenhall-street, London, E.C.

No. 4 on Page 288 is of a Chippendale character; it is in mahogany, with a beautiful cut-through pediment. Formerly in the Honorable East India Company's House in Leadenhall Street, London, E.C.

Sheraton speaking of a Bookcase Door somewhat similar to No. 8 on Page 287 says: "In the execution of these doors, the candid and ingenious workman may exercise his judgment both by varying some parts of the figures, and taking other parts entirely away, when the door is thought to have too much work. This door relates to No. 36 on Page 154.

SHERATON CHAIR SPLATS and TURNING   Late 18th Century.

"The first thing to be done is to draw on a board an oval of the full length and breadth of the door. Then take half the oval on the short diameter and glue on blocks of deal at a little distance from each other, to form a caul; then, on the short diameter, glue on a couple of blocks, one to stop the ends of the veneer with at the time of gluing, and the other, being bevelled off, serves to force the joints of the veneer close and to keep all fast till sufficiently dry. Observe, the half-oval is formed by the blocks of the astragal, and not the rabbet; therefore consider how broad a piece of veneer will make the astragals for one door, or for half a door. For a whole door which takes eight quarter ovals, it will require the veneer to be 1¼-ins. broad, allowing for the thickness of a sash saw to

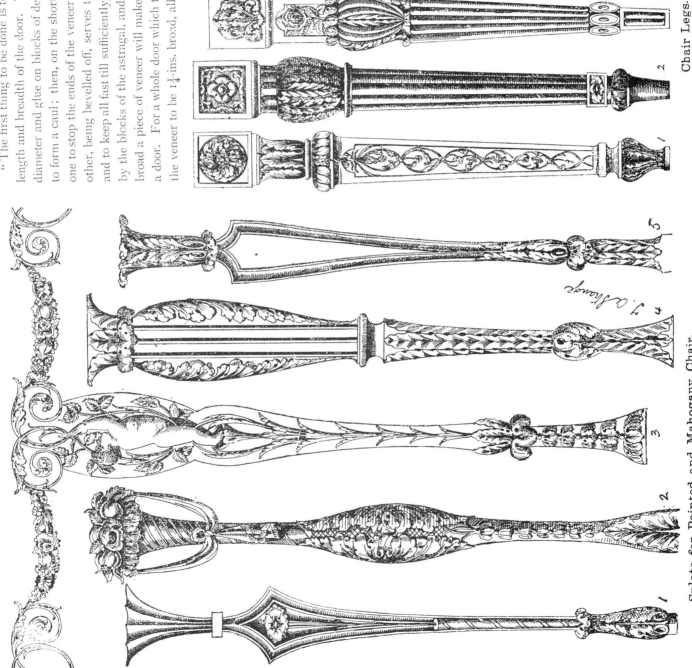

Chair Legs.

Splats for Painted and Mahogany Chair.

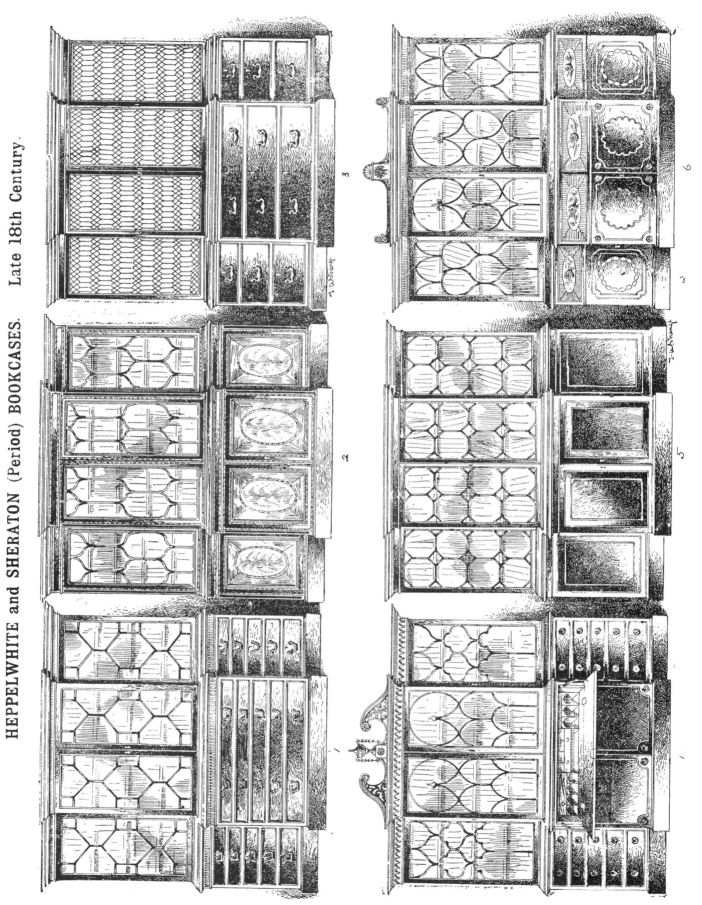

HEPPELWHITE and SHERATON (Period) BOOKCASES and BUREAU BOOKCASES.

HEPPELWHITE BOOKCASES, BOOKCASE CABINETS and CABINET BUREAU.

This is a Sheraton Bookcase.

HEPPELWHITE and SHERATON BOOKCASES.   Late 18th Century.

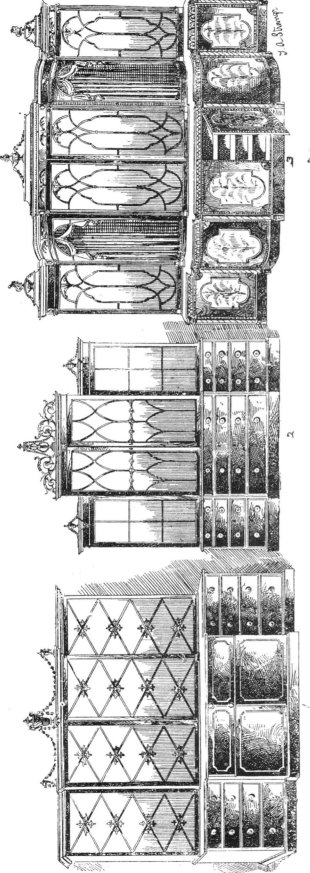

cut them off with. Veneers of this breadth may, by proper management, be glued quite close; and if the veneer be straight baited, and all of one kind no joint will appear in the astragal. Two half ovals thus glued up, will make astragals for a pair of doors, which, after they are taken out of the cauls and cleaned off a little, may be glued one upon the other, and then glued on a board, to hold them fast for working the astragals on the edge; which may easily be done, by forming a neat astragal in a piece of soft steel, and fixing it in a notched piece of wood, and then work it as a gauge; but before you work it, run on a gauge for the thickness of the astragal, cut it off with a sash saw, by turning the board on which the sweep-pieces are glued on an edge; then having sawn one astragal off, plane the edge of your stuff again, and proceed as before.

For gluing up the rabbet part, it must be observed that a piece of dry veneer equal to the thickness of the rabbet must be forced tight into the caul; and then proceed as before in gluing two thicknesses of veneer for the rabbet part, which will leave sufficient hiding for the glass, on supposition that the astragal was glued in five.

See Page 290.

A Gentleman's Secretary.

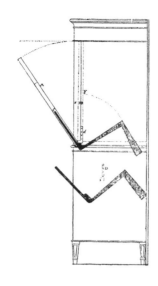

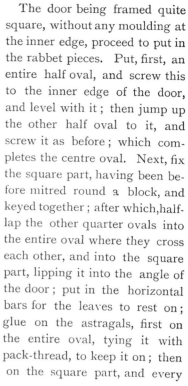

The door being framed quite square, without any moulding at the inner edge, proceed to put in the rabbet pieces. Put, first, an entire half oval, and screw this to the inner edge of the door, and level with it; then jump up the other half oval to it, and screw it as before; which completes the centre oval. Next, fix the square part, having been before mitred round a block, and keyed together; after which, half-lap the other quarter ovals into the entire oval where they cross each other, and into the square part, lipping it into the angle of the door; put in the horizontal bars for the leaves to rest on; glue on the astragals, first on the entire oval, tying it with pack-thread, to keep it on; then the straight one on the edge of the framing, fitting it to the oval; lastly, mitre the astragal on the square part, and every other particular will follow of course.

No. 1 on Page 288 is in mahogany. The pediment is carved with quadroon and bead ornament, with fir cones and vases turned and carved on the top; the projecting lower part has a revolving cover, and draw-out desk, which forms a writing-table, with drawers and pigeon-holes at back. Paintings of floral ornament, and brass handles. From Felday, Dorking.

Nos. 1, 2, 4 and 5 Bookcases on Page 289 are Heppelwhite's. No. 3 is Sheraton's. Particulars as under.

THE LIBRARY CASE. — The elliptic breaks of this bookcase will produce a good effect in the whole.

The doors in the upper part are intended to have fluted green silk behind, and a drapery at top.

The pilasters are supposed to be glued to the stile of the door, and are hinged as in common.

The lower middle part contains clothes-press shelves, and every other part may be fitted up for books; or the lower elliptic breaks may be formed into a nest of drawers, as there is depth enough.

The half columns on the lower doors are glued to the stile, and

See Page 292.

See Pages 294 to 301.

Feet and Inches

SHERATON BEDSTEADS.   Late 18th Century.

the doors hinged as in common; but for the sake of shewing the design to advantage, the open door is drawn as if the columns were separate.

The young workman should observe that the whole is to be made in six carcasses, and screwed together, and then the plinth should be made to fit it, of one entire frame and screwed down on to the carcasses; as also is the cornice and its frieze.

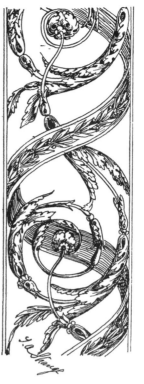

Borders for Pier-Tables.

is supported by that means ; for the hinge is made very strong, about three-quarters thick at the dove-tail end, and tapered off to about a quarter thick at the joint, and where it is screwed to the fall. The hinge is made in two parts, as D and *b*. D has a centre pin, and is screwed on to the inside

The Gentleman's Secretary on Page 290 is Sheraton's, particulars of which are as follows :

This piece is intended for a gentleman to write at, to keep his own accounts, and serve as a library. The style of finishing it is neat, and sometimes approaching to elegance, being at times made of satin wood, with japanned ornaments.

THE MANUFACTURING PART.—The great thing to be observed in this, is the management of the fall A, or writing part, which is lined with green cloth. This fall is hung by an iron balance hinge B, so that when the fall is raised up by the hand a little above an angle of forty-five degrees, or in the position it is shewn at A, it falls to of itself by the balancing power of B.

When A is in a horizontal position, B is at F, the inside of the pilaster, on which is glued a piece of cloth to prevent the iron from rattling. B stopping at F it is evident how firmly the fall

Pediments.

See Pages 301 and 302.

SHERATON ORNAMENT. Late 18th Century.

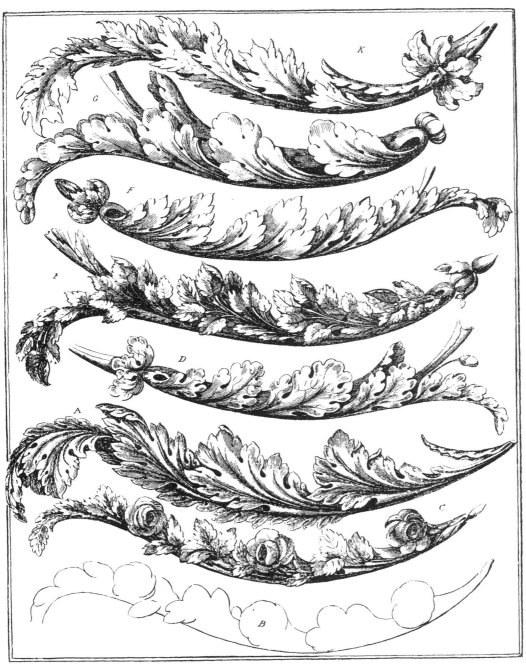

Ornament for Copying.

of the pilaster, as at *d*; *b* is all in one piece, and is screwed on to the fall, having a centre hole to receive the above-mentioned pin in the other part of the hinge.

It is necessary to observe that there is a vacuity behind both the upper and lower pilasters in which the iron balance operates, so that nothing is seen but the mere joint of the hinge.

Again, it is requisite to observe, that a hollow must be worked on the upper side of the under carcass, to give place to the circular motion of the under angle of the fall, as it turns upon its hinge from a perpendicular to a horizontal form. This hollow may be observed in the plate. The space 1 contains the fall when it is up; 2 is an open space, which affords room for the rings on the small drawers; and 3 is the pilaster. The ornamented frieze under the cornice is, in reality, a drawer, which springs out when the bolt of the fall lock is relieved. This is done by a spring bolt let into the partition under the drawer, which is forced up by the bolt of the fall lock into the under edge of drawer; and when the fall is unlocked this spring bolt returns to its place in the partition, and a common spring screwed on to the drawer back sends it forward, so that it may be drawn out independent of a ring or handle.

When the fall is up, there appear two panels in the form of those below. As for any other particular, it must be understood by a workman.

Observe, the dimensions of every part may be accurately taken from the profile by the scale.

The Secretary in right-hand corner of Page 290 is Heppelwhite's.

SHERATON ORNAMENT.   Late 18th Century.

The double Bedstead on Page 291 is Sheraton's.

THE SUMMER BED IN TWO COMPARTMENTS.—These beds are intended for a nobleman or gentleman and his lady to sleep in separately in hot weather. Some beds for this purpose have been made entirely in one, except in bed-clothing, being confined in two drawers, running on rollers, capable of being drawn out on each side by servants in order to make them. But the preference for this design for the purpose, must be obvious to every one in two or three particulars.

First the passage up the middle, which is about 22-ins. in width, gives room for the circulation of air, and likewise affords an easy access to the servants when they make the beds.

Centre for a Pembroke Table.

Secondly, the passage gives opportunity for curtains to enclose each compartment, if necessary on account of any sudden change of weather.

Thirdly, it makes the whole considerably more ornamental, uniform and light.

The manufacturing part may easily be under-

Centre for Pier Table.

stood from the design by any workman ; I shall, however, point out a few particulars. The arch which springs from the Ionic columns should be glued up in thickness round a caul, and an architrave put on each side afterwards. The arch should be tenoned into the columns, with iron plates screwed on, so that it may be taken off when the bed is required to come down. In this arch a drapery is fixed, with a tassel in the centre, and a vase above. The head-board is framed

See Page 302.

296

all in one length, and the two inner sides of the bed tenoned into the head-rail, and screwed. The tester is made in one, in which are two domes, one over each compartment. It may, however, be made without domes, but not with so good effect. In the middle of the tester, perpendicular to the sides of the passage, are fixed two rods, for the curtains above mentioned. These rods are hid by

the end of the bed, it being merely a geometrical elevation.

The Duchesse on Page 291 is Sheraton's.

THE DUCHESSE.—The French have what they term duchesse beds, whence I suppose we have derived our ideas of a duchesse. What is sometimes named a duchesse amongst us, is merely two barjier chairs fastened to a

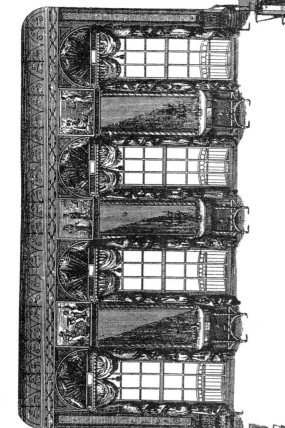

valances, and between the valances is formed a panel, by sewing on variegated margins to suit the rest of the upholstery work. The ornamented margins, and the oval with crests in the centre of the counterpanes, may all be printed to any pattern at a manufactory which has been lately established for such purposes.

The scale shews the sizes which apply to every part of

See Page 303.

stool in the middle ; sometimes, indeed, we add a slight tester and covering, but even this is very different from theirs.   The French duchesse beds are more stately.   The tester is full and fixed to the wall, with drapery hanging down to the bedding and floor.   The head part is formed something like the back of a chair ; at the foot there are short stump pillars ; and the whole frame of the bed being detached from the tester, may be moved to any part to loll upon.   The duchesse which is here given, is intended to answer three different purposes.   The ends, when detached from the middle stool, may serve as small sofas.   When they are connected together without the tester, and a squab or cushion made to fit over the whole, it will then serve to rest or loll upon.   When it is used as a bed, four short pillars are screwed to each back foot, and a straight lath extends across from pillar to pillar at each end.   From these pillars are fixed the sweep iron rods which form the tester, and which support the drapery and covering which is thrown over the whole.   The little dome or top is made separate and

See Page 303.

HEPPELWHITE, SHEARER and SHERATON (Period) SIDEBOARDS.   Late 18th Century.

entire of itself, with the cornice mitred round, and the tassels fixed to it as shewn in the design, and the whole is placed loose on without any fastenings.

They are made narrow, between two and three feet wide, and seldom above it. Everything is made exceeding light about the tester. The stool is fixed to each chair with straps and buttons, and the whole thus finished produces a pleasing appearance.

The Bedstead in right-hand corner of Page 291 is Sheraton's.

THE BED.—This design requires no explanation, except that which relates to the tester. The cove of the tester is to be formed by ribs ; one at each mitre,

See Page 304.

HEPPELWHITE, SHEARER and SHERATON (Period) SIDEBOARDS. Late 18th Century.

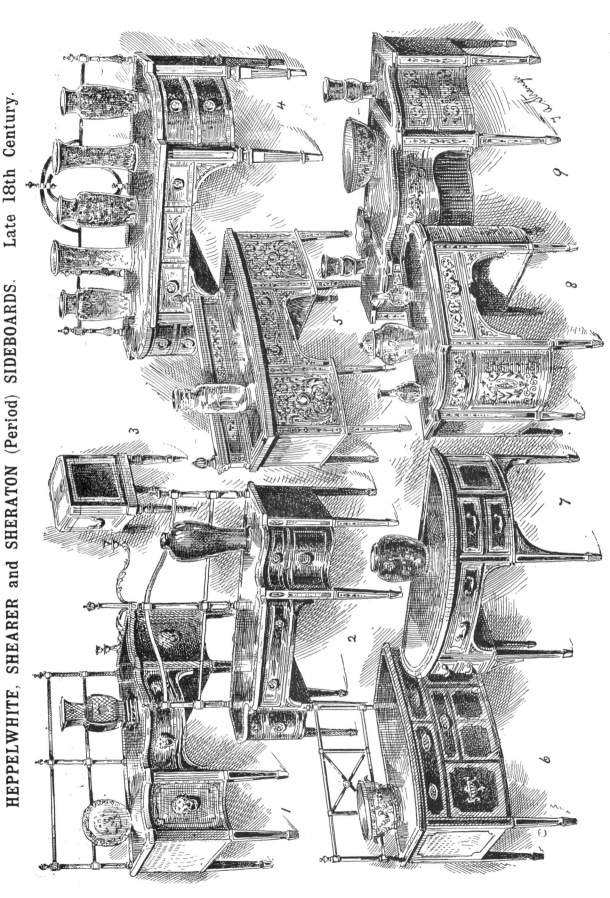

and other short ones joined to them, with the rest about five inches apart from each other. At the upper part of the cove is a square tester into which the ribs are fixed. On the edge of this tester, which is made very light, is fixed a small moulding mitred all round. The cove being formed, the ribs may be covered with strong board-paper, both inside and out, which may either be japanned to match the furniture, or it may be covered with the furniture itself. The circular part above the cove is nothing more than a straight board fixed on to the upper tester. For the sake of easy conveyance, the cove may be made in four parts, mitreing at each corner, and the ornament intended to be at each mitre on the outside running entirely up the feathers, will hide the joint.

See Page 304.

See Page 304.

SHERATON SIDEBOARDS. Late 18th Century.

I shall, therefore, omit it here, and proceed to give some hints relative to the manufacturing part. The dome is supported with iron rods of about an inch diameter, curved regularly down to each pillar, where they are fixed with a strong screw and nut. These iron rods are covered and entirely hid by a valance, which comes in a regular sweep, and meets in a point at the vases on the pillars, as the design shews. Behind this valance, which continues all round, the drapery is drawn up by pulleys, and tied up by a silken cord and tassels at the head of the pillars. The head-boards of these beds are framed and stuffed, and covered to suit the hangings, and the frame is white and gold, if the pillars and cornice are. The bed-frame is sometimes ornamented, and has drapery valances below.

The swags of silk line that appear on the drapery should be fastened to the back part of the cornice, in order that they may hang easy. The pillars are to be japanned. The panel that hides the screws is made to slip into a groove at the bottom, and being bevelled off behind at the top, when raised up a little from their place, by pressing the front, can easily be taken away to come at the screws. The valance and drapery both together slip on to a lath as in common.

The French State-Bed on Page 292 is Sheraton's.

THE FRENCH STATE-BED.—Beds of this kind have been introduced of late with great success in England.

The style of finishing them, with the management of the domes, is already described in general terms, in preceding page,

See Page 305.

SHERATON (Period) CLOCKS.   Late 18th Century.

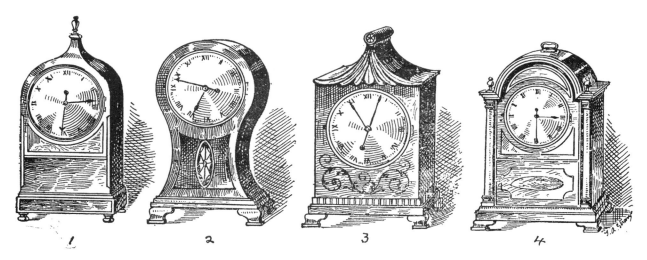

Observe that grooves are made in the pillars to receive the head-boards, and screwed at the top, by which means the whole is kept firm, and is easily taken to pieces. Square bolsters are now often introduced, with margins of various colours stitched all round. The counterpane has also these margins; they are also fringed at bottom, and have sometimes a drapery tied up in cords and tassels on the side.

THE DRAPERY on Page 295.—Little can be said of this, as every part explains itself, as represented in the drawing. It is, however, necessary to observe that the French strapping and tassels in the right-hand design is no part of the cornice, as some cabinet-makers have already mistaken it to be. It is the upholsterer's work, and is sewed on within the vallance or ground of the drapery.

These curtains are drawn on French rods. When the cords are drawn the curtains meet in the centre at the same time, but are no way raised from the floor. When the same cord is drawn the reverse way, each curtain flies open, and comes to their place on each side, as they are now represented. The cord passes on a side pulley fixed on the right-hand.

To effect this, the rod is made in a particular manner, having two pulleys at one end, and a single one at the other, which cannot well be described in words without a drawing of it.

THE ORNAMENT FOR COPYING on Page 293.—K, is the thistle leaf, sharply pointed and irregular. G, is the roman leaf, round and massy. F, the parsley leaf, light and rather sharp pointed. E, the rose leaf, formed into groups. D, the oak leaf, broad and massy, scolloped on the edge with small partings. A, is a fancy leaf, rather sharp, with large partings. C, roses and leaves alternately.

SHERATON LONG CLOCKS.

THE INTERIOR on Page 296.—In the drawing-room which is here shown, everything will appear easily understood to a workman in town, who is accustomed to see such apartments; but for a stranger, and those workmen who reside in the country, it will be proper to point out a few particulars.

The pier-tables have marble tops and gold frames, or white and gold. The glasses are often made to appear to come down to the stretcher of the table; that is, a piece of glass is fixed in behind the pier-table, separate from the upper glass, which then appears to be the continuation of the same glass, and by reflection makes the table to appear double. This small piece of glass may be fixed either in the dado of the room, or in the frame of the table.

The arches above the windows are merely artificial, being only wooden frames put up, strained with canvas; after which the same kind of stuff of which the curtains are made is formed to appear like a fan, and drapery tacked on to it.

The pannelling on the walls are done in paper, with ornamented borders of various colours.

The figures above the glasses are paintings in clare-obscure. The sofas are bordered off in three compartments, and covered with figured silk or satin. The ovals may be printed separately, and sewn on. These sofas may have cushions to fill their backs, together with bolsters at each end. In France, where their drawing-rooms are fitted up in the most splendid manner, they use a set of small and plainer chairs, reserving the others merely for ornament.

The commode opposite the fire-place has four doors; its legs are intended to stand a little clear of the wings; and the top is marble, to match the pier-tables. In the frieze part of the commode is a tablet in the centre, made of an exquisite composition in imitation of statuary marble. These are to be had, of any figure, or on any subject, at Mr Wedgwood's, near Soho Square. They are let into the wood, and project a little forward. The commode should be painted to suit furniture, and the legs and other parts in gold to harmonize with the sofas, tables, and chairs.

THE INTERIORS on PAGE 297.—With respect to the section, it is only necessary to observe that the pier-table under the glass is richly ornamented in gold. The top is marble, and also the shelf at each end; the back of it is composed of three panels of glass, the Chinese figure sitting on a cushion is metal and painted. The candle branches are gilt metal, and the panels are painted in the style of the Chinese, the whole producing a brilliant effect.

304

The view contains an ottoman, or long seat, extending the whole width of the room, and returning at each end about five feet. The Chinese columns are on the front of this seat, and mark out its boundaries. The upholstery work is very richly executed in figured satin, with extremely rich borders, all worked to suit the style of the room. Within this ottoman are two grand tripod candle-stands, with heating urns at the top, that the seat may be kept in a proper temperature in cold weather. On the front of the ottoman before the columns are two censers containing perfumes, by which an agreeable smell may be diffused to every part of the room preventing that of a contrary nature, which is the consequence of lighting a number of candles.

The chimney-piece is rich, adorned with a valuable time-piece, and two lights supported by two Chinese figures; on each side of the fire-place is also a Chinese figure, answerable to those which support a table on the opposite side, under which is seated a Chinese figure. Over each table, the fire-place, and in the centre of the ottoman, is a glass, which by their reflections greatly enliven the whole. The subjects painted on the panels of each wall are Chinese views and little scenes. The carpet is worked in one entire piece with a border round it, and the whole in effect, though it may appear extravagant to a vulgar eye, is but suitable to the dignity of the proprietor.

The Sideboards on Pages 298 and 299 have been gathered from various contemporary sources.

THE SIDEBOARD, WITH VASE KNIFE-CASES on Page 301.—The pedestal parts of this sideboard may be made separate, and then screwed to the sideboard. The top extends the whole length in one entire piece, and is screwed down to the pedestals. The hollow plinths of the vases are worked in one length and mitred round. The top of the plinth is then blocked on at the under side, and the vase part is made to screw into it, so that the vases may occasionally be taken off. A cross band is meant to be mitred all round the hollow plinths, coming forward to the edge of the top; so that if the top be veneered, it will only require the length between the two plinths. Within the front is a tambour cupboard, which is both useful and has a good effect in its appearance; almost every workman will know how to manage this, so that I need not explain it. The ornament behind is brass, intended as a stay to silver plate, and has branches for three lights. The circle in the centre may have a glass lustre hung within it as an ornament.

THE SIDEBOARD TABLES, and Tables of this kind in general.—The sideboard, No. 3 on Page 301, has a brass rod to it, which is used to set large dishes against, and to support a couple of candle or lamp branches in the middle, which, when lighted, give a very brilliant effect to the silver ware. The branches are each of them fixed in one socket, which slides up and down on the same rod to any height, and fixed anywhere by turning a screw. These rods have sometimes returns at each end of the sideboard; and sometimes they are made straight, the whole length of the sideboard, and have a narrow shelf in the middle, made of full half-inch mahogany, for the purpose of setting smaller dishes on, and sometimes small silver ware.

The right-hand drawer, as in common, contains the cellarette, which is often made to draw out separate from the rest. It is partitioned and lined with lead, to hold nine or ten wine bottles, as shown in Nos. 1 and 2.

The drawer on the left is generally plain, but sometimes divided into two; the back division being lined with baize, to hold plates, having a cover hinged to enclose the whole. The front division is lined with lead, so that it may hold water to wash glasses: which may be made to take out, or have a plug-hole to let off the dirty water. The left-hand drawer is, however, sometimes made very short, to give place to a pot-cupboard behind, which opens by a door at the end of the sideboard. This door is made to hide itself in the end rail as much as possible, both for look and secrecy. For which reason a turn-buckle is not used, but a thumb-spring, which catches at the bottom of the door, and has a communication through the rail, so that by a touch of the finger the door flies open, owing to the resistance of a common spring fixed to the rabbet which the door falls against, as is denoted by Figure A. F is for the finger, B is the brass plate let into the rail, L is the lever, p is the spring that presses the lever upwards, and c is the end of it which catches the under edge of the door as it passes over it and strikes into a plate with a hole in it, and s is the spring screwed to the rabbet which throws the door out when F is pushed upwards.

But the reader must here observe that the shape of this sideboard will not admit of a cupboard of this sort in the end rail. Those which are square at the ends, and only a little shaped in front, are fittest for this purpose.

In large circular sideboards, the left-hand drawer has sometimes been fitted up as a plate-warmer, having a rack in the middle to put the plates in, and lined with strong tin all round, and on the underside of the sideboard top, to prevent the heat from injuring it. In this case the bottom of the drawer is made partly open, under which is fixed a small narrow drawer to contain a heater, which gives warmth to the plates the same as in a pedestal.

SHERATON.   Late 18th Century.

In spacious dining-rooms the sideboards are often made without drawers of any sort, having simply a rail a little ornamented, and pedestals with vases at each end, which produce a grand effect.   One pedestal is used as a plate-warmer, and is lined with tin ; the other as a pot-cupboard, and sometimes it contains a cellarette for wine. ,The vases are used for water for the use of the butler, and sometimes as knife-cases.   They are sometimes made of copper, japanned, but generally of mahogany.

There are other sideboards for small dining-rooms, made without either drawers or pedestals ; but have generally a wine-cooler to stand under them, hooped with brass, partitioned and lined with lead for wine bottles, the same as the above-mentioned cellarette drawers.

The sideboard Nos. 1 and 2 shews two patterns, one at each end.   That on the left is intended to have four marble shelves at each end enclosed by two backs and open in front.   These shelves are used in grand sideboards to place the small silver ware on.   The pattern on the right is intended to have legs turned the whole length, or rounded so far as the framing and turned below it, with carved leaves and flutes.   The division beyond the cellarette drawer is meant for a pot cupboard.

It is not usual to make side-boards hollow in front, but in some circumstances it is evident that advantages will arise from it.   If a side-board be required nine or ten feet long, as in some noblemen's houses, and if the breadth of it be in proportion to the length, it will not be easy for a butler to reach across it.   I therefore think, in this case, a hollow front would obviate the difficulty, and at the same time have a very good effect by taking off part of the appearance of the great length of such a sideboard.   Besides, if the sideboard be near the entering door of the dining-room, the hollow front will sometimes secure the butler from the jostles of the other servants.

A SIDEBOARD.—This design is intended to have a brass rod behind containing lights in the centre and at each end.

There is also a narrow mahogany shelf about three inches and a half wide fixed against the middle of the rod at the back ; on which shelf a channel is worked by a plane, for the purpose of keeping up small dishes placed in the spaces between the larger ones which rest on the sideboard top.

The frame of this table is richly carved out of solid wood, and the ornament of that part of the legs which cross the frame is formed in imitation of a truss leaf.

The vase under the table may be of mahogany, and fitted up in the inside to hold wine bottles, or it may be considered merely as ornamental.

The Sideboards on Page 300 are from Sheraton's book.

THE PULPIT,—The design of introducing a pulpit into this work was to afford some assistance to the cabinet-maker, who in the country is generally employed on such occasions.   In erecting a pulpit of this kind three particulars ought principally to be regarded.   First, the plan ; secondly, the manner of conducting the steps and hand-rail round the column ; and, lastly, to fix the whole firm, so that it may not by shaking produce a disagreeable sensation to the preacher.

The plan of this pulpit is a regular hexagon, which to me is the most beautiful and compact of any.   One of its sides is occupied by the door, and one for the back of the preacher, another to rest his arm, and the remaining three for the cushion. The plan of the steps is a circle, which is most convenient when there is a want of room.   The plan should be divided according to the number of steps necessary for attaining to a proper height, which in this case is twelve, as 1, 2, 3, etc., in the plan.

A section should then be drawn, and the height of the risers adjusted to the number of the steps, as in the section a, b, c, etc.

Draw the semi-plan P, and divide the circumference into eight equal parts, as 1, 2, 3, 4, etc., because, that in the plan there are so many steps contained in its semi.   Draw from 1, 2, 3, 4, etc., lines perpendicular, and continue them to the uppermost steps.   From a, the first step, draw a line to a on the plan P.   Do the same from b to b, c to c, and so of all the others, which will describe the steps and risers as they revolve on a cylinder.   The face mould for the hand-rail, when it is cut out of the solid, is found as follows (see Page 301) :—Draw a quarter plan as there described, divide the chord line into any number of equal parts, as 1, 3, 5 ; from which raise perpendiculars to intersect the circumference ; draw next the rake or pitch-board of the steps at Figure R, by taking the breadth of the step on the plan, and repeating it 1, 2, 3, 4 ; then take the height of four risers, as from x to y, and draw the line y 4, which line will be the chord for the face mould ;

SHERATON.　Late 18th Century.

therefore take y 4, and divide it into six, as in the plan of the hand-rail. Take the perpendicular heights as 1, 2, 3, 4 and 5, 6 of the plan, and transfer them to the correspondent perpendiculars on the face mould, which will give points through which the curve is to pass, to form the face mould, as the figure shews. Three of these lengths will be wanted to complete the hand-rail, including the ramp and knee.

These hand-rails are, however, sometimes glued up in thin pieces round a cylinder in one entire length, after which a cross banding is put on the top, and rounded off. In this case a cylinder is formed of deal, and the line of the steps is traced out as described, which is the guide for the thin mahogany to be bent round. In fixing the steps, I presume it will be found the best method to mortice and dovetail the risers of each step into the pillar ; this may be done by making the mortice so much wider than the breadth of the riser as the dovetail is intended to be in depth, so that when the riser is put into the mortice it may be forced up to its place by a wedge driven in at the under edge of the riser. By this means it will be impossible that the steps should work when they are tongued and blocked together. The soffits of the steps are in the form of an ogee, answerable to the brackets, and are fitted up separately afterwards.

In fixing the pillar it must be noticed that it is first tenoned into transverse pieces of oak timber, which are sunk a good depth into the ground, so that when the clay is beat in solidly about the pillar it cannot work ; yet it is easy to conceive that in the pulpit it will be liable to spring when the preacher is in it ; to prevent which I have introduced a light small column, situated in the centre of the pulpit, and connected with it by a cove, on which the pulpit rests. The sound-board is made as light as possible, which furnishes in an octave cove at the top, and is fixed to the pillar by a strong screw and nut, together with a tenon, which is sunk into the sound-board. The banisters of the hand-rail may be straight bars of brass made very light, dove-tailed into the ends of the steps, and let into a plate of thin iron at top, which is screwed the under side of the hand-rail.

Observe that on the left side of the plate is a scale of feet and inches, from which the various measurements may be taken.

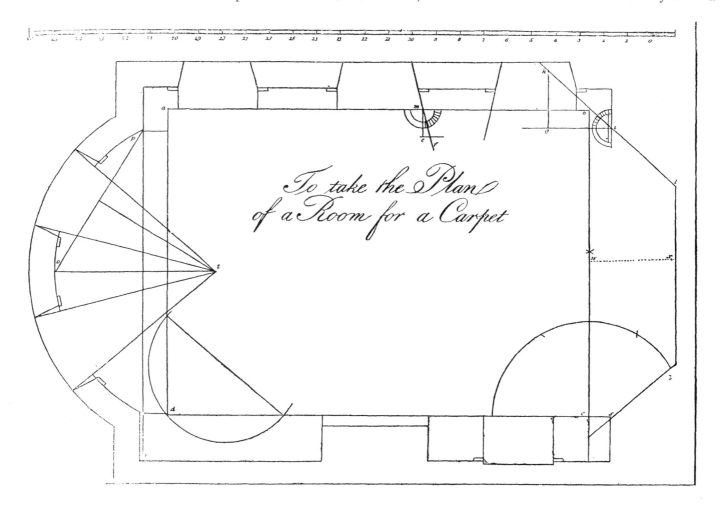

SHERATON PULPIT.   Late 18th Century.

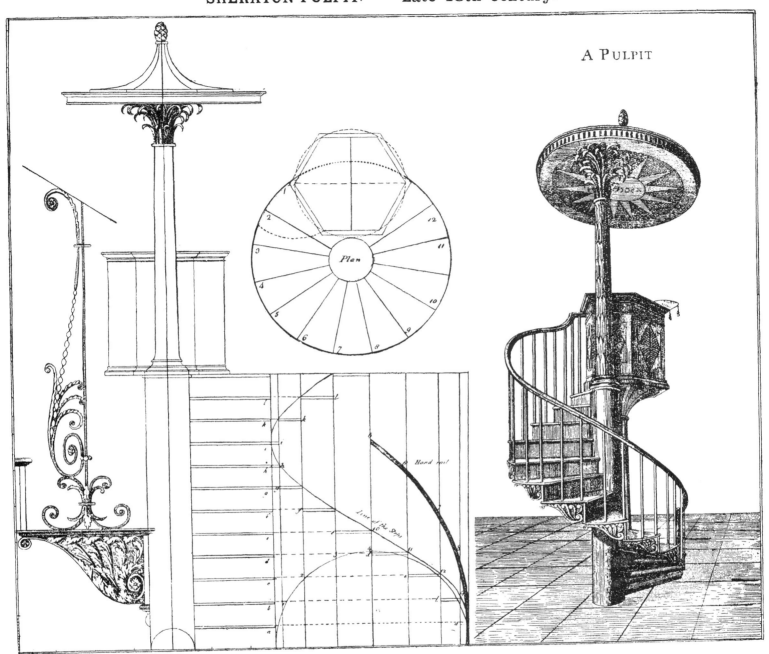

A PULPIT

To take the plan of a room in an accurate manner, so that a carpet may be properly cut by it.

OPERATION.—The room being cleared of every obstruction, and the floor swept clean, proceed as follows :—

First, take a chalk line, and by it strike a line parallel to that side of the room which seems freest from irregularities, as *d c* in Plate IV. Then by Problem III., Page 38, raise a perpendicular from *c* continued to *b*. Proceed next to the other end of the room, as at *d*, and by the second method of Problem III, if most convenient, raise another perpendicular continued to *a*. Draw then a line from *a* to *b*, exactly parallel to *d c*, the opposite side of the room. Then will the angles *a b c d* form a true parallelogram, proportioned to the size of the room, by which the principal distortions or irregularities of any of the sides of the room will at once appear. For instance, the angle *v* is somewhat out, as the line parallel to *a d* plainly shews; and in this manner any other angle of the room, whether obtuse or acute, may be ascertained.

Secondly, let the hexagon end of the room be next considered ; and let it be observed that the plan-taker is supposed to have no square, or straight rule, but only a case of instruments and line. Therefore, in order to know how much the side *i l* bevels off from a square, take the line and strike it by the side *i l* of the hexagon, and continue the line at pleasure beyond *h*. Take then the brass protractor, and place the centre of its base to *i*, as the figure shews. Make a pencil mark over 90, on the arch of the instru-

ment, and from *i* draw a straight line across the pencil mark to *g* at pleasure. Take the side *i l* of the hexagon, and place it from *i* to *h*. Draw *g h* parallel to the base of the protractor, or to *b c*; then will *g h* shew how much *i l* is out of square, as required. Examine then the other side of the hexagon by the same rule, and if there be any variation from the opposite side, it will easily be discovered. Proceed to the windows, and find the rake of the jambs in the same manner as before; only observe, that the protractor cannot be placed to the architraves because of their irregularity; and therefore it must be placed on the line *a b* at *m*, after the line *f* is drawn from the jamb cutting at *m*. From *m* draw a perpendicular to *e*, and

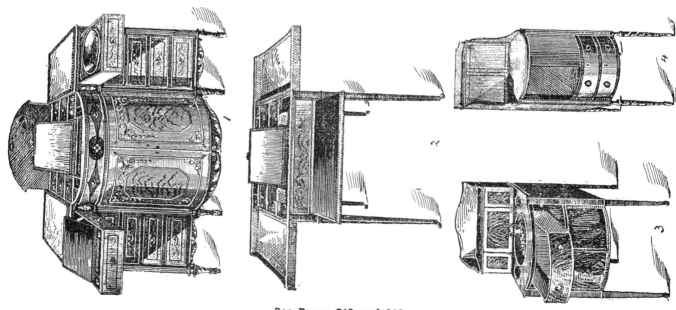

See Pages 312 and 316.

SHERATON LADY'S CABINET DRESSING-TABLE, etc.   Late 18th Century.

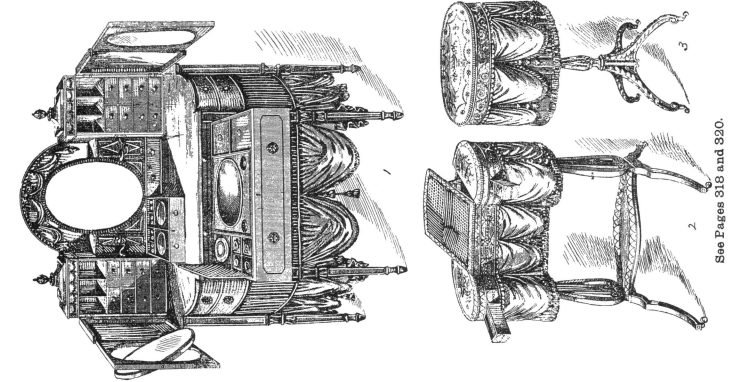

See Pages 318 and 320.

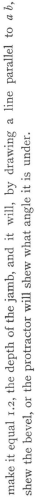

make it equal 1.2, the depth of the jamb, and it will, by drawing a line parallel to *a b*, shew the bevel, or the protractor will shew what angle it is under.

Lastly, proceed to the circular end of the room, with its windows; and in order to find the centre of the arch *v o p*, draw *p v* at its foot, and parallel with *a d*. On the middle of *p v* raise a perpendicular, and continue it to *t* at pleasure. Draw then the chord *o p*, and bisect it as at *n*, whence raise a perpendicular, cutting *o t* in *t*, which will be the centre. From the opening of each window draw the several radii, as shewn in the figure, by which it will be easily seen how much the jambs vary from these central lines.

The room being thus lined out, take a sheet of paper, and lay down a scale of feet and inches that will comprehend the longest part of the room. Measure then, with your common rule, the sides and ends of the parallelogram which was chalked out on the floor, and whatever these measure by the rule, take the same number of feet, inches, and parts from the scale, and draw the parallelogram on the paper in the same manner as was done on the floor; and in this way go on, taking off every dimension

See Page 320.

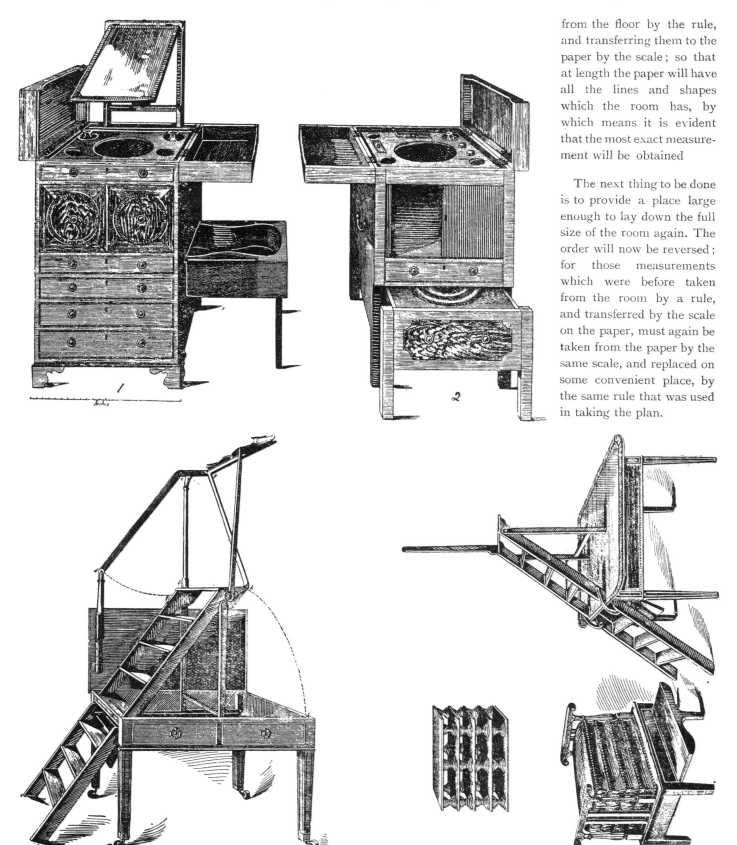

from the floor by the rule, and transferring them to the paper by the scale; so that at length the paper will have all the lines and shapes which the room has, by which means it is evident that the most exact measurement will be obtained

The next thing to be done is to provide a place large enough to lay down the full size of the room again. The order will now be reversed; for those measurements which were before taken from the room by a rule, and transferred by the scale on the paper, must again be taken from the paper by the same scale, and replaced on some convenient place, by the same rule that was used in taking the plan.

See Page 321.

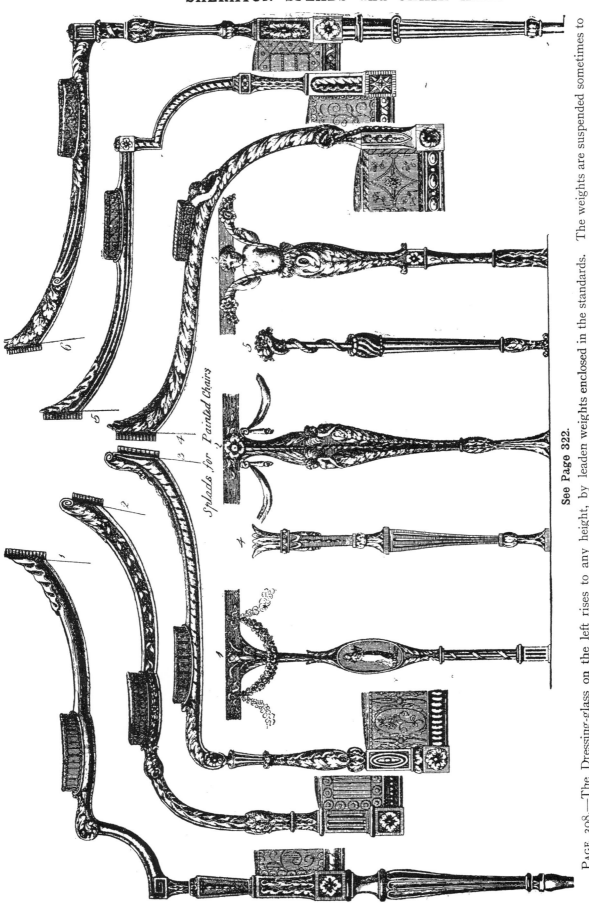

Splads for Painted Chairs

See Page 322.

PAGE 308.—The Dressing-glass on the left rises to any height, by leaden weights enclosed in the standards. The weights are suspended sometimes to tambour glued on to webbing, which passes over a brass roller at the top and fixes to a piece of thin wood tamboured to match it. Through this piece of thin wood is put an iron pin, with a thin plate to it to screw it fast : which pin goes through the side of the glass and fastens by a nut at the inside, so that when the glass is raised it may be turned to any direction. But some use a kind of coloured strong webbing, without the tambour, which makes it less troublesome, and less liable to injury, though it does not look so neat. There is a brass handle behind the ornamented top to raise the glass by. The boxes on each side are intended to hold conveniences for dressing. On these there is a comb tray on the left side, and a pin-cushion on the right. When the dressing-boxes are not in use they are intended to turn behind the glass. For this purpose they are fixed to a brass socket, which turns upon a short brass rod, and by a screw they may be raised up or lowered at pleasure. (Continued on Page 316.)

SHERATON' CHAIR-BACKS.   Late 18th Century.

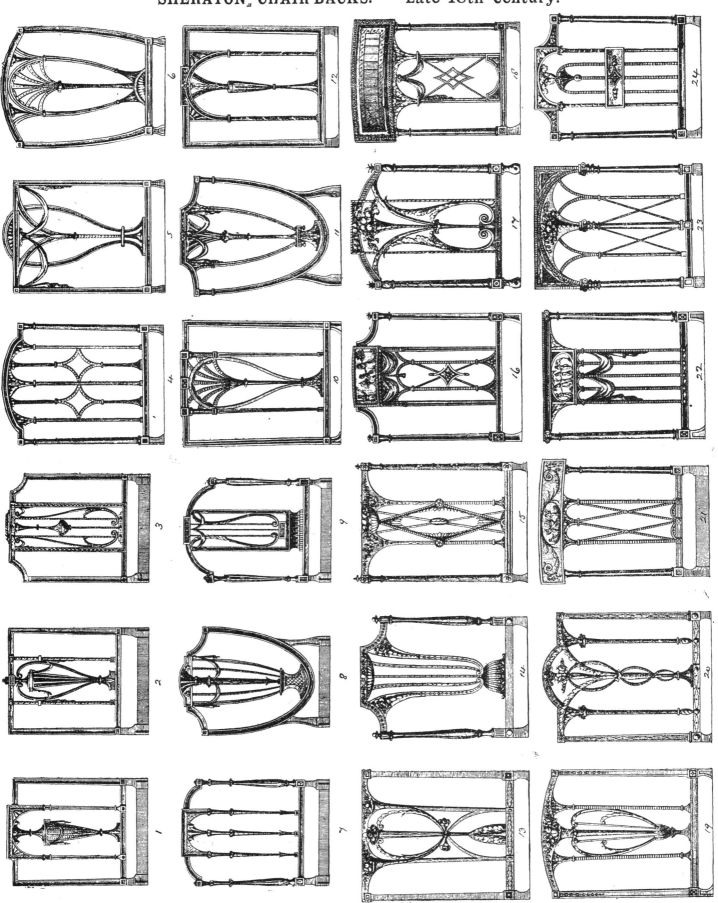

See Page 322.

SHERATON SETTEES.   Late 18th Century.

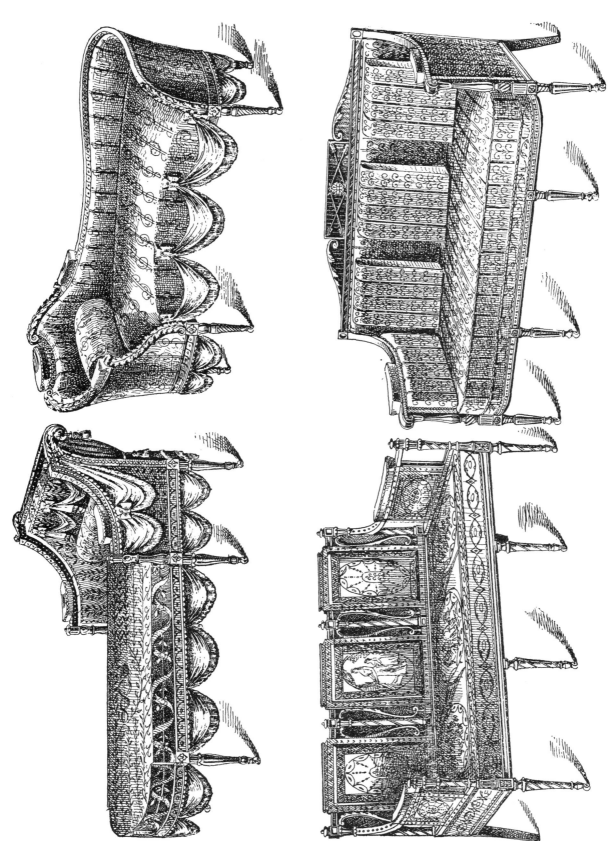

These are done in white and gold, or japanned. The loose cushions at the back are generally made to fill the whole length, which would have taken four; but I could not make the design so striking with four, because they would not have been distinguished from the back of the sofa by a common observer. These cushions serve at times for bolsters, being placed against the arms to loll against. The seat is stuffed up in front about three inches high above the rail, denoted by the figure of the sprig running longways; all above that is a squab, which may be taken off occasionally. If the top rail be thought to have too much work, it can be finished in a straight rail, as the design shows.

SHERATON CHAIRS. Late 18th Century.

See Page 322.

SHERATON LEGS OF PIER AND CARD TABLES, and TRIPOD CANDLESTANDS.

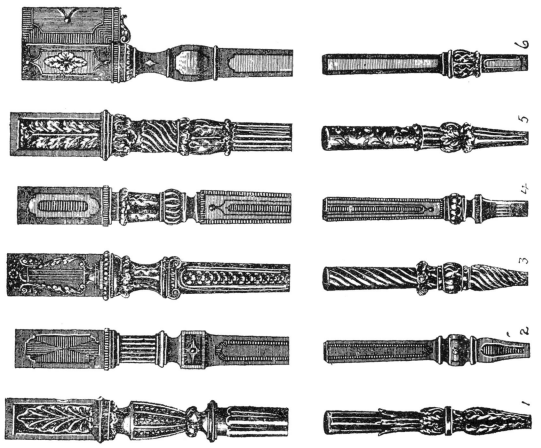

The other dressing-glass has a convenience for writing as well as for dressing, which convenience rises by a little horse. The dressing-boxes are made with close covers, and a slider encloses the whole, so that when the whole is turned up nothing can come out of its place. The glass does not rise as the other, but fixes in centres, so as to move in any position either back or forward.

And observe, that when the dressing-flap is turned up it locks into the top-rail, and the glass of course falls to its own place. The under-side of the flap being the front when turned up, it may be japanned and banded. The lower parts of the standards are shaped like a lyre, and to form the strings, brass wire is let in, which has a pretty effect.

DRESSING COMMODE, PAGE 308.— With respect to the dressing part of this Commode (No. 1), it may be made either fixed fast or to be brought forward in the manner of a drawer with leapers to keep it to its place. If it is made to be fixed fast,

the doors may be opened to form the knee-hole. The top which covers and encloses the dressing part slides down behind. A bottle of water, and a pot to receive it when dirty, can both be kept in the cupboard part.

The Dressing-table (No. 2) can require no explanation, except what relates to the size, which from front to back is eighteen inches, thirty-four the whole height, and two feet four the length of the front.

The drawer in the Wash-hand Stand (No. 3) is lined with lead, into which the basin is emptied. The upper part, which contains the cistern, takes off occasionally. Below the drawer is a cupboard. Observe that in the design the drawer-back is supposed to be behind the basin; but before the drawer is wholly taken away the basin must be taken out.

The Pot Cupboard (No. 4) is used in genteel bedrooms, and is sometimes finished in satin wood, and in a style a little elevated above their use. The two drawers below the cupboard are real. The partitions may be cross-banded,

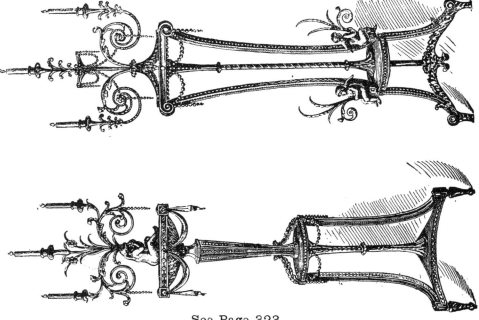

See Page 323.

SHERATON SCREENS. Late 18th Century.

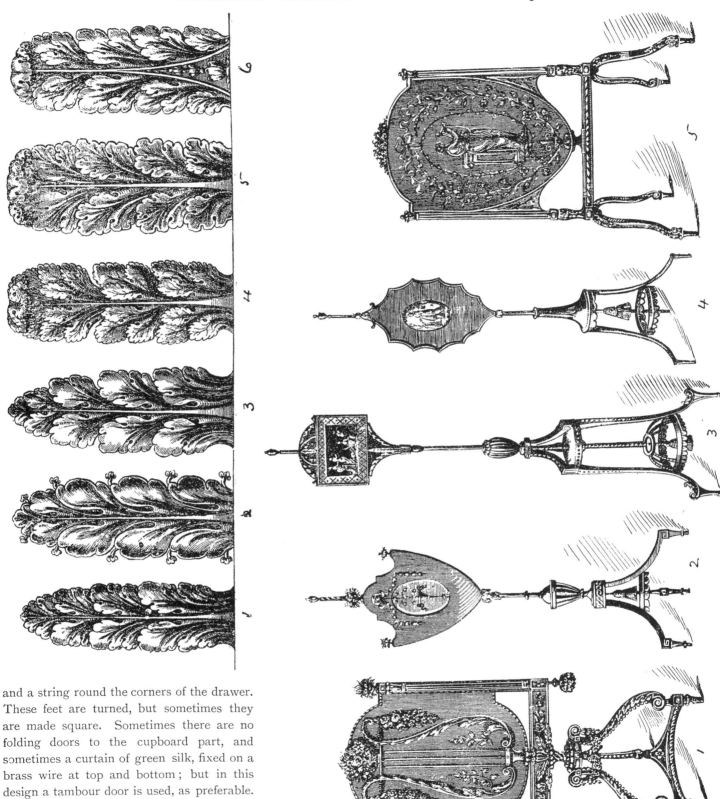

and a string round the corners of the drawer. These feet are turned, but sometimes they are made square. Sometimes there are no folding doors to the cupboard part, and sometimes a curtain of green silk, fixed on a brass wire at top and bottom; but in this design a tambour door is used, as preferable. The upper cupboard contains shelves, and is intended to keep medicines to be taken in the night, or to hold other little articles which servants are not permitted to overlook.

See Page 323.

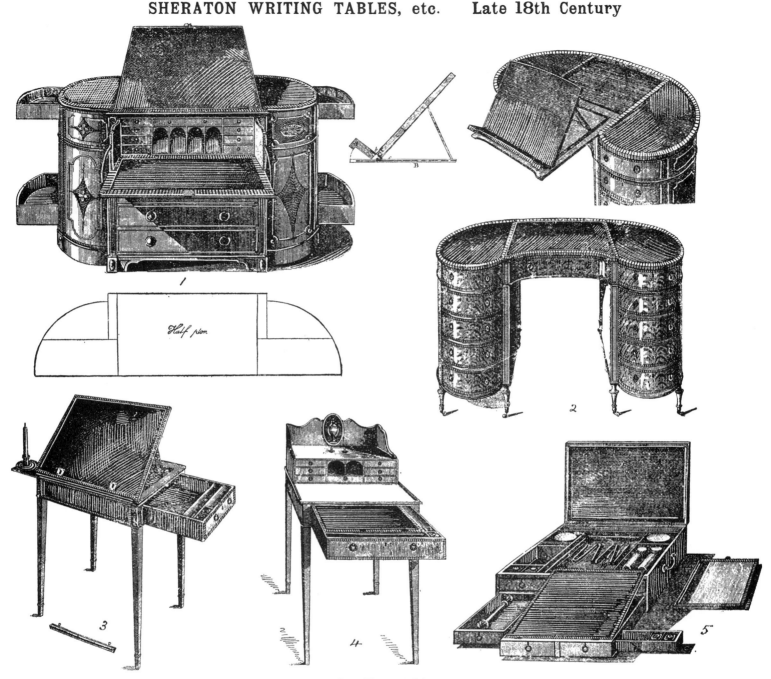

Half plan

1

2

3

4

5

See Page 324.

See Page 324.

PAGE 309.—LADY'S CABINET DRESSING TABLE (No. 1).—This table contains every requisite for a lady to dress at.   The style of finishing them is neat and somewhat elegant.   With respect to the manufacturing part, and what it contains, these may be learned from the design itself, which here shews the parts entirely laid open.   I shall, therefore, only mention two or three particulars.   When the washing-drawer is in, a slider which is above it may be drawn out to write on occasionally. The ink and sand are in the right-hand drawer under the centre dressing-glass.   Behind the drapery, which is tacked to a rabbet, and fringed or gimped to cover the nails, is a shelf on which may stand any vessel to receive the dirty water. Above the drapery are tambour cupboards, one at each end, and one in the centre under the drawer.   Above the tambour at each end are real drawers, which are fitted up to hold every article necessary in dressing.   The drawers in the cabinet part are intended to hold all the ornaments of dress, as rings, drops, etc.   Behind the centre glass is drapery; it may be real to suit that below, or it may only be painted in imitation of it.   The glass swings to any position, on centre pins fixed on the shelf above the candle branches.   The side glasses fold in behind the doors, and the doors themselves, when shut, appear solid, with ovals in the panels, and ornamented to suit the other parts.   Observe, the whole plan of the top is not in the plate, it

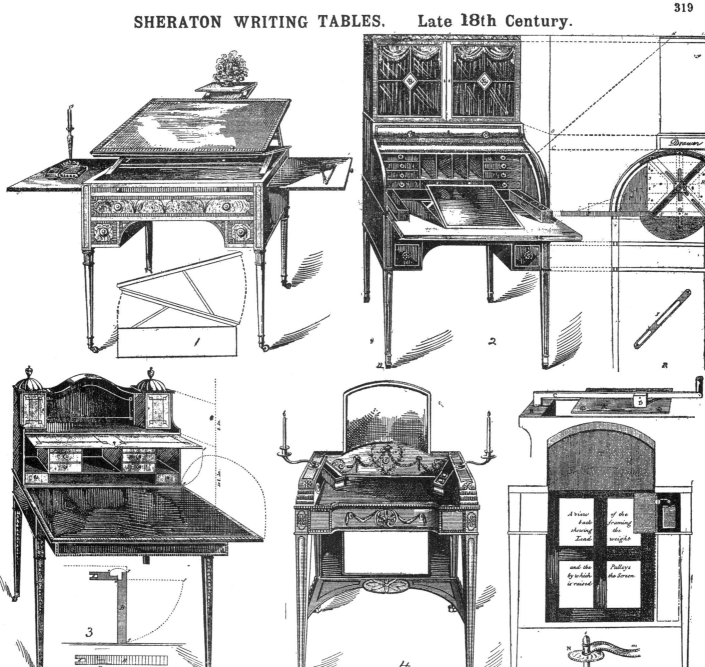

See Page 324.

being required to be two feet over. The perspective lines shown at the circular end are as follows:—When the plan is made, divide the curve into parts, as shewn, and from these divisions on the ground line draw lines to the centre *s*. Then turn up the ordinates to the ground line, and from the points where they cut on that line, draw lines to the distance, as shewn, which will cut the visuals at 6, 7, 8, 9, and so on, finding points to direct the curve by.

The Table on the left (No. 2) is intended to afford conveniences for writing, by having a part of the top hinged in front to rise up. This rising top when it is let down locks into the frame, and secures the bag where the work is. The standards on which the frame rests have transverse pieces tenoned on, which screw to the under side of the frame. The drapery which hides the work-bag is tacked to a rabbet at the under edge of the frame all round.

The design on the right (No. 3) is simply a work-table ; the upper frame, to which the top is hinged, is about two inches broad, made separate. The pillar is fixed to the bottom of the bag, which is a round frame made of wainscot, with a stretcher across each way, for the purpose of fixing the pillar to it, and to strengthen the frame. The upper frame, already mentioned, is connected with the lower one by small upright pieces tenoned in, after which the bag is formed of silk and tacked to each frame, and ornamented on the outside with drapery.

SHERATON.　Late 18th Century.

The upper middle part of the Wardrobe on Page 309 contains six or seven clothes-press shelves, generally made about six or six inches and a half deep, with green baize tacked to the inside of the front to cover the clothes with. The lower part consists of real drawers. The wings have each of them arms, to hang the clothes on, made of beech, with a swivel in their centre, which slips on to an iron rod fixed by plates screwed on to each side of the wings as expressed in the design. The whole is made in four separate carcases ; the wings by themselves, and the upper and lower middle parts separate. The plinth is made all in one frame, and likewise the cornice with its frieze, and being screwed to each carcass, the whole is kept firm. Observe, that in the wings a bead is put up for the doors to fall against when they are shut to ; by which means are cleared the knuckles of the hinges on the doors of the middle part. It should also be observed that as the surbase cannot go round the out ends of each wing on account of opening the doors, the moulding is returned against the front of each door. The surbase on the middle part returns, and stops against the inner end of the wing ; and the edge of the door of each wing, with the surbase which is on them, are scribed on to the aforesaid return, which then appears as an internal mitre, and gives place to the opening of the door. The scale, applied to the middle part, gives its height and length. The wings are two feet and sixteen or seventeen inches deep ; and the depth of the middle part about twenty-three inches.

PAGE 310.—CORNER BASIN STANDS (Nos. 1, 2 and 3).—The right-hand basin-stand contains a cupboard and a real drawer below it ; by the top folding down the basin is enclosed and hid when it is not in use. The left-hand top is fixed to the side of the basin-stand by a rule joint, the same as the flap of a Pembroke table ; but instead of iron the hinges are made of brass. The right-hand top is hinged to the other by common butt-hinges, by which means it will fold against the other, and both may be turned down together. When the tops are in their place, there then appears a rule joint on both sides. The front edges of the tops are hollowed and beaded, which hang a little over, so that the fingers may get hold to raise them up. Short tenons are put to the under edge of the right-hand top, to keep it in its place on the end of the lower part.

The Basin-stand on the left has a rim round the top, and a tambour door to enclose the whole of the upper part, in which is a small cistern. The lower part has a shelf in the middle, on which stands a vessel to receive the dirty water conveyed by a pipe from the basin. These sort are made large, and the basin being brought close to the front gives plenty of room. The advantage of this kind of basin-stand is, that they may stand in a genteel room without giving offence to the eye, their appearance being somewhat like a cabinet.

LADY'S DRESSING TABLE (No. 4).—The style of finishing these tables is neat. They are often made of satin wood, and banded ; but sometimes they are made of mahogany. The size of this table, which is here three feet, should be increased in its length near six inches when these folding side glasses are introduced. The reason of this is, that a lady may have more room to sit between them to dress. It should, in this case, be made about two inches wider. But observe, the size here given is that which is used when only the rising back glass is introduced ; and this has been the common way of finishing them. These side glasses are an addition of my own, which I take to be an improvement ; judging that, when they are finished in this manner, they will answer the end of a Rudd's table, at a less expense. The glass behind rises up like that of a shaving stand. Those on the side fold down past each other, being hinged to a sliding stretcher, which is capable of being pushed backward or forward. If the right-hand glass be pushed to the back it will then fold down, and the other keeping its place will do the same. A and B in the plan shew these glasses in their places ; e is the back glass and t is the top, which is hinged to a piece of wood which runs in a groove at each end, so that when the top is drawn fully up, it will fall down on the frame. The other folding top on each side have each of them a small tenon near the front, as may be seen at the edge of the left-hand one. These tenons being let into the middle part are the means of securing each side-top when they are folded down, and the middle part is put down upon them, so that the lock in the middle secures the three tops. The drawer on the right is the depth of two fronts, as is easily seen ; the use of which is to put caps in. The left-hand fronts are in two real drawers for the purpose of laying small things in. The cupboard in the knee-hole has its front reeded in the hollow part to imitate tambour, and the circular door in the centre is veneered and quartered. This cupboard will take a lady's hat as they wear them now. The other dressing conveniences are obvious in the plan.

BED STEPS (Nos. 5 and 6).—The design on the right contains a bidet behind, which runs in as a drawer. For the purpose of raising the bidet drawer to a proper height, the case is made double, one fitting within the other, as shewn in the plate ; for provided the outer case is made nine inches deep, the inner one, being at least eight, would, when raised up, make it eighteen inches high, which is sufficient. The inner case is kept up by a couple of wooden springs, one at each end, which are so made and fixed to the inside of the outer case, that the thumb may relieve them so that the bidet will settle down even with the edge of the case. The second step, which forms the night table part, draws out, and the step which covers it rises up and falls against the upper step, which forms a pot cupboard. The steps and risers are usually covered with carpet, and the sides caned.

SHERATON.   Late 18th Century.

The design on the left, when the top is down, forms only two steps.   The front of the upper step is hinged to the top, and the top to the back; and to keep it in its place when down, the workman will observe that a groove is cut in both ends, not in a straight direction, but near the bottom; the groove is perpendicular to the seat; a pin is then fixed to the under side of the front at each end, which works in the aforesaid grooves, and the perpendicular part of the groove, which is obvious in the design, assists in throwing the front upright when it is down upon the seat.

Of the Corner Night Tables (Nos. 7 and 8) on Page 310, that on the right requires no explanation, except that the doors may be hinged to turn in, if it is thought most convenient.   The table on the left is intended to answer the purpose of a wash-hand stand occasionally.   To answer this end the top part is framed together of itself, and fixed by an iron or strong wooden pin into the back corner of the lower part, which contains a socket, so that the top part can be turned to one side, as shewn in the design, or as much further as is necessary to clear the hole.   Observe also, that on the front is fixed a groove, in which a pin passes that is fixed to the front of the bottom of the upper part, and prevents the top part from turning quite off from the bottom, which would endanger the pin on which the top part turns; it should have castors at the brackets, that when the night table is wanted it may be drawn a little forward from the corner of the room to give place for turning round the upper part.   It should be about thirty-four inches to the top of the basin itself; the height of the seat sixteen inches and a half; and its other dimensions are known from the plan.   The bottom drawer may be made neat, and drawn out by means of a dovetail groove in the middle of the drawer, and a piece to fit it fixed across the bottom of the carcass.

PAGE 311.—The Bidet Dressing Table has a real drawer under the cupboard part, and the rest are sham.   The right-hand cupboard door opens by a spring catch communicated to the patera handle in the centre.   The water bottle is supported by a round box, made of very thin wood, glued and canvassed over to strengthen it, and fixed to the top.   The bidet legs turn up with a joint.   The design shews only legs at one end, but the other legs are supposed to be folded up till the whole is taken out; and when used, the legs are kept in their place by iron hooks and eyes.   The scale shews the size of the front, and its depth from front to back is sixteen inches and a half.   The frame, to which the glass is hinged is fourteen inches in width.

The Night Table (No. 2) requires no explanation, and I shall only observe that the covers with rings on them are meant for a tooth-brush, and the ivory boxes on the right for tooth-powder.   The scale for the dressing table shews the size of the night table applied to the front, and its depth from front to back is eighteen inches.

PAGE 311.—The design of the Library Steps and Table was taken from steps that have been made by Mr. Campbell, Upholsterer to the Prince of Wales.   They were first made for the King, and highly approved of by him, as every way answering the intended purpose.   There are other kinds of library steps which I have seen, made by other persons, but, in my opinion, these must have the decided preference, both as to simplicity and firmness when they are set up.   The steps may be put up in half a minute, and the whole may be taken down and enclosed within the table frame in about the same time.   The table, when enclosed, serves as a library table, and has a rising flap, supported by a horse, to write on.   The size of the table is three feet ten inches long, thirty-three inches high, and two feet one inch in width.   When the steps are out they rise thirty-three inches perpendicular from the top of the table-frame, and the whole height of the last step is five feet five perpendicular from the ground.   The perpendicular height of the hand-rail is three feet one inch above the last step; and observe, that on g, which is iron, is fixed a small flap on which a book may rest, so that a gentleman, when he is looking at any book in his library, may note down a passage from it without the trouble of going down again.   The method of folding the whole up is as follows:—The triangular iron bracket g is unlocked by a catch which keeps it firm to the hand-rail, and the desk flap is fixed to it being turned over to the inside, the whole comes forward and lies level upon the upper steps.   The standard b may then be raised out of its socket, and, having a joint at the top, it turns up to d, as shewn by the dotted curve line.   The short standard d e is then, by relieving a spring, pressed down below the edge of the table top; and the hand-rail and standard b having been folded together, as mentioned before, they both rest on the iron socket fastened to the front edge of the upper steps.   The horse o is folded by the side of the upper steps, and then both they and the horse fall down within the table frame; and it must be observed, that in folding down the steps the hand-rail and standard, which rested for a while on the socket fastened to the front of the steps, fall into another socket of the same kind fastened to the under side of the table top, where they remain, and fall within the table frame when the top is folded down.   Lastly, the lower steps a are turned up to a horizontal position, and being hinged to a slider which runs in a groove, the whole slips in as a drawer, and is enclosed by the flap p, which turns up and appears as the front of a drawer.

The Library Steps are considerably more simple than those already described; and though not so generally useful, will come vastly cheaper. The upper flight of steps turn down upon the under ones, both of which rise up and slide in as a drawer, after which a flap, which is shewn in the design, is turned up, and has the appearance of a drawer front. Observe, that the resting post at the top folds down to the side of the steps by means of an iron joint. The horse has green cloth under its feet to prevent its scratching the top. The design shews that the two steps are connected together by hinges, so made as to clear the edge of the table top; and also, that there is a sliding board to which the under flight is hinged, which sliding board runs in a groove. The length of the table is three feet six inches, its width twenty-two inches. The table is thirty inches high, the upper flight is thirty perpendicular, and the resting post thirty-three.

PAGE 311.—The upper figure of the Chamber Horse shews the inside when the leather is off, which consists of five wainscot inch boards, clamped at the ends; to which are fixed strong wire twisted round a block in regular gradation, so that when the wire is compressed by the weight of those who exercise, each turn of it may clear itself and fall within each other. The top board is stuffed with hair as a chair seat, and the leather is fixed to each board with brass nails, tacked all round. The leather at each end is cut in slits to give vent to the air, which would otherwise resist the motion downwards. The workman should also observe that a wooden or iron pin is fixed at each end of the middle board, for the purpose of guiding the whole seat as it plays up and down. This pin runs between the two upright pieces which are framed into the arms at each end, as the design shews. The length of the horse is twenty-nine inches, the width twenty, its height thirty-two. To the top of the foot-board is eight inches, and to the board whereon the seat is fixed thirteen.

PAGE 312.—The Splads are all intended for japanning, except No. 4, which may be worked in mahogany. The Elbows are meant chiefly to be carved and gilt; but the mere outlines of any of them will serve as patterns either for painted or mahogany chairs, by leaving out the ornaments for the mahogany, and retaining some of them, or even all of them may be adapted for painting. It may be proper to observe that as high as the stuffing of the seat a rabbet should be left on the stump to stuff against; which is easily done, as the stump is made smaller above the rail. The cushions on the arms are formed by cutting a rabbet in the arm, or leaving the wood a little above the surface. Some, however, bring the rabbet square down at each end, covering the wood entirely, except a fillet, which is left at the bottom and continues round the cushion.

PAGE 313.—CHAIR BACKS:—Little needs to be observed respecting Nos. 16, 17, 18, 22, 23, 24, as the plate of itself sufficiently expresses what they are; if, however, any of these be thought too crowded with work, they may be reduced to a state sufficiently plain without doing the least injury to the outline of the whole, as in the following manner:—

No. 16 is intended for painting, but may have the drapery left out under the top rail, by means of substituting a plain upright bar in the middle.

No. 17 may be reduced by taking away the side foliage, and making the bottom of the banister plain.

No. 18 may be either a drawing-room chair painted, or it may be made a handsome parlour chair, by taking out the top drapery and making the bottom of the banister plain; if for a parlour chair, the top rail is intended to be stuffed and covered with red or green leather, or it may be entirely of mahogany panelled out of the solid; but if a drawing-room chair it must be stuffed and covered to suit the seat.

No. 22 is a painted chair, with the back feet at top, formed in imitation of the Ionic capital. The drapery in this also may be taken away without hurt done to the general outline.

No. 23 is a painted chair, and may be subject to a variety of alterations; it may be executed with good effect without anything except the three composite columns, and two arches in the top rail. The remaining part of the rail on each side of the basket of flowers may be neatly panelled in the painting; or the diamond part may be retrenched, and the two smaller pillars with their arches retained.

No. 24 cannot well be subject to any alteration, excepting that the ornament in the arch may be turned into a straight bar.

PAGE 315.—These Drawing-room Chairs are finished in white and gold, or the ornaments may be japanned; but the French finish them in mahogany, with gilt mouldings. The figures in the tablets above the front rails are on French printed silk or satin, sewed on to the stuffing, with borders round them. The seat and back are of the same kind, as is the ornamented tablet at the top of the left-hand chair. The top rail is panelled out, and a small gold bead mitred round, and the printed silk is pasted on. Chairs of this kind have an effect which far exceeds any conception we can have of them from an uncoloured engraving, or even a coloured one.

SHERATON. Late 18th Century.

PAGE 316.—The Tripod Candlesticks are used in drawing-rooms, for the convenience of affording additional light to such parts of the room where it would neither be ornamental nor easy to introduce any other kind. The style of finishing these for noblemen's drawing-rooms is exceeding rich. Sometimes they are finished in white and gold, and sometimes all gold, to suit the other furniture. In inferior drawing-rooms they are japanned answerable to the furniture. Persons unacquainted with the manufacturing part of these stands may apprehend them to be slight and easily broken ; but this objection vanishes when it is considered that the scrolls are made of strong wire, and the ornaments cemented to them. I could not shew to advantage more than three lights, but, in reality, there are four ; one at the centre, and one at each angle. The top of the left stand is a round vase, which can be turned and have the square handles put on afterwards. The handles should be placed parallel to two of the feet. The top of the right one is a concave spherical triangle, having all its sides equal. As to any other part, the workman's own notions will suggest everything necessary in their manufacture.

PAGE 317.—The Lyre Fire Screen is constructed upon an entire new plan, it being designed to turn upon a swivel, which fixes to the vase and passes through the bottom rail, so that the screen may be turned to any position without moving the stand. The screen part, which rises between the standards or pillars, is suspended by a weight in the tassels, which are communicated to the screen by a line passing through the pillars and over a pulley fixed to their top. There must be a dovetail groove in each standard, and the screen made to fit into these ; so that the standards may keep their proper place, and not fly open at the top. Observe that the ornament on the tops of the pillars or standards rise up with the screen, being fixed to it, and detached from the pillars. It is intended that the lyre ornament be carved in bas relief, gilt and burnished ; which, when planted on to a blue silk or satin ground, cannot fail to produce a fine effect.

The other screen (No. 5) being common, needs no explanation, only that it is suspended by little springs fixed in the dovetail grooves of the standards. In respect to the general size of horse fire screens, about eighteen or nineteen inches may be allowed for the breadth, and three feet six or seven inches for their height.

The Tripod Fire Screens (Nos. 2, 3, and 4) are so termed because they have three feet or legs. The middle screen may be finished in white and gold or japanned ; and the other two of mahogany or japanned. The rods of these screens are all supposed to have a hole through them, and a pulley let in near the top, on which the line passes, and a weight being enclosed in the tassel, the screen is balanced to any height. The rods are often made square, which indeed best suits those which have pulleys, while those that are made round have only rings and springs. Such screens as have very fine prints, or worked satin, commonly have a glass before them. In which case a frame is made, with a rabbet to receive the glass, and another to receive the straining frame, to prevent it from breaking the glass ; and to enclose the straining frame a bead is mitred round.

PAGE 318.—LIBRARY TABLE WITH A WRITING DRAWER.—This Table (No. 1) is intended either to sit or stand and write at. The height of the secretary drawer is adjusted for sitting, and the top of the table is high enough to stand and write on, especially if the middle top be raised by a horse, as shewn in the design. This table will also prove very useful to draw on ; for when the middle part is up for drawing upon, there remains sufficient room at each end of the table on which to place the necessary implements for drawing ; besides the drawers at each end may be fitted up to hold colours of various kinds ; I mean the two upper ones, for there are drawers quite down to the plinth. The drawers under the secretary will hold the large sheets of drawing paper, together with the tee squares ; and as it will not be necessary to make the drawers under the secretary the entire width of the table, the opposite front being made sham to have the same appearance, the whole of it may be hinged at bottom and locked at the top, and the inside will allow depths for books. This sham front being a considerable width, it would hazard the hinges to let it rest wholly on them when turned down, and therefore there should be iron rule-joints at each end as stays. To these conveniences there are also four cupboards enclosed with doors, as shewn in the design ; and the whole finished in this manner, I venture to affirm, will prove as useful a table as has ever been devised or published. In respect to the manufacturing part, it will be best to make it in two parts. The upper part containing the secretary, and two drawers at each end ; and the lower part, four drawers under the secretary, a bookcase behind, and four drawers at each end, the lowermost of which is shewn in the design. The top should be framed of inch and a quarter wainscot, containing a well for the desk part which may be made to rise on the front as well as at the back, by forming a double horse ; but in this design it is only intended to rise at the back by a single horse, and hinged to the cross-band at the front. The cupboard doors may either be framed and panelled, or glued up to their sweep in narrow slips of inch mahogany, and clamped ; not by tonguing, but by a square joint, and pins driven through the clamps. The management of the circular base-moulding and plinth may be learned in Page 332.

SHERATON. Late 18th Century.

No. 2, Page 318, is a Kidney Table, on account of its resemblance to that intestine part of animals so called. Its use, however, is the same as that already described. The drawers which appear in the design are all real, and are strung and cross-banded, with the grain of the mahogany laid up and down. The pilasters are panelled or cross-banded, and the feet below turned. The view of it above shews the end panelled, and the back may be so too, or it may be plain. With respect to the manufacturing part, I need not say anything after what has been said on the other, except to explain the reading desk which slides out, as shewn above. Observe, B is the profile of the frame which slides out, in the edge of which there is a groove shewn by the black stroke, and a tongue is put into the edge of the well part to suit it. F is the desk part which rises at the same time to stop the book; *b* is a tumbler hinge let in flush with the top, and hid by the cloth or leather; *c* is a common but-hinge let in the edge of F, and upon the frame B, so that when F falls to B, A does also The length of the table is four feet, its width two, and its height thirty-two inches.

The left-hand Table (No. 3) is to write and read at. The top is lined with leather or green cloth, and cross-banded. To stop the book there are two brass plates let in, with key holes; and in the moulding, which is to stop the book, are two pins, with heads and shoulders, by which the moulding is effectually secured.

The right-hand Table (No. 4) is meant to write at only. The top part takes off from the under part, which having a bead let in at the back and ends of the top, prevents the top part from moving out of its place. This table being made for the convenience of moving from one room to another, there is a handle fixed on to the upper shelf, as the drawing shews In the drawer is a slider to write on, and on the right-hand of it ink, sand, and pens.

The Lady's Travelling-box (No. 5) is intended to accommodate her in her travels with conveniences for writing, dressing, and working. The front is divided into the appearance of six small drawers; the upper three sham, and the under real. The writing drawer takes up two of these fronts in length, and contains an ink drawer, and a top hinged to the front, lined with green cloth. The top being hinged at front, by pushing in drawer, it will rise to any pitch. The other drawer on the left, which only takes up one front, holds a kind of windlass or roller, for the purpose of fixing and winding up lace as it is worked. The middle vacuity, which holds the scissors and other articles of that nature, takes out, which gives access to a convenience below it for holding small things. The boxes on each side hold powder, pomatum, scent-bottles, rings, &c. The dressing-glass, which is here represented out of the box, fits into the vacuity above the scissor-case.

Page 319.—The Drawing Table (No. 1) will be found highly useful to such as draw, it being designed from my own experience of what is necessary for those who practise this art. The top of this table is made to rise by a double horse, that the designer may stand if he please, or he may sit, and have the top raised to any direction. As it is sometimes necessary to copy from models or flower-pots, &c., a small flap s made to draw out of the top, which may be raised by a little horse to suit any direction the top may be in, so that the model or flower-pot may stand level. The sliders at each end are necessary for the instruments of drawing, and for a light to stand on. The long drawer holds paper, square, and board, and those drawers which form the knee-hole are fitted up for colours.

The use of the Cylinder Desk and Bookcase (No. 2) is plain, both from the title and design. The style of finishing them is somewhat elegant, being made of satin-wood, cross-banded, and varnished. This design shews green silk fluting behind the glass, and drapery put on at top before the fluting is tacked to, which has a good look when properly managed. The square figure of the door is much in fashion now. The ornament in the diamond part is meant to be carved and gilt, laid on to some sort of silk ground. The rim round the top is intended to be brass; it may, however, be done in wood.

The manufacturing part of this piece is a little intricate to a stranger, for which reason it will require as particular a description as I can give to make it tolerably well understood. First, observe the slider is communicated with the cylinder by an iron trammel, as I., so that when the former comes forward, the latter rises up and shews the nest of the small drawers and letter holes, as appears in the design. When, therefore, the slider is pushed home even with the front, the cylinder is brought close to it at the same time. In this state the lock of the long drawer under the slider secures both the drawer itself and also the slider at the same time in the following manner:—D is the long drawer under the slider, P the partition above it, and S is the slider; C is a spring-bolt let into the partition. When, therefore, the drawer lock-bolt is out, as it rises it drives C, the spring-bolt into the slider; and when the drawer is unlocked, then C falls down to its place in the partition, and the slider can be pulled out. The trammel I. is a piece of iron near a quarter thick, and inch and quarter broad, with grooves cut through, as shewn at I. S, in the profile, is the slider; and *g*, 12, *h*, the cylinder. The trammel T is fixed to the cylinder at *h* by a screw, not drove tight up, but so as the trammel will pass round easy. Again, at the slider S

SHERATON.　Late 18th Century.

a screw is put through the groove in the trammel, which works on the neck of the screw, and its head keeps the trammel in its place; so that it must be observed that the grooves or slits in the iron trammel are not much above a quarter of an inch in width.　When the slider is pushed in about half-way, the trammel will be at u, and its end will be below the slider, as the plate shews; but when the slider is home to its place, the trammel will be at T and g.　The centre piece with four holes is a square plate of iron, having a centre pin which works in the upper slit of the trammel.　It is let into the end of the cylinder, and fixed with four screws.　To find the place of this centre lay the trammel upon the end, as T h, in the position that it will be in when the slider is out, and, with a pencil, mark the inside of the slits in the trammel.　Again, place the trammel on the end as it will be when the slider is in, as at T g, and do as before; and where these pencil marks intersect each other will be the place of the centre plate.　The figures 1, 2, 3, 4, shew the place of the small drawers.　The triangular dotted lines with three holes is a piece of thin wood screwed on to the end, to which is fixed the nest of small drawers, forming a vacuity for the trammel to work in.　F is a three-eighth piece veneered and cross-banded, and cut behind to give room for the trammel.　This piece both keeps the slider to its place and hides the trammel.　The next thing to be observed is, that the lower frame, containing two heights of drawers, is put together separate from the upper part, which takes the cylinder.　The ends of the cylinder part are tenoned with the slip tenons into the lower frame and glued.　The shaded part at A shews the rail cut out to let the trammel work.　The back is framed in two panels, and the back legs are rabbetted out to let the back framing come down to the lower drawer.　The slider is framed of mahogany, with a broad rail at each end about nine inches, and one at the front about three and a half.　In the inside of the framing a rabbet is cut to receive a thin bottom.　The bottom being fixed in, a slip is put at each end to receive the horse which supports the desk part.　The ink and pen drawers at each end of the slider have a small moulding mitred round them to keep them fast, without their being glued on.　Observe, there is a sham drawer front fastened on to the slider, which, of course, goes in with it, and which contains the depth of these ink and pen drawers, so that they are not required to be taken out when the slider goes in.　The cylinder is jointed to its sweep in narrow slips of straight-baited hard mahogany, and afterwards veneered.　If the veneer be of a pliable kind it may be laid with a hammer, by first shrinking and tempering the veneer well, which must not be by water, but thin glue.　If the veneer be very cross and unpliable, as many curls of mahogany are, it is vain to attempt the hammer.　A caul in this case is the surest and best method, though it be attended with considerably more trouble than the hammer.　To prepare for laying it with a caul, proceed as follows:—Take five or six pieces of three-inch deal, and sweep them to fit the inside of the cylinder.　Fix these upon a board answerable to the length of the cylinder.　Then have as many cauls for the outside of the cylinder, which may be made out of the same pieces as those for the inside.　Take then quarter mahogany for a caul to cover the whole veneer and heat it well.　Put the caul screws across the bench, and slip in the board with the round cauls screwed to it; and proceed, in every other particular, as the nature of the thing will necessarily dictate.

The Table No. 3 on Page 319 is intended for writing on, and to hold a few small books in the back of the upper part.　Within the door at each end, under the domes, are formed small cabinets of drawers, etc. The front of the upper part, which encloses the nest of drawers and letter holes, slides in under the top, and when drawn sufficiently out falls down in the curve f g, and locks into the fold-

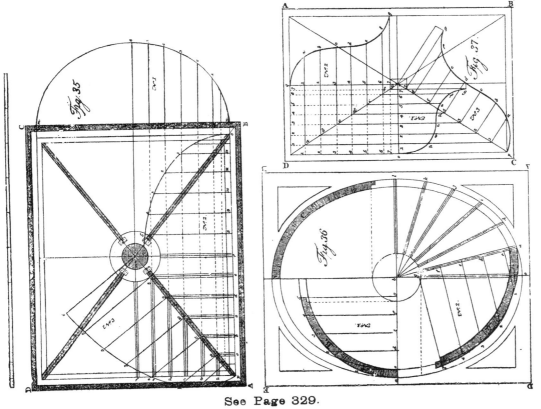

See Page 329.

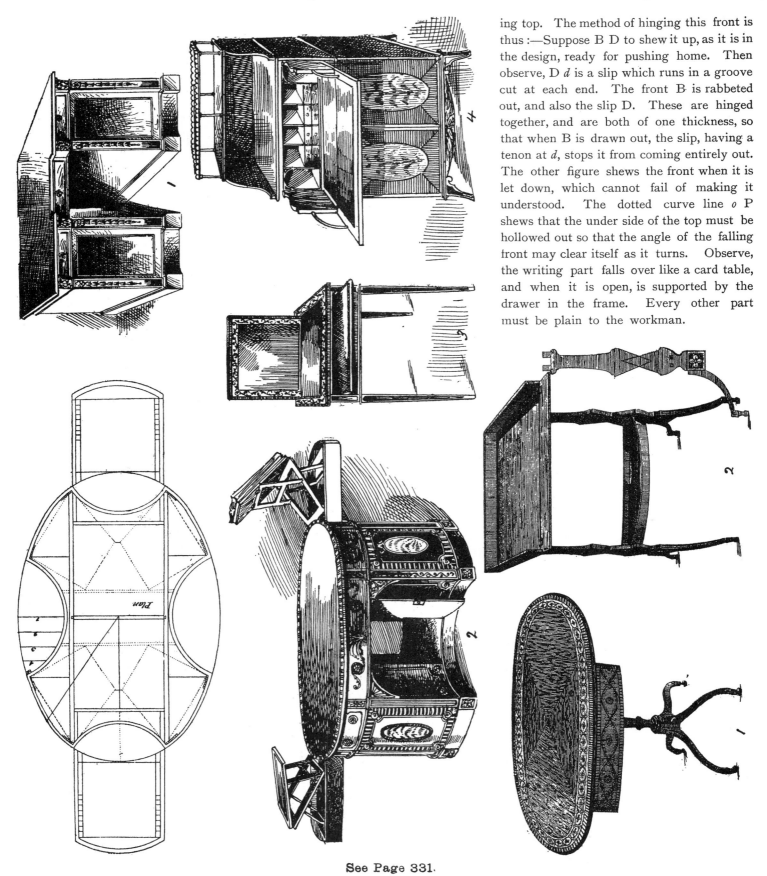

ing top.   The method of hinging this front is thus :—Suppose B D to shew it up, as it is in the design, ready for pushing home.   Then observe, D *d* is a slip which runs in a groove cut at each end.   The front B is rabbeted out, and also the slip D.   These are hinged together, and are both of one thickness, so that when B is drawn out, the slip, having a tenon at *d*, stops it from coming entirely out. The other figure shews the front when it is let down, which cannot fail of making it understood.   The dotted curve line *o* P shews that the under side of the top must be hollowed out so that the angle of the falling front may clear itself as it turns.   Observe, the writing part falls over like a card table, and when it is open, is supported by the drawer in the frame.   Every other part must be plain to the workman.

See Page 331.

SHERATON CABINETS and TABLES. Late 18th Century.

For particulars see Page 333.

The convenience of this Lady's Writing Table (No. 4 on Page 319) is, that a lady, when writing at it, may both receive the benefit of the fire and have her face screened from its scorching heat. The style of finishing them is neat, and rather elegant. They are frequently made of satin wood, cross-banded, japanned, and the top lined with green leather. The manufacturing part is a little perplexing to a stranger, and therefore I have been particular in shewing as much as I well could on the plate. Observe, that in the side boxes the ink drawer is on the right, and the pen drawer on the left. These both fly out of themselves, by the force of a common spring, when the knob on which the candle branch is fixed is pressed. Figure A is the spring which is let in under the candle branch; C is a lever which is pressed to B, the end of the drawers,

SHERATON PIER TABLES and KNIFE BOXES. Late 18th Century.

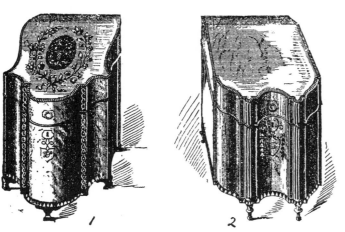

See Page 334.

by a spring rising from D; N is a part of the candle branch, and e is the knob just mentioned, which is capable of being pressed down; therefore if P be screwed into E by pressing e, C rises and relieves B, which immediately starts out, by a common spring fixed on the inside of the boxes. Observe a patera in the centre of the back amidst the ornament. This patera communicates to a spring of precisely the same kind as A; which spring keeps down the screen when the weights are up; and by touching the said patera, which has a knob in its centre like e, the spring is relieved, and the weights of course send up the screen, being somewhat assisted by a spring at the bottom, which may be seen in the design. Figure T shews the lead weight, how the pulleys are fixed, and the manner of framing the screen before it is covered with stuff. The workman will observe that a thin piece of mahogany slides out in a groove, to afford access to the weights, and afterwards enclose them. There is a drawer under the top, which extends the whole of the space between the legs. The scale shews the length of the table, *b* its height, *a* the depth of the drawer, *b c* the depth of the side boxes, and *e d* the height of the swell of the screen part; the width of the table is twenty inches.

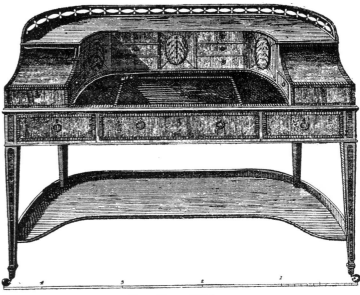

See Page 334.

PAGE 325.—THE NATURE AND CONSTRUCTION OF HIP AND ELLIPTIC DOMES FOR BEDS.—Domes of various kinds have for many ages past been introduced into elegant and magnificent buildings, on account of their graceful effect and majestic appearance. I am of opinion that the notion of employing domes for the roofs of grand buildings was first suggested by the appearance of the hemisphere surrounding our earth or horizon, forming a canopy or roof to the globe; which, if it were so, domes had their origin from a truly sublime and magnificent idea. The use of domes for the tops of beds is of much later date than for buildings; but it is certain, whoever he was that first employed domes for the tops of beds must be considered as a person of enlarged ideas, as no other top or roof for a genteel bed can equal them; therefore we see them generally used for state beds, where both grandeur and effect are essentially requisite. The term Dome generally implies a vaulted, arched, or spherical roof. Some derive it from *domus*, a house; and others from the barbarous Latin *doma*, a roof or open porch. When an arched roof is raised from a square or oblong plan, it is called a Hip Dome, because they require mitre ribs at each angle, uniting in a centre at top. But those domes which take their rise from an oval plan are called Elliptic; and lastly, those which have an octagon or hexagon for their plan may be styled Polygonal Domes.

To construct a Hip Dome :—Let A B C D (Fig. 35) be the under tester, upon which another tester is to be fixed to receive the ribs of the dome. Draw the diagonals D B and A C, and their intersection will be the centre for the dome. Draw a right line through line centre parallel to A B; draw another line through the centre at right angles with it, then will the diagonal lines be the plans of the hip ribs, and those at right angles to each other will be the plans for the centre ribs. Draw a circle from the centre of the dome of about eight inches radius, as the figure shows, which is intended as a ground for ornament in the centre of the dome at the inside, and also to combine together the hip and centre ribs. Proceed next to consider the height of the dome as may be required. Let 7.6 at No. 1 be the perpendicular height of it, and let *m n* be the width of the dome. Then draw a semi-ellipsis to pass through the points *m* 6 *n*. Divide half of this semi-ellipsis into as many equal parts as it may be thought necessary to have ribs in that space, which, in this example, is six. Draw on these sub-divisions perpendicular lines, as the figure shows, and sub divide the last space, from which raise a perpendicular as before. Proceed to No. 2, and divide half the length of the dome, as *f o*, into the same number of equal parts as half the width was divided into. From the divisions raise perpendiculars at pleasure. Take the length of the several perpendiculars from No. 1, and place them on the corresponding perpendiculars at No. 2, and draw a curve line through each point; then will the ellipsis thus produced be the outside shape of all the long ribs, the same as No. 1 is of the short ribs. Lastly, proceed to No. 3, which is for the four hip ribs. Draw the dotted lines from 8, 9, 10, 11, 12 at No. 1, till they cut the diagonal line *g h* at the corresponding numbers. From these intersections, raise perpendiculars at pleasure, as before. Transfer the length of each perpendicular line from either No. 1 or 2 to No. 3 on each perpendicular as numbered, and drawing a curve line through each point as before, it will produce an ellipsis for the outside shape of each hip rib.

The next thing to be considered is the length required for each rib, according to their distance from each angle of the dome. A little thought will make this easily understood; for if No. 3 was placed in an upright position, being considered as a frame, and if the portion of the curve from *n* to 1 at No. 1 was placed upright to it, the two points, 1 in No. 1, and 1 in No. 3, would coincide, and the point 2 of No. 1 would coincide with 2 at No. 3, and so of all the rest. Hence from *n* to 1 of No. 1 is the length of the first short rib, whose plan is at *a*; from *n* to 2 is the second short rib, whose plan is at *b*; from *n* to 3 is the third short rib, its plan at *c*; from *n* to 4 is the fourth short rib, its plan at *d*; and from *n* to 5 is the fifth short rib, its plan at *e*. The long ribs are taken from No. 2, in the same manner, each of which has its plan laid down at No. 3, as *a*, *b*, *c*, *d*, *e*, *f*, so that I need not say anything more on this part of the subject. For the length of the hip ribs, take from *p* to 5 at No. 3, and allow three-quarters of an inch for dovetailing into the centre block.

SHERATON DRESSING CHESTS and WASHSTAND.   Late 18th Century.

1

2

every rib, excepting the one that is upon each semi-diameter, must have a winding form, both inside and outside, in proportion to the length of the oval with its breadth.   Determine, next, how much the dome is to rise from the tester, which, in this example, I consider to be equal to half the short diameter ; and therefore the arch of the rib B is a quadrant of a circle drawn from the centre b.   This arch will serve for two ribs, that is B and its opposite.   Likewise from the arch B we determine the outline of every other rib thus : divide the semi-diameter $a\ b$ into five and a half equal parts, and raise perpendiculars till they touch the arch B.   Divide the plan of the rib $a\ b$ at No. 2 into the same number of equal parts, and raise perpendiculars at pleasure ; to which perpendiculars transfer the several lengths of those at No. 1 to the corresponding ones at No. 2, as $a\ c\ d\ e\ f\ g$; by which the rib A will be formed.   The ribs for $h\ i\ j$ and k are formed in the same manner, and therefore it is unnecessary to describe these.   Observe : C, on the plan of the elliptic tester, is for the long centre rib and its opposite, as will easily be understood by inspecting the figures, and a little reflection on the subject.   These domes may be made in four parts, the same as hip domes, if required.   The ribs of these domes are all dovetailed into a centre block, which may be circular or elliptical to suit the dome, and which serves for the ground of a carved and gilt patera for the inside of the dome, as has already been mentioned on hip domes.   When the ribs are all completely fixed, the spaces between them may be filled up by gluing white deal in ; and when the pieces of deal are worked down to the ribs, the whole will form an agreeable dome, which should be covered with canvas, and painted to suit the furniture, or

To construct an Elliptical Dome :—Let A B, D E (Fig. 36), be the plan of the tester, whose inside forms a true ellipsis by the help of angle pieces framed in, which must be evident to every workman.   The oval being thus formed according to the inside length and breadth of the tester, and the two diameters being already drawn, proceed with one quarter of the dome thus : draw the plan of the upper tester, into which the ribs are to be fixed, as the second elliptic line shews.   Divide then the portion of the ellipsis between o and l into as many equal parts as it is required to have ribs in one quarter of the dome, as at o, a, h, i, j, k, l, tending to the centre b.   From these centre lines draw parallel lines on each side, which shall determine the thickness of the ribs, and at the same time shew how broad each rib will be required, in order to give it its proper twist so as to suit its ellipsis ; for here it must be observed, that

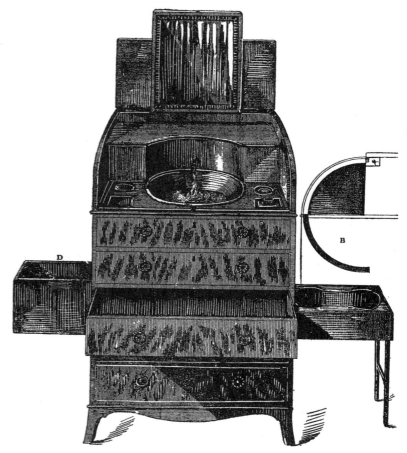

See Page 334.

SHERATON BEDSTEAD.   Late 18th Century.

Bedstead in Sheraton's Empire Style

otherwise covered with the same kind of stuff. And, if so, it will be unnecessary to cover it with canvas ; but as the stuff must be put on the dome in so many breadths, cut so as to answer its shape, a gimp may be stitched on to hide the tacks and give the dome a more rich appearance. But if the dome be large, it may have a small gilt moulding in place of the gimp, which is fixed to the dome by gilt-headed screws. For the inside of the dome, it will be requisite to have a gilt moulding, to hide the joining of the under and the upper tester, and to serve as an architrave to the dome. The triangular compartments at each corner of the tester, occasioned by the manner of framing it to suit the dome, should have small mouldings put on to suit that shape, which will take off the flat appearance it would otherwise have, and add to the effect of the whole. As for any other particular with respect to ornaments, what has already been observed on hip domes may be applied here.

With respect to the dome described by Fig. 37, I do not think it necessary to go through an explanation of it after what has been said on Fig. 35, which, if the reader has fully understood, he cannot fail to be acquainted with the lines laid down in Fig. 37, merely from inspection, especially as I have marked each corresponding line with similar letters and numbers.

PAGE 326.—The Library Table (No. 2) is intended for a gentleman to write on, or to read at, having desk drawers at each end, and is generally employed in studies or library rooms. The style of finishing it ought to be in the medium of that which may be termed plain or grand, as neither suits their situation. Mahogany is the most suitable wood, and the ornaments should be carved or inlaid what little there is ; japanned ornaments are not suitable, as these tables frequently meet with a little harsh usage. The strength, solidity, and effect of brass mouldings are very suitable to such a design, when expense is no object. For instance, the pilasters might be a little sunk, or panelled out, and brass heads mitred round in a margin, and solid flutes of the same metal let in. The astragal which separates the upper and lower parts might be of brass ; and likewise the edge of the top, together with the patera in the upper panel, as shewn on the left hand. The top is lined with leather or green cloth, and the whole rests and is moved on castors hid by the plinth.

The top should be framed in inch and quarter wainscot, in the figure of a long hexagon, which best suits the shape of the oval. The panels, which are tongued in, should be of at least three quarters hard mahogany, about nine inches square, and the stiles three and a half broad. The top being thus framed of very dry wood, it should be planed over, and stand for some time at a moderate distance from a fire, after which it may be glued together, and when hardened it ought to be planed over again, and remain in that state till the lower part is finished. If these methods are not pursued, the panels will shrink, and their joints will draw down the leather or cloth, so that the figure of the framed top will appear, especially when it is lined with leather. Next, it must be considered how to glue on the mahogany to the framing so as to make the surbase moulding appear of solid wood. First, plough the four short sides of the hexagon, and then tongue in suitable mahogany lengthways, meeting in a straight joint in the centre of the top ; and lastly, after the tonguing is dry, glue in straight joint pieces on the two long sides of the hexagon, and when dry, the top will be prepared for cutting to its elliptic shape.

The manner of framing the upper and lower parts of the carcase must be learned from the plan. The upper part, framed in an entire oval, contains the desk drawers ; and, if thought necessary, two short ones may be obtained over the side niches. The cupboard part is framed in two, each of which has a niche at the end, and one-third of the side niches ; for the niches are all of them divided into three panels, and the middle panels of the side ones serve as doors by which an open passage is gained through the table. There are four cupboards in the whole, divided in the manner specified by the dotted lines in the plan, one or two of which may be fitted up in a nest of small drawers and letter-holes. The plinth is framed entire of itself, and the base moulding stands up a little to receive the whole and hide the joint.

In putting on the base moulding there are two or three methods which I would offer as the best I know of. The frame being made so thick as to take the projection of the base, it must then be rabbeted out of the solid to receive it. This being done, proceed to glue the base in three or four thicknesses, confining them to their place by hand screws, or other devices of that nature ; but observe to let the base project further out than the deal plinth that it may receive the mahogany veneer which is to be glued on lengthways to hide the deal. After the whole is glued fast to its place, the veneer on the plinth and the base must be cleaned off level with each other. The convex parts of the base moulding may be worked wtth hollows and rounds ; and after these are finished, the niches should be worked down to them by a tool made on purpose.

Another method of gluing the base mouldings is as follows :—Prepare the inch deal, and make the cauls to fit the end and niches of the plinth, after which take straight baited three-eighths Spanish wood, and work the hollow part of the base separate from the torus ; then, from quarter stuff of the same kind, cut off slips for the torus ; heat the caul well, and both wet and heat the slips which will then easily bend. When the hollow part is well tempered, and also the torus, begin at one end and by a thin chip run glue in between them ; and as you go on drive in nails about every inch, having between the nails and the moulding a thin slip of wainscot well heated. Observe to let the moulding pass beyond the caul at each end that a pack-string may be tied to keep it to its place when it is taken out. The torus may then be worked before it is glued on the plinth.

A third method is to make the plinth itself the caul, and first work the hollows, and soak them in water a whole night. Next morning take a hand-iron and heat it well, and over the curved side of which bend the hollow as near as may be to sweep. Having already a stop screwed on to the plinth, jump one end of the moulding to it, and glue as you go on, at the same time fixing small hand screws to draw it to, or brads may be put through the square part to assist in this business, if necessary, for these will be covered by the torus. After the hollow is sufficiently dry, the torus being worked off and well soaked, and bent round the iron as above, it will glue to the hollow without the smallest difficulty, by first jumping it against the stop before mentioned ; and after it is brought pretty near, take another stop and screw it against the end of the torus, which will draw it down without further trouble. These two methods are founded on experiment ; for, at my request, it was performed by some cabinet-makers to my full satisfaction ; therefore, should either of these methods fail in the hands of any, it must be owing to some defect in the management.

The Pembroke Table (No. 1 at bottom of Page 326) is for a gentleman or a lady to breakfast on. The style of finishing these tables is very neat, sometimes bordering upon elegance, being at times made of satin wood, and having richly japanned borders round their tops, with ornamented drawer fronts. The manufacturing part of this table differs but very little from those in common use. The fly brackets which support the flaps are made and fixed in the same manner as any other, only I apprehend it best to make a dovetail groove in the front for the drawer sides, at a distance from each end of the drawer front equal to the thickness of the bracket and the inner lining, so that the front laps over and covers the whole, as appears in the design. In this case the lock-bolt shoots up into the top of the table. The top and frame may be connected to the pillar and claws either by a square block glued up, or by a couple of pieces about four inches broad, half-lapped into each other at right angles, and double tenoned into the pillar, and screwed to the bottom of the frame, as the profile of the pillar and claw is intended to suggest. The workman is desired to observe that the top of the table, as shewn in the design, is not meant to represent a regular ellipsis, as they are generally made a little fuller out at each corner of the bed. The reason of this is that the flaps, when turned down, may better hide the joint rail.

The title of the French Work Table (No. 2 at bottom of Page 326) sufficiently indicates its use. The style of finishing them is neat, being commonly made of satin wood with a brass moulding round the edge of the rim. The front part of the rim is hinged to the top, in the same way as the front of a secretary or desk drawer ; so that when it is turned up it fastens by two thumb springs as they do. The brass moulding is mitred upon the edge of the rim when the front is up, and after it is hinged ; which being cut through with a thin saw, the moulding, on the return of the front, will be fair with that on the end. The shelf below is shaped something like a boat. The bottom of it is made of inch stuff, and double tenoned into the standards, as the profile plainly shews. The top of each standard has also double tenons, to which cross bars are morticed and screwed to the under side of the top. The scale shews the proportions of the standard and the height of the table ; its breadth is fourteen or fifteen inches. The boat part, which serves as a convenience for sewing implements, is six inches over the middle and three at each end.

The Lady's Secretary (No. 4, Page 326) is sometimes finished in black rose-wood and tulip cross-banding, together with brass mouldings, which produce a fine effect. The upper shelf is intended to be marble, supported with brass pillars, and a brass ornamented rim round the top. The lower part may be fitted up in drawers on one side, and the other with a shelf to hold a lady's hat or the like.

SHERATON. Late 18th Century.

The Screen Table (No. 3) is intended for a lady to write or work at near the fire; the screen part behind securing her face from its injuries. There is a drawer below the slider, and the slider is lined with green cloth. The back feet are grooved out for the screen to slide in; in each of which grooves is fixed a spring to balance the screen by. The top is first cross-banded all round; then a border is put on, so broad as to fall exactly where the joint of the screen will be in the top. Beyond that again is put a narrower cross banding. When the screen is down the top appears uniform, without any joint, at least not so as to be offensive to the eye. The straining frame of the screen is made of thin wainscot, and framed in four panels. When the said frame is covered in the manner of any other screen, slips are got out and grooved and mitred round, and a part of the top which rises up with the screen is glued on to the slip, and as of course the top will project over behind, so it affords hold for the hand to raise the screen by.

PAGE 327.—The Lady's Cabinet (1st article) is made entirely in one part. The legs and columns are therefore all in one piece. The inside of the cabinet is made separate, and slips in between the legs, and a piece of narrow wood, as a band, is fitted to fill the space up to the column, as the design shews. The marble shelves, with frets at each end, are for a tea equipage. Above and below these shelves are drawers which turn out by a hinge. Above and below the front are also drawers. The drawer below may be made to support the front when turned down to write on, or may be supported by brass joints, as shewn in the design for the inside of the cabinet. The plans of each cabinet show their length and breadth; it remains only to mention their height, which is four feet, and four feet two inches.

PAGE 327.—The Cabinet in the top right-hand corner is, I presume, as new as the fire-screen, and will have a better effect in the execution than in the design. The front of the cabinet is hinged to a sliding piece which runs in a groove, upon the same principle as the writing table No. 2 on Page 318. The front being turned down to a horizontal position, it may then be slipped in till it stops. To support the front thus turned down, there are two sliders which come out of the plinth on which the cabinet rests. These sliders come out by relieving a spring which is fixed in their side, and having a common spring behind, they are forced out so that the fingers may lay hold to draw them quite out. They are lined with green cloth both at top and bottom to prevent them from scratching both the front and top of the cabinet. The inside of the front is also lined with green cloth to write on. The inside of the cabinet is fitted up in a manner shown in the cabinet next to it. Above the falling front is a drawer, to the under side of which the front locks, so that the drawer and front are either locked or opened at one time. Above the drawer is an ornamented frieze, japanned; and round the top, which is marble, is a brass edging. The flower pot at the top, and that on the stretcher, are supposed to be real, not carved. The columns stand clear as shewn by the plan; and they are intended to have brass bases and capitals, with wooden shafts fluted. The candle branches turn to any form in a socket, and the whole may be taken away, as they are only screwed into a nut fixed into the legs of the table. There is a brass fret fixed at each end, which finishes at the standards of the candle branches. The lower frame contains a drawer in front, and the legs being octagon, are intended to be veneered crossways as far as to the carving, which may be gilt to suit the bases and caps of the column.

The use of the Cabinet in the lower left-hand corner (Page 327) is to accommodate a lady with conveniences for writing, reading, and holding trinkets and similar articles. The style of finishing them is elegant, being often richly japanned, and veneered with the finest satin-wood. The manufacturing part is not very difficult, but will admit of the following remarks. The middle drawer over the knee-hole has a slider to write on, and those on each side are plain. The doors under them are hung with pin-hinges, and in the inside there is one shelf in each. The cupboard within the knee-hole is fitted up in small drawers, and sometimes only a shelf. The pilasters or half-columns are put on after the carcass is made. The corner ones are planed square first, and then rabbeted out to receive the angle of the carcass, and afterwards deal is glued in a slight manner into the rabbet, that it may be easily taken out after the column is turned. The centre door of the upper part is square at the top, opening under the astragal which finishes the cove part. The pilasters on the door frame, and the drapery is formed and sewed to the silk, and both are tacked into a rabbet together. Behind the silk door are sliding shelves for small books. The wings are fitted up as shewn in the design on the right or with more small drawers, having only two or three letter holes at the top.

The centre Secretaire on Page 327 is a small one for a lady, with falling front and writing drawer.

PAGE 328.—The two top Pier Tables are merely for ornament under a glass; they are generally made very light, and the style of finishing them is rich and elegant. Sometimes the tops are solid marble, but most commonly veneered in rich satin, or other valuable wood, with a cross-band on the outside, a border about two inches richly japanned, and a narrow cross-band beyond it to go all round. The frames are commonly gold, or white and burnished gold. Stretching-rails have of late been introduced to these tables, and it must be owned that it is with good effect, as they take off the long appearance of the legs and make the under part appear more furnished ; besides, they afford an opportunity of fixing a vase or basket of flowers, which, with their reflection when there is a glass behind, produce a brilliant appearance. Some, in place of a stretcher, have a thin marble shelf, with a brass rim round it, supported by a light frame ; in which case the top ought to be of marble also.

Of the Card Tables (the lower two) on page 328, it is scarcely necessary to say anything, especially as the quarter plans shew how they must be framed ; and therefore I shall only observe that the ornaments may be japanned on the frames and carved in the legs. As to the method of managing the tops, I take it to be the best to rip up dry deal, or faulty mahogany, into four inch widths, and joint them up. It matters not whether the pieces are whole lengths provided the jump-joints be crossed. Some tongue the jump-joints for strength. After the tops are dry, hard mahogany is tongued into the ends of the deal, then slips are glued on to the front and back, that the whole may appear solid mahogany, if a moulding is to be worked on the edge ; but if the edge be cross-banded, there is in this case no need for tonguing in mahogany.

Of the Knife Cases little need be said. It is only wanted to be observed that the corner pilasters of the left-hand case have small flutes of white holly or other coloured wood et in, and the middle pilasters have very narrow cross-bands all round, with the panels japanned in small flowers. The top is sometimes japanned, and sometimes has only an inlaid patera. The half columns of the right hand case are sometimes fluted out, and sometimes the flutes are let in. The feet may be turned and twisted, which will have a good effect.

PAGE 329.—These Lady's Drawing and Writing Tables are finished neat, either in mahogany or satin wood, with a brass rim round the top part. The upper part is made separate from the under part, and fixes on to it by pins. The rising desk in the middle may be made to slide* forward, which will then serve to draw upon ; and the small drawers below the coves at each end will be found convenient for colours. The drawer in the middle of the front serves to put the drawings in. The top is lined with green leather or cloth. The scale shews the size of every part in the front, and the breadth is two feet three inches. The height of the upper part is eight inches.

PAGE 330.—These Dressing Chests are also on a new plan, particularly as the common slider generally used for merely writing on is turned into a shallow drawer, which contains a little writing flap which rises behind by a horse, and places for ink, sand, and pens, and also dressing boxes. When the drawer is in, it appears like a common slider, with a partition above and below, as that with the convex front. There is therefore no slip under the top, as the drawer sides must run close up to it. The drawer below of course must lock up into the under edge of the dressing drawer, and the dressing drawer into the top, which is done at one time, by the bolt of the under lock forcing up that of the upper one. The height of these chests is always governed by the slider, which runs thirty-two or thirty-three inches from the floor ; and their breadth is twenty-two or twenty-three inches.

These Cylinder Wash-hand Tables (Page 330) are always made of mahogany, and having a cylinder to rise up to hide the washing apparatus, they look neat in any genteel dressing-room. They also contain a bidet on the right near the front and D, a water drawer on the left near the back, so that when the two are pushed home they pass by each other. The drawer on the front, which appears partly out, runs above the bidet and the water drawer. The two heights of sham drawers above contain the cylinder, and the two heights of sham drawers below contain the bidet and water drawer. The basin has a plug hole at the bottom, by which the water is conveyed off into the drawer D, which is lined with lead. The top of the cistern is hinged, and can be turned up at any time to fill it with fresh water. The glass rises up behind, in the same manner as that of a shaving stand, and when the glass is down, the top can be turned down also ; and the cylinder being raised to meet it, the whole is enclosed. The motion of the cylinder is guided by two quadrant pieces, one at each end of it, which are hinged to the top in which the basin hangs. This is shown by A in the profile, which, when the cylinder is let fall to its place, will be at B. When the cylinder is raised up to A, it catches at C, which is a spring of the same kind as those put on Secretary drawers. The bidet drawer is sometimes made to take quite out, having four legs to rest on. The end of the piece of work is cut out so as the feet can go in without being folded up. This, in the design, is stopped from coming quite out, and the framed legs, which appear, fold under the drawer and slip in along with it.

The use of the Universal Table on the next page is both to answer the purpose of a breakfast and a dining table. When both the leaves are slipped under the bed, it will then serve as a breakfast table ; when one leaf is out, as in this view, it will accommodate five persons as a dining table ; and if both are out, it will admit of eight, being near seven feet long, and

*See the directions given for the Kidney Table, Page 324.

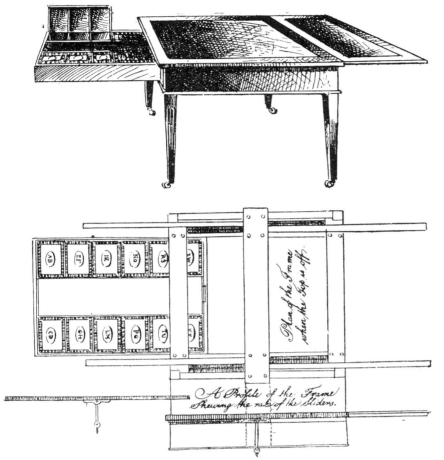

three feet six inches in width. The drawer s divided into six boxes at each side, as in the plan, and are found useful for different sorts of tea and sugar, and sometimes for notes, or the like. In this drawer is a slider lined with green cloth to write on. The style of finishing them is plain and simple, with straight tapered legs, socket castors, and an astragal round the frame. This table should be made of particularly good and well-seasoned mahogany, as a great deal depends upon its not being liable to cast. In the best kind of these tables the tops are framed and panelled; the bed into two panels, and the flaps each into one, with a white string round each panel to hide the joint. The framing is three inches broad, and mitred at the corners; and the panels are sometimes glued up in three thicknesses, the middle piece being laid with the grain across, and the other two lengthways of the panel to prevent its warping. The panels are, however, often put in of solid stuff, without this kind of gluing. When the panels are tongued into the framing, and the mitres are fitted to, the tops should stand to shrink as much as possible before they are glued for good. There are different methods of securing the mitres of the framing. Some make simply a straight mitre, which they can shoot with a plane, after which they put a couple of wooden pins in. Others, again, having fitted the mitres to by a plane, they slip into a tenon. But the strongest method is to mortice and tenon the mitres together, having a square joint at the under, and a mitre joint at the upper side. This method, however, is the most tedious of the three, and where the price will not allow of much time, the above methods are more ready, and, if managed with care, are sufficiently strong. In gluing the mitres, it will be proper, first, to glue on the outside of each mitre a piece of deal in the shape of a wedge, which will take a hand-screw, so that when they are putting together the glue may be brought out, and the mitres made close. The frame, as shewn in the plan, is made exactly square, either of faulty mahogany or of wainscot veneered. In making this frame a box is formed at each end about three inches in width, containing two sliders a piece, which run past each other in the said box, as shewn in the plan. In the bottom of each box are put two pieces, with plough grooves in them, and raking contrary to each other. In the line N O on these raking pieces the sliders run, and are stopped from coming too far out by a pin fixed in the under edge of the slider; which pin runs in the plough grooves already mentioned, denoted in the plan by a dark line. The raking line of the sliders is found by taking the width of the flap, as from S to M, and making the line incline in that width equal to the thickness of the flap. This may be easily understood by placing a rule from the outer point M of the flap to S in the inner point, which then will be parallel to the raking line. The sliding pieces being in a right line their whole length at the under edge, of course their upper edge must be bevelled off, so that when they are drawn fully out they may be even, and in an exact line with the top of the frame. The frame and tops being thus prepared, they are connected together by an iron screw and nut, as at A, which is about the substance of a bed screw. This screw is jointed into a plate, which plate is let into the under side of the bed, level with it; though I have described it at A with its thickness out, merely that the plate might be shewn. At B the bed A is represented on the frame, and the iron screw passing through the rail of the table, is confined to its place by the nut, which is let into the under edge of the rail by a centre bit. And observe, in making this centre-bit hole for the nut, it must be sunk deeper than its thickness, that bed may have liberty to rise a little, and so give place to the flaps when they are wanted to be pushed in. It must be noticed also, from the plan of the frame, that there is a middle piece about five inches broad, and of equal thickness with the flaps, screwed down to the frame with four screws at each end. This middle piece answers three purposes ; it secures the frame, stops the flaps when they are pushed in, and prevents the sliding pieces from tilting. Before the bed is finally fixed to its place, there must be four pieces of green cloth let into the under side of it to prevent the flaps from rubbing as they slide under. Upon the edges of the flaps a hollow is worked all round, leaving a quarter of an inch square, for no other purpose than to take off the clumsy appearance of the two thicknesses when the flaps are under the bed. At the under side of the flaps must be gouged out finger-holes to draw them out by. The drawer is next to be considered, which is sometimes made with two fronts and to draw out both ways, as in the plan. On each front of the drawer is a lock for the convenience of securing it at either end ; for in case one flap be drawn out, then the drawer can be locked or pulled out at the contrary front, without the trouble of pushing the flap in to come at the drawer. The covers of each box before mentioned may have an oval of dark wood and the alphabet cut out of ivory or white wood let into them, as in plan ; or they may be white ovals and black letters ; the use of which is to distinguish the contents of each box. Lastly, the slider to write on is made exactly half the inside length of the drawer ; so that when it is pushed home to either front, there is immediately access to six of the boxes. And here I would observe that sometimes the flaps of these tables have round corners, but they do not answer the bed so well when they are in. And, to save expense, the tops have been found to answer the purpose in solid wood, without being framed. When they are made in this manner, particular regard should be had to placing the heart side of the wood outward, which naturally draws round of itself, and may therefore be expected to keep true, notwithstanding its unfavourable situation.

(N.B.—The heart side of a board is easily known by planing the end, and observing the circular traces of the grain, which always tend outwards.)

PAGE 337.—FIG. 33. To find the lines for working the Mouldings of a Clock Bracket, &c., when the front moulding projects more than the ends. Operation—Let $a\,o\,b\,d$ be the plan of the clock bracket. From the centre of $a\,o$ draw the mitre lines to b and d, and from the centre let fall a perpendicular, as at f. From this perpendicular draw a profile of the cavetto and astragal, according to the projection intended for the ends of the bracket. From the spring of the cavetto on the top of the necking raise a perpendicular up to the line $a\,o$; then, from the upper part of the cavetto, as from 1, raise another perpendicular up to 1 on $a\,o$. Divide the intermediate space into any number of equal parts, as at 1, 2, 3, 4, etc. From these draw perpendiculars to the mitre line, and continue them downwards till they touch the cavetto at 2, 3, 4, etc. Lastly draw from the utmost projection of the astragal, or necking, a perpendicular, cutting the mitre line at 5 ; then from 5, 4, 3, 2, 1, on the cavetto draw parallels out at pleasure to No. 1. Take in your compasses $d\,o$ from the plan of the bracket, and place it from d to p, No. 1. From p let fall a perpendicular ; then from the plan, as before, take 1.1 and place it from 1 on the perpendicular line p to 1 on the parallel line. Again, take the line 2.2 from the plan, and place it on the parallel line 2 to 2 at No. 1, and so of all the rest, forming so many points, by which a profile of the front cavetto may be formed, and which will mitre in with the end cavetto, if the mouldings are exactly worked to these profiles, and the mitres be accurately cut. How the mitres are to be cut is seen by the mitre lines on the plan. In Plate II, Fig. 12, an example of the same kind is shewn, as it may be performed by the Sector. Let the Quadrant A D be considered as one of the cavettoes to be mitred together. Then let it be proposed that another cavetto is to mitre to the former, whose projection shall be equal to 1.10. Proceed then to draw this cavetto by the same directions as are given in page † for drawing an Oval ; after which the cavettoes are to be worked according to these curves. The length of the mitre for the least projecting cavetto is from 99 to 10, and that of the largest projecting cavetto is from 10 to A, and the mitre line is 9.10. By these methods it is evident that any moulding of different projections, and consisting of various members, may be worked, and cut so as to mitre exactly together.

Of working and mitring raking Mouldings. Let No. 1, Fig. 34, be a level ovolo in a broken pediment. Make its projection equal to its height. Divide the height of the ovolo into any number of equal parts, and from these divisions draw parallel lines, as is shewn in the figure. Next, from 1.2, the extreme points of the ovolo, draw two parallel lines, according to the rake of the pediment described below, which will of course increase the height of the ovolo as 3.4. Draw then the perpendicular or a line square from either of the raking lines, as at No. 2. Divide this line into the same number of equal parts, and from these divisions draw lines parallel to the raking part, and continue them out at pleasure. Take then 5.5 from No. 1, and transfer this opening of the compasses to 5.5 on No. 2, and also at No. 3, marking where it extends to. Again, take in your compasses 4.4 from No. 1, and transfer this also to 4.4 on Nos. 2 and 3, marking it as before ; proceeding in the same manner with the rest ; by which, points will be found to enable us to draw the raking ovolo, so that it will mitre with the level one at No. 1 ; and also the returning ovolo at No. 3, thus found, will mitre in with the raking

†Sheraton's Directions for Drawing Ovals, etc., have been left out for want of space.

Of mitring a Comb Tray, or any thing of the same nature

Fig. 32.

Fig. 33

The method of finding the lines for working the mouldings of a Clock Bracket, when the front moulding projects more than the ends

N.º 1.

Fig. 34

The method of working and mitring raking mouldings.

Fig. 35

Half of the Tuscan Pediment

Fig. 36.

Centre of shaft

Diameter

moulding No. 2. In the same manner may be found the raking and returning cyma-recta mouldings described in Fig. 35, which it is unnecessary to say anything about, after what has been said on the ovolo.

Fig. 36.—As I have in this Section described the methods of drawing and mitring mouldings of different projections, and also of drawing and mitring raking with level mouldings, it may be proper here to describe the proportion of the Tuscan raking Pediment, and the manner of drawing it. It is true, according to an orderly arrangement, the Pediment should come after the column; but this is of small consequence, if it can as well be understood in this place. The intention of a close p e d i m e n t, whether raking or circular is not only to ornament the front door or entrance of any building, but likewise to shelter such as seek admittance from inclement weather. For this purpose the raking close pediment of any order is best calculated; for whilst we are sheltered from rain or snow by the bold projections of the several members of each order, especially the Doric, the descending showers easily and quickly glide off on each side, on account of the rake of such pediments. It is therefore improper to have open pediments of any order at the exterior entrance of buildings: and it is considered by architects as improper to have close ones over interior entrances or door-ways, where they are only employed as ornamental. The pitch of the Tuscan pediment is the same with the other Orders, for in this respect they are all uniformly the same; but their intercoluminations, or spaces between the pillars, or pilasters, together with other particulars, vary according to the respective order to which they belong; which I shall mention afterwards, in treating on the Orders. To proportion and, draw the Tuscan order, proceed thus: Observe, that Fig. 36 is exactly half the pediment only; and therefore, in drawing a whole pediment, the divisions specified in the figure must be laid on each way from the central line. And observe, likewise that the frieze and architrave are not drawn to the cornice, because they are not wanted in describing the pediment. Operation.—Lay down three diameters from the centre of the pediment to the centre of the shaft, as at 1, 2, 3 in the figure. Divide a diameter into eight equal parts, and take three of these and place them each way from the centre line of the shaft which gives the upper diameter of the column, as the figure shews. Again divide a diameter into four, as that distinguished by the writing in the figure, and take three of those parts for the perpendicular height of the cornice; at this height draw a parallel line at pleasure sufficient for the whole length of the pediment as the upper line with the numbers.   Then take the perpendicular height of the cornice, and place it from the outside line of the shaft on the line continued out from the under edge of the cornice, which will determine its projection, as is easily seen by the level scale line h.   Raise a perpendicular line from the whole projection, as g, till it cuts the upper parallel line ; then will this line serve as a scale for the heights of each member in the cornice, the proportions of which are easily seen by the aliquot parts on the scale ; but if not rightly understood, the reader may suspend his judgment till the Tuscan Order is described.   Divide the upper parallel line, which is equal to one half of the whole length, into nine equal parts, and give four of these for the pitch of the pediment, as the figures 1, 2, 3, 4 shew.   Draw then a right line from 4 to the utmost projection of the level cornice, and proceed to draw each member of the level cornice, as the scale lines direct.   Note the two upper lines, containing the nine divisions represent the upper fillet of the level cyma-recta.   The next thing to be done, is to proportion the members of the raking cornice by those of the level one.   To do this draw a line square from the pitch of the pediment, and continue it till it passes through the level cornice.   Then take the skew measurement of the lower fillet of the level cyma-recta, as $a\ b$, and transfer this to the raking cyma-recta downwards from a to b.   Again take $b\ c$ from the level corona, and transfer it from b to c for the raking corona.   Lastly, take c, d, e, f, in the same manner, and transfer them one after another for the raking mouldings, as before ; after which, draw lines through the several points parallel to the pitch or raking line, and the pediment will be completed for shading, if required.

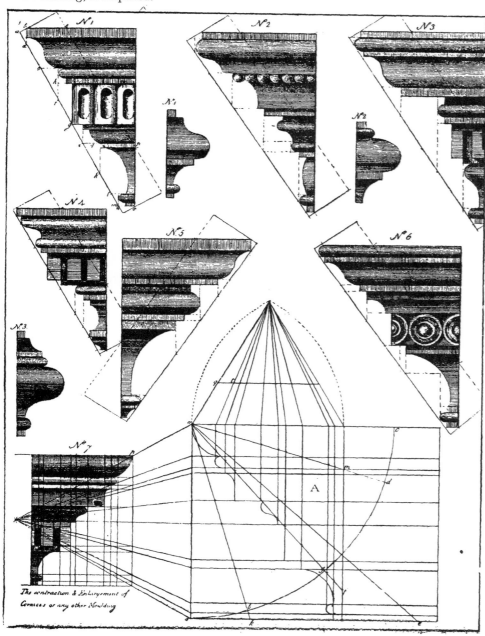

The contraction & Enlargement of Cornices or any other Moulding

In the Cornices on this page the spring is shewn, and the proper gauging is pointed out. The width and thickness also of the mahogany is shewn. The astragal, in Nos. 3 and 5, can be worked separate, and glued on afterwards. The pateras, in No. 6 are turned and planted on.

The method of gauging and working Cornices.—The explanation of this may be thought, by some, an unnecessary business ; but from the bungling manner in which I have seen many workmen proceed to stick cornices, I am certain that a few hints will be of service, especially to the inexperienced. For this purpose I have, in No. 1, lettered each gauge-point, and I shall proceed, as supposing that it is necessary that the whole should be taught. When the pattern of any cornice is given to be worked, take the drawing and strike a line $a\ n$ to touch as near as may be each member. From this front line strike one at each end square from it, so as to take in the whole extent of the Cornice. Then draw another line parallel to that on the front, to shew the necessary thickness of the mahogany, and proceed as follows : Let the stuff be sawn out broad enough to plane to $b\ o$; after which plane it true on both sides, and glue on deal of the breadth of $e\ p$, and

SHERATON   Late 18th Century.

thick enough to make out the whole spring of the cornice. After the glue is dry, plane the mahogany to the exact breadth of *b o*. After striking a square line across the mahogany, extend the compasses from *a* to *a*, and to *c, f, g*, etc., and lay all these points on the square line, and run a gauge through each of them. Run then a gauge from *a* to *b*, and from *n* to *o*; and taking a bevel, fix the handle of it exactly by the front line, and let the inside of the blade of it correspond with *o p*. With the bevel thus fixed, plane down the wood behind till it fit the bevel in every place, and be brought down to *o*. Take then a square, and plane down the wood at *b* and *e* till the square fit in every place, and the wood is brought down to *b*. After this lay the Cornice on the side *o p*, and shoot off the wood *a, a, b*; then lay it on the side *b e*, and shoot off the wood at *n o* to *m*. The Cornice being thus properly sprung, fasten it down on the side *a p*, and proceed to rabbet out the several squares. Begin at *c* and rabbet down to *f*; at *h* run on a side gauge, and entering in by a snipe's bill, work down to *i*, the fluting being laid on afterwards; at *q* run on a side gauge each way for the square of the ovolo. From *i* rabbet down to *k*, and at *l* down to *m*; and thus it is evident that the whole Cornice, of whatever kind, cannot fail of being correctly worked.

The Method of Contracting and Enlarging Cornices.—Suppose A to be a Cornice already drawn or worked, and it be required to draw and work one a third, fourth, or any other proportion narrower than A, and at the same time, to contract its projection in proportion to its height : Take the compasses and extend them to *a o*, the whole height of the Cornice A, and with this opening sweep an arch each way, and where they intersect, to that point draw right-lines from *o* and *a*, forming an equilateral triangle. In the same manner proceed with the projection of A, as shewn in the figure. To the summits of those triangles draw lines from the several heights and projections of each member. If the Cornice to be drawn is to be one-third less, then divide any one side of the triangles into three equal parts, and take one part from *o* to *p*, and let fall a perpendicular from *p*; and from where this perpendicular cuts each line draw parallels, which will give the height of each member in exact proportion. For the projections : *o q* is one-third of the side of the triangle, as before; draw a parallel line at *q*, which will give the several projections sought. Take *q t*, and transfer this to *p r*, and so of the rest, till you have laid on each projection : after which let fall perpendiculars, as shewn at No. 7, and proceed to draw the outlines of each member within their proper squares, and the Cornice will be contracted in the most accurate manner.

Enlarging Cornices.—Suppose now the Cornice A is required to be higher than what it is at present. Draw parallel lines from each member, and having fixed the compasses to the height proposed, fix one foot at *o*, and move the other till it touch anywhere on the line *a k*, as at *k*; draw a line from *c* to *k*, and where this line intersects with each parallel before drawn, will be the several heights of the mouldings as required. To find the projection, proceed thus :—sweep the arch *a c*, cutting *o k* at *b*; take *a b* and place it from *c* to *d*, and from *d* draw a line to *o*, and *o m* will then be the whole projection of the Cornice proportionable to the height *o k*; consequently where the line *o m* intersects, each perpendicular raised from the several projections of A, will be the several projections sought; *o m* is then a scale line for the projections, and *o k* for the heights of each member ; and having these, the Cornice can then be drawn on a separate paper, in the same manner as A was drawn at first. By continuing the parallel lines of A to the right, as shewn in the plate, by letting fall its perpendiculars to any length, it is evident that A may be enlarged as much as we please, by drawing the line *o k* more oblique, as at *e*, which then makes it rather more than one-third higher. Then, by extending the compasses from *a* to where *o e* cuts the arch, and by replacing this opening from *c* to *g*, and striking a line from *o* to *g* through to *f*, *o f* will be its projection as before ; on which principles *o f* will be in a ratio with *o e*. This the workman can prove, for by comparing *o f* with the length of the projection of A, he will find it rather more than one-third longer ; and by comparing *o e* with *o a*, he will find it rather more than one-third longer also. Thus it is evident that any Cornice or moulding whatever, and however complex, may be contracted and enlarged as we please, and that with the greatest mathematical nicety.

The Harlequin Pembroke Table on Page 342 serves not only as a breakfast, but also as a writing table, very suitable for a lady. It is termed a Harlequin Table, for no other reason but because, in exhibitions of that sort, there is generally a great deal of machinery introduced in the scenery. Tables like this have already been made, but not according to the improved plan of the machinery here proposed. In this, however, I assume very little originality or merit to myself, except what is due to the manner of shewing and describing the mechanism of it ; the rest is due to a friend, from whom I received my first ideas of it. The particular advantages arising from the machinery are as follows : First, the nest of drawers, or till, shewn in the design, can be raised to any height, gradually, until at length the whole is out. Second, when the whole is out, as represented in the design, it cannot be taken away, because of three stops which keep it in ; two at one end, and one at the other, according to the grooves in No. 1. Thirdly, but if necessity require that the till should be taken quite away from the rest of the table, in order to come at the machinery, then one of these stops at one end is so constructed that it can be slipped back, and, the till being raised up at the same end where the stop is slipped back, the two at the other end of course will relieve themselves, so that the till can be taken quite away. Fourthly, when the till is replaced, the stop can

SHERATON HARLEQUIN TABLE. Late 18th Century.

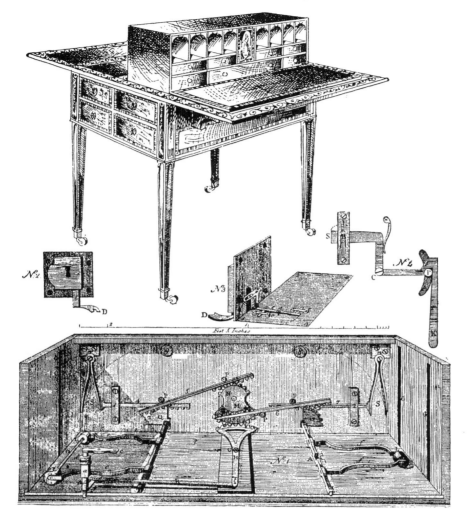

be pushed into the groove again by the finger, which returns again into the groove by the force of a small spring. Fifthly, the till being let down again until it is perfectly even with the rest of the table-top, it can then be secured in its place by means of another stop at the bottom, so that if the whole table were turned upside down the till would still keep its place. Sixthly, although the till be raised and lowered by turning the fly bracket which supports the flap, yet the bracket is made to lose this effect or power by the turn of a key, and the bracket may then be drawn out to support the flap without raising the till, and the table can then be used, as in common, to breakfast upon. These are all the advantages that are necessary, or that can be looked for in tables of this sort, to render them complete, and to obtain the approbation of the ingenious. But it will now be requisite to shew in what manner the machinery operates so as to effect these; and, likewise, to give some description of its parts, that the workman may be able to form a proper idea of the whole.

The first and great thing to be attended to is, to shew the manner of raising the till by turning the fly bracket. To accomplish this, I have given a perspective view of the whole machinery at No. 1. Supposing the till to be taken out, and the fly brackets and inner lining away from the framing $a\ b$ is an upright iron axis, made in two parts, and connected together by a round pin at the joint b; of course, if the winch c be turned round, the axis a will turn round with it by the above pin, without moving the lower part of the axis b. Whence it is evident, that if the winch c be screwed to the under edge of the fly bracket, which bracket is shewn in the design, it will turn round without affecting any part of the machinery. This is the cause why the flap of the top can be up whilst the till is down. But if the square socket a be pressed down past the joint b, the two parts of the axis will then be confined together, and therefore if the winch c be moved this way, it is evident that the machinery will instantly be put in motion in the following manner: The winch c being screwed to the fly bracket, and turned square out, it describes by its passage a quadrant of a circle; and the arm s of the crank rod being fixed fast into the same axis $a\ b$, consequently it will describe the same curve as the bracket: and as the crank rod R is jointed into its arm at s and at t, in moving the arm the rod R is pushed forward to j, and the horizontal cog wheel H turns to the left hand on the centre C. It being then turned to the left, as expressed by the dotted line at q it follows that the upright cog wheel N must be turned to the right hand; and if this be turned to the right hand, then must also the quadrant cog wheel Q on the left turn to the right with it; and, because the axis A is fixed fast in the wheel Q, and the crooked levers $e\ e$ into A, consequently the rollers L L, fixed by the rod o to these levers, will describe a quadrant of a circle, as denoted by the dotted line on the roller 9; because the connecting cog rod 5 makes Q move in the same curve as N does. Again, if N, the upper part of the upright cog wheel, move to the right, then must M, the lower part of it, move to the left; and being connected with the cog rod 6, and it again to the right hand quadrant cog wheel Q, it follows, as before, that the levers $f\ f$, and the roller L, will describe a quadrant of a circle to the left hand, as at 8. The reader must easily see now, that when the winch c is turned by the fly bracket, that every part of the machinery will be put in motion, and that the levers and rollers, in approaching gradually to 8 and 9, must necessarily raise up the till. But it must also be observed, that the motion of the levers f

SHERATON.   Late 18th Century.

and *e e* is greatly promoted by the power of the common steel springs S S; for, when the till is down, these are always charged; that is, the sides of the springs are nearly close to each other, and these being connected with what may be termed the auxiliary, or assistant cog rods, 4 and 7, and consequently pressing against their ends, the quadrant cog wheels Q Q are thereby made to revolve, and the levers and rollers are raised almost as much by this means as by the other machinery. It must also be noticed, that as these springs and auxiliary rods greatly assist the other power in raising the till, so do they also check the sudden fall of it, by a constant resistance against the pressure of it, so that the passage of the till downwards is made by this means smooth and easy.   Observe *p, p, p, p,* are brass pulleys fixed to keep the cog rods in their place, and *w w* are pieces of wood to keep the springs firm to their centre.   The reason why there are but three rollers, and two of them at one end, is obvious; because the till must rest truer on three points than on four.   It cannot totter on this account when it is fully raised, because there are two stops at that end where there is only one roller, which run in the grooves G G; and if the stops chuck up to the end of the grooves when the till is up, it is impossible that it can totter, considering that the other end is upon two rollers.   And here let it be noted, that if the workman find any inconvenience owing to the double roller *o* being at the same end with the axis *b b,* it can be removed by putting the double roller where the single one is, which makes no difference with any other part of the machinery.   And observe, that when the rollers are nearly perpendicular to their axis A A, they enter upon an inclined plane, or on thin pieces of wood planed off like a wedge, of the width of the rollers, and whose thin end is glued to meet the rollers as they rise, so that the till can thereby be raised as high as we please.   These wedges being glued on the under side of the till to suit exactly the place of the rollers, the projection of the wedges below the till makes it necessary that there should be a vacuity in the axis A A, for them to fall into when the till is down; because, in this situation, the till rests on the three rollers, which are nearly on a level with the axis A A.   And as the wedges above mentioned must lie across the axis A A when the till is down, every workman must see the necessity of a vacuity, or otherwise the till would not settle to its place.

The next thing in order is to shew how one of the stops can be relieved, or slipped back, so that the till may be taken quite away.   The construction of this stop is shewn by No. 4, which supposes that we see the under side of the till.   A hole is cut through the till, which hole is drawn by a compass, having one foot at C the centre.   P is a round pin, which comes through to the inside of the bottom of the till.   K is a tin key which hooks this pin.   In applying this key to the pin, the writing slider, shown in the design, must be pushed in, and the front part which covers the letter holes turned up to its place; and there being a groove across the under side of the slider, exactly where the pin comes, and the slider giving a little way for the thickness of the aforesaid key, the groove just mentioned admits the key over the head of the pin P; then when the key s drawn back again, P moves towards A by the centre C; and S, the stop which projects beyond the till, is by this means drawn within.   B is a plate screwed on to the till to keep the stop firm.   Again, when the till is down to its place, it is necessary that it should be stopped there also, as has been already said.   The apparatus for this is shewn at No. 3, which is a different view of the same lock as at No. 2.   1, 2, 3, 4 is supposed to be a part of the bottom, not of the till, but that whereon the machinery is placed at No. 1.   *t s* is a kind of trammel with slits in it, moving on a centre at *s.*   A pin is fixed to the bolt of the lock, and there being a passage for the pin cut out of the lock plate, as shewn in the design, this pin moves

Sheraton Tables.   Late 18th or early 19th Century

up and down, according as the key is turned. *a* is a kind of lever, with two arms, moving at the centre *a*. *c c* are staples which are fastened to the under side of the till, and as the bolt of the lock shoots downwards, the trammel *t s* throws the arms of the lever out of the staples which are fixed to the underside of the till; by which means the till is relieved, and can then be raised by drawing out the fly bracket. And here the workman must be careful to observe, that when the bolt *b* No. 1 is shot, as it now appears, the till is always relieved, and the bracket at the same time has power to raise the till; because the fork D works in the groove *d* of the axis *a b* at No. 1, and thereby presses the socket *a* to *b*, and gives the winch *c* power over the machinery. And observe, further, that when the bolt *b* at No, 2 is up, as it is shewn at No. 3, then it is evident that the arms of the stop lever will pass through the before-mentioned staples at the under side of the till and secure it, while at the same time the bracket will lose its power over the machinery ; because the socket *a*, at No. 1, is thereby raised above *b*, and of course as *b* turns on a pin, the winch *c* cannot affect the crank rod *s* R, and therefore no part of the machinery is moved. Thus it is, I think, sufficiently clear that the till can be stopped and relieved when it is either up or down, and also that the bracket can be drawn out to support the flap, while at the same time the till is both down and stopped, so that the whole may be used as a common breakfast table. It remains now to give some hints respecting the manufacturing part.

The Table Top.—The size of the table when opened is four feet, and two feet seven inches long; and the rails eight and a quarter deep. The whole top is divided into four compartments, to answer the opening for the till. Round these compartments is a japanned border, to fill up the space which lies between the end of the table and the till. The border must be continued all round alike, to make the panels appear uniform and of equal size. The bed of the top should be framed in two panels of three-quarters mahogany well seasoned, and the breadth of the stiles to suit the opening of the till. A panel of half-inch stuff should be tongued into the other part of the bed where the till does not rise. Then, for the sake of the astragal which is to be worked on the edge of the top all round, a piece should be tongued in, the long way of the grain, into each end of the bed. And observe, that as the bed of the table will frequently have to be taken off in the course of the work, it is best to put small tenons into the under side of it, and mortices into the rails all round, by which means the bed will be kept to a certain place, and taken easy off at any time. A black string is put next the till, all round the inside of the border to hide the joint. In putting this black string on at the opening of the till the inside of the mahogany frame should be rabbetted out to take a slip of black veneer, about three-eighths wide; and it being left to stand above the framing the thickness of the veneer, this black slip cannot be shot by a rabbet plane to the thickness of a neat string, and the veneer must be jumped to it. The use of this is, that when the till rises it may not take any part of the string away with it, which it certainly would do if it were put on merely as a corner string.

The Till,—The carcass of the till is made of half-inch mahogany; the partitions and letter holes of thin quarter stuff, and black beads put on their edges, all of which must be kept back about half an inch from the edge of the carcass, to give place to the writing slider, part of which turns up as a front to the inside of the till, and part of it remains in it; and, as part of the writing slider remains in the bottom of the till below the drawers, consequently there must be a joint in the slider to answer it, which joint is hinged at each end before the cross band is put on for the green cloth. The workman may make the hinges himself to suit that purpose. They may be made as common desk-fall hinges, only the knuckles of the hinge are made a little higher than common to receive a thin veneer; which, when screwed on, the veneer for the band of the cloth lies upon and covers the straps, so that a part of the knuckle is only seen; but observe, that the ends of the veneer, each meeting at the knuckle, must be cut in a sloping direction, so that they and the brass knuckle between them will be exactly in the form, and of the same nature, as the rule joint of a fly bracket for a Pembroke table; and therefore it must be evident to every workman that the front will turn up square. The slider is stopped into the till by a couple of pins which run in grooves; and when it is pushed home, before it can turn up, a hollow must be worked in the bottom of the till, to give room for the angle of the rising part of the slider to turn in. When the slider is turned up, it is kept in its place by a spring catch, which strikes into a plate put on at the under side of the top of the till. And observe, that when the front is up, it should be rather within the carcass of the till, both for the purpose of letting the till go easy down, and to admit of a slip of thin green cloth at each end, so that when the front is turned upon the top of the Pembroke table, it may not scratch it. Another method may, however, be proposed, and which will be attended with less trouble, only with this disadvantage, that it takes off a little of the height of the drawers. The slider, being made in two parts, may be hinged in the manner of a card-table top, which, when it is folded over, can be pushed to its place. But observe that the under top must be made so much broader than the upper one, as will admit of its being stopped in after the manner of the other, so that when it is drawn out the upper top will rise and clear the drawer fronts. If the slider be made in this manner, the drawers can then be brought within a little of the front edge, and what remains serves to give place to a couple of thumb-nail holes to draw out the slider by.

SHERATON. Late 18th Century.

(N.B.—The prospect door is made to run in at the top, like a drawer, upon the same principles as the front of the cabinet on page 327.)

The Frame of the Table.—The legs are made a little stronger than usual, because the table is pretty heavy altogether. Both the end rails are divided into four drawers each, in appearance; but, in reality, there are but two in the whole; for observe, that, for the sake of strength in the frame, the lower drawer of the left hand is made real, and that above it is a sham; but at the other end, which is not seen in the design, the upper drawer is real, and the under one a sham. A middle rail is tenoned, of inch stuff, into each end rail. Against this rail the upright part of the machinery is fixed, as shewn at No. 1; and as this rail stands within the edge of the top framing about an inch, it contains the whole projection of every part of the machinery, so that the till passes without obstruction. The inner lining for the fly brackets to fall against, is not less than three-quarters thick when planed; and it must be the whole breadth of the end rails, *i.e.*, eight and a quarter. The fly bracket makes up the remaining thickness of the foot, and comes down low enough to answer the height of the upper cross band of the lower drawer. The part remaining below the bracket is veneered the whole length with satin wood, and cross-banded to match the drawer fronts. The workman, in making the fly bracket to which the winch c is screwed, must observe to make a shoulder pin on the turning part of it at the under edge; and this shoulder will require to be double the usual thickness, that the iron winch c may be let into the bracket without injuring the rule joint, or interfering with the wire of its centre. The lock at No. 2 or 3 is put on at the inside of the inner lining, so near to the axis a b at No. 1, as that the fork D of the lock shall extend to the groove d in the socket of the axis a b, which will then determine the place of the key-hole, as shewn in the design.

The Pediments.—With respect to these pediments little can be said, as the designs themselves shew in what manner they should be executed. No. 1 should have the facia, or ground board, glued up in three thicknesses, having the middle piece with the grain right up and down. The foliage ornaments are cut out along with the astragal, and planted on; and the whole may easily be made to take off from the cornice, by having a tenon at each end and one in the centre. No. 2: the tablet part is intended to have a cross band round it, and the drapery may be japanned. The astragal on the top of it is meant to return over the ogee. The square of the ogee may come forward, level with the tablet, to prevent too great a projection. No. 3: in the centre there are two pilasters to project a little from the ground, which are fluted. The panels at each end are intended to be fanned the reverse way, or with the rounds out.

We now come to Sheraton's later style. In 1803 he published "The Cabinet Dictionary"; also in 1804-1807 "The Cabinet Maker, Upholsterer, and General Artists' Encyclopedia" (with coloured plates). Nos. 1 and 2 on Page 244 he calls "Curricule" Chairs. The word curricule he describes in his dictionary as a "chaise of two wheels drawn by two horses." No. 2 on Page 344 may be thirty-two inches high in the back, and to slope a little lower to the front of the arm, and in the front two feet over all. No 1 on the same page is not more than twenty-eight inches high, and should be made narrow in front; but the depth from back to front must not be less than two feet. No. 7 on Page 347 he describes as an "Easy Chair, stuffed all over; it is intended for sick persons, being both easy and warm, for the side wings coming quite forward keep out the cold air, which may be totally excluded from the person asleep by laying some kind of covering over the whole chair." He calls Nos. 9 and 10 on Page 344 "Herculaneums." "Hall Chairs," he mentions, "are generally made of mahogany, with turned seats, and the crest or arms of the family painted on the back."

Sheraton, in his "Cabinet Dictionary," makes the following remarks about Chair-makers: "In the chair branch it requires a particular turn in the handling of the slopes, to make them agreeable and easy. It is very remarkable the difference of some chairs of precisely the same pattern, when executed by different chair-makers, arising chiefly from the want of taste concerning the beauty of an outline, of which we judge by the eye, more than the rigid rules of geometry." He further adds, "The kind of mahogany employed in chair making ought to be Spanish or Cuba, of a clean straight grain; wood of this quality will rub bright, and keep cleaner than any Honduras wood. Yet there is wood of the last quality, if properly selected for chair making, to which there can be no material objection; and where lightness is preferred, as is sometimes the case, it will demand the preference." And again he adds, "It appears from some of the later specimens of French chairs, some of which we have been favoured with a view of, that they follow the antique taste, and introduce into their arms and legs various heads of animals; and that mahogany is the chief wood used in their best chairs, into which they bring in portions of ornamental brass; and, in my opinion, not without a proper effect, when due restraint is laid on the quantity."

No. 4 on Page 347 is a Conversation Chair. The manner of conversing amongst some of the highest circles of company, on some occasions, is copied from the French by lounging on a chair. It should be observed that they are made extraordinary long between back and front, for the purpose of space for the fashionable posture; and also that they are narrow in front and back, as an accommodation to this mode of conversing.

SHERATON CHAIRS. Early 19th Century.

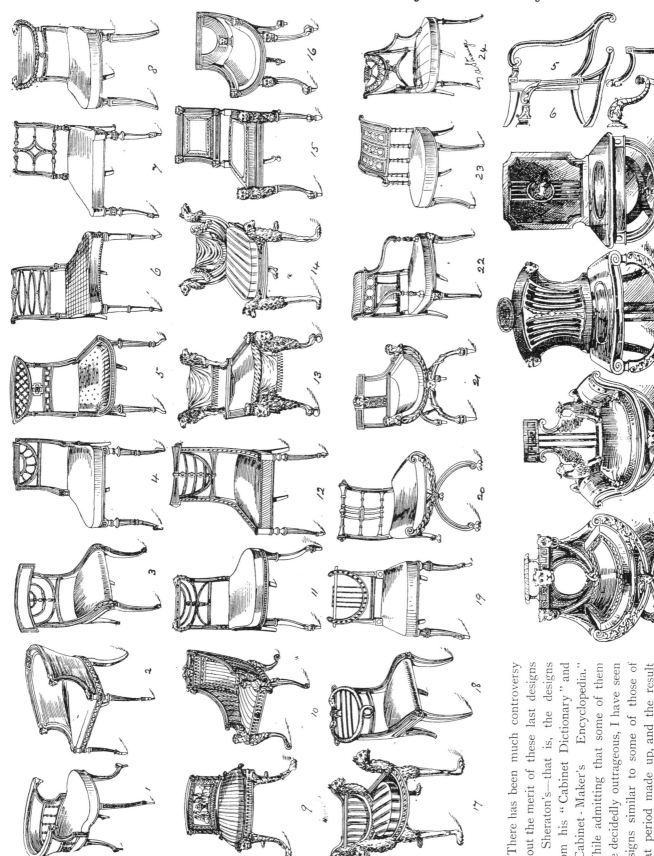

There has been much controversy about the merit of these last designs of Sheraton's—that is, the designs from his "Cabinet Dictionary" and "Cabinet-Maker's Encyclopedia." While admitting that some of them are decidedly outrageous, I have seen designs similar to some of those of that period made up, and the result appeared to me satisfactory this applies more especially to the Writing Tables.

SHERATON CHAIRS. Early 19th Century.

Late 18th Century HALL CHAIRS and Early 19th Century SHERATON SOFAS.

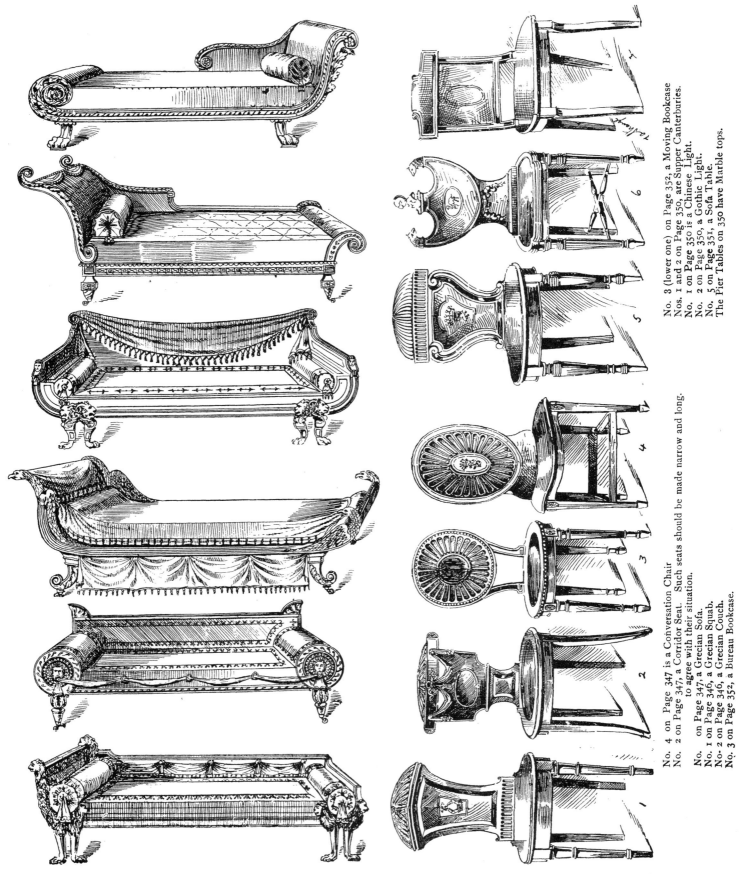

Sofas.   Hall Chairs.

No. 4 on Page 347 is a Conversation Chair
No. 2 on Page 347, a Corridor Seat. Such seats should be made narrow and long.
to agree with their situation.

No.   on Page 347, a Grecian Sofa.
No. 1 on Page 346, a Grecian Squab.
No. 2 on Page 346, a Grecian Couch.
No. 3 on Page 352, a Bureau Bookcase.

No. 3 (lower one) on Page 352, a Moving Bookcase
Nos. 1 and 2 on Page 350, are Supper Canterburies.
No. 1 on Page 350 is a Chinese Light.
No. 2 on Page 350, a Gothic Light.
No. 5 on Page 351, a Sofa Table.
The Pier Tables on 350 have Marble tops.

SHERATON CHAIRS, SOFAS, etc.   Early 18th Century.

Sofas on Pages 346 and 347.—The chief difficulty in these designs is the stuffing part, and doubtless requires an upholsterer of taste and abilty to finish them properly. The frames may be finished either in white and gold or carved in mahogany.

The Sideboards on page 348 are those that are used for a dining-room equipage, on which the silver plate is placed. No. 1 is a Cellaret Sideboard with a cupboard at each end, which may be either plain or have drawers. The fronts of the Cellarets are hung on a centre, which is connected with a square case within, where the bottles of wine are kept, except those in immediate use, which are placed in a circular case on the inside of the front, as expressed in the design. The most fashionable sideboards at present, are those without cellarets or any kind of drawers, having massive ornamented legs and moulded frames.

Buffet on Page 348.—The Buffet was anciently an apartment separated from the rest of the room by small pillars or balusters. Their use was for holding china and glass, with other articles of a similar nature. The lower part of the Buffet on Page 348 is enclosed with doors, having silk curtains with worked brass or wire before them. The upright border round the top of lower part is of brass, together with those round the china shelves. These shelves are supported at each end with four brass

Buffet.

Sideboard Tables.

columns made very light; the lights at each end may be of brass and taken away occasionally. As these Buffets would suit well to be placed one on each side of the fireplace of a breakfast room, they might very conveniently hold such branches. There is a Gothic drapery under the cornice, and a fringe above it.

The Sofa Table, No. 5 on page 351, is used before a sofa, and is generally made between five and six feet long, and from twenty-two inches to two feet broad. The one with a rising top is a Sofa Writing Table.

In cabinet making "Commode" applies to pieces of furniture, chiefly for ornament, to stand under a glass in a drawing-room. It is sometimes used more agreeably to its derivation, and signifies such Commodes as are used by ladies to dress at, in

SHERATON SIDEBOARDS. Early 19th Century.

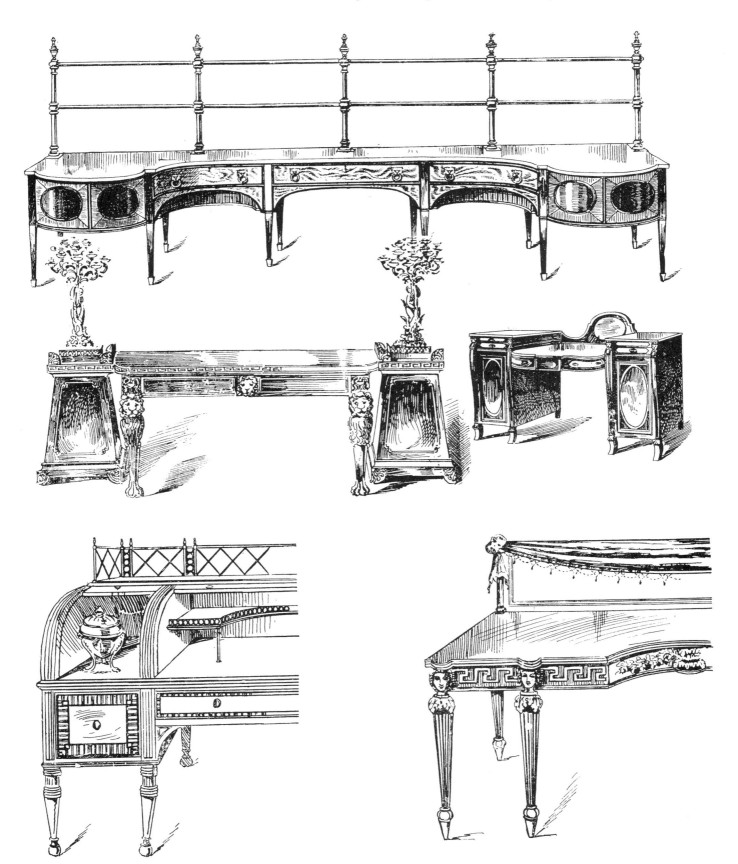

350

SHERATON DUMB-WAITERS, PIER-TABLES, etc.   Early 19th Century.

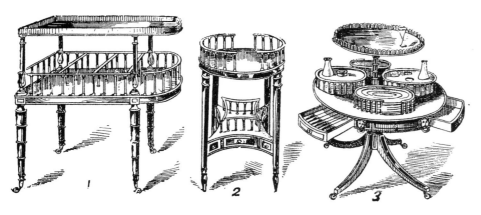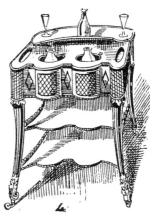

Dumb-Waiters.

which there is a drawer fitted up with suitable conveniences for the purpose. The Commode No. 1 on Page 362 is adapted to stand under a large glass either in a pier or at the end of a room. The ornaments in the top and at the bottom frieze are brass inlaid, which on a dark ground, will have a good effect. The upper frieze is of cross-banding, and is formed into drawers, or it may be without, which is commonly the case when such Commodes are used chiefly as ornaments. The doors may be framed, first square, and curved pieces of thin mahogany put in after, and

then the hollows mitred round of the same stuff afterwards, and veneered and cross-banded. The trellis-work before the silk curtains is of brass, either wrought wire or cut from sheet brass, and half-lapped in the intersections and soldered.

Nos. 2 and 4 at bottom of Page 352 are Pouch Tables.—Sheraton thus describes a Pouch Table in his "Cabinet Dictionary": "A table with a bag, used by ladies to work at, in which bag they deposit their fancy needlework. The work bags of both these tables are suspended to a frame which draws forward, in which frame is a lock which shuts its bolt up into the under edge of the rail of the top.

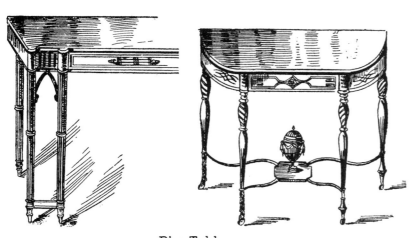

Pier-Tables.

SHERATON LIBRARY and SOFA TABLES, etc.   Early 19th Century.

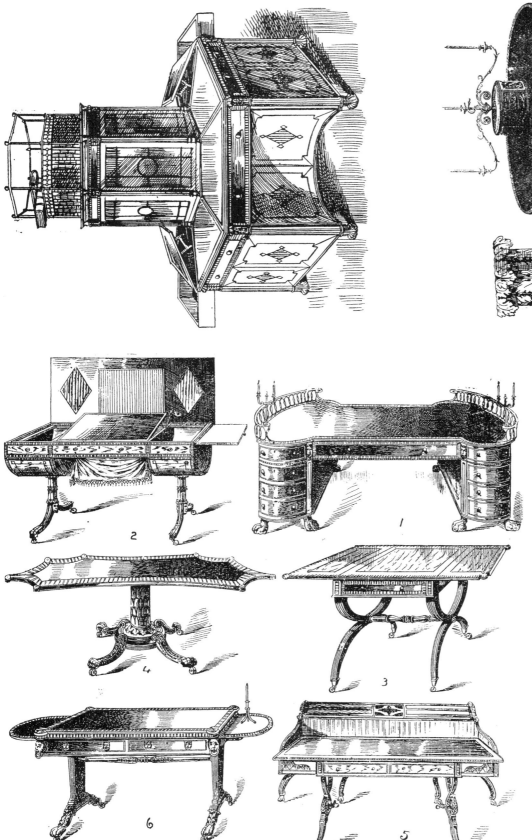

They are also used as chess tables occasionally ; the design on the right shews the top with the chess-board down, contrary to that on the left, which is also capable of being drawn out and turned down." Sheraton further adds, " The frets on the edges of both tables are of brass, and the ground ought to be of black rose-wood when they are required to be elegant, otherwise they may be very neatly made of mahogany."

The Library Table, No. 5 on Page 352, is in the "Antique Style." It has only three real drawers : one in the centre between each leg. If, however, the sides of the drawers be

SHERATON WRITING-TABLES, CABINETS, and WORK TABLES.

For further Designs of Sheraton see Page 251.

made to incline to the centre of the table, and made to run on slips grooved into the bottoms, there is room for six drawers. This table is best suited for gilding, on account of the carving introduced into the design.

No. 3 on Page 341 is a Library Table. The toes and castors are cast in one piece of brass. The nest of drawers in the centre rise by two small springs placed opposite to each other, which are constructed on the model of baize door springs, and cannot but be understood by any workman who is acquainted with hanging a door of that kind. In this Table there are four real drawers made with square sides.

No. 3 on Page 351 is called a Pembroke Table, a name given to a kind of breakfast table from the name of the lady who first gave orders for one of them. The size of such tables is from three feet eight inches to four feet wide, that is when open; and from two feet ten inches to three feet long when the flaps are down. The width of the bed should never be less than one foot nine inches; but in general they are from one foot ten inches to two feet one inch, and their height never more than two feet four inches, including castors.

The Sisters' Cylinder Bookcase, No. 2 on Page 352, is intended to stand in the centre of the room for the use of two ladies who may both write and read at it together. The upper part is fitted up for books all round; but in order to receive the depth of the books on each front, the ends must be made sham books as far from the fronts as to receive the depth of a small volume. From these backs must be a partition, which will part the shelves the other way, so that each bookcase, front wise, will hold two depths

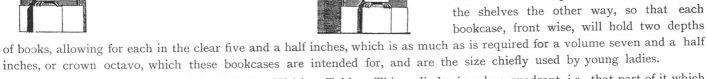

of books, allowing for each in the clear five and a half inches, which is as much as is required for a volume seven and a half inches, or crown octavo, which these bookcases are intended for, and are the size chiefly used by young ladies.

No. 2 on Page 341 is a Lady's Cylinder Writing Table.—This cylinder is only a quadrant, i.e., that part of it which moves is so. But it is intended to stand in the centre of the room. It is made to appear alike on each side. Therefore the cylinder is parted in two at the top, and the front one falls down to let the slides come forward. The lock of this table is in the edge of the cylinder, and when it is down in its place there are two flush plate rings let into it by which it is raised up; and the link plates being on the edge of the back cylinder, they meet together and lock at the top. The brass rod extending to the two ends of the cylinder is for a candle branch, as is represented. This branch, if required, may be taken off occasionally by unscrewing the nut at each end of the rod. Lastly, the circular flaps at each end are made to coincide with the lower part of the cylinder ends, which are made to receive them, so that when they are let down they appear to be the ends themselves. They are supported by brass joints in the form of a bracket, made for the purpose, and must be let into the end to keep clear of the flap when it is let down.

WILLIAM PAIN, DOORS and ORNAMENTS. Late 18th Century.

WILLIAM PAIN, CHIMNEY-PIECES, etc. of Late 18th Century.

William Pain published many works on architecture, etc.; among others, "The Practical Builder," in 1776; "The British Palladio," in 1786; "The Carpenter and Joiner's Repository"; "The Carpenter's Pocket Dictionary"; "The Practical House Carpenter," in 1805. His designs are decidedly classic, reminding one of the Adam style. His sons carried out a great many buildings in Ireland.

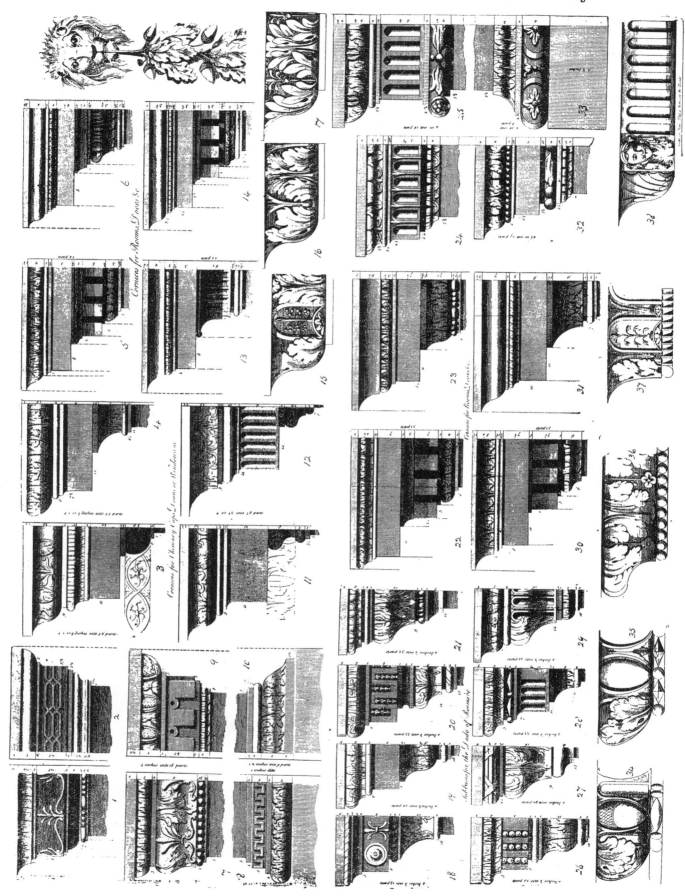

WILLIAM PAIN, CEILINGS, FRIEZES, etc. Late 18th Century.

The Library Case, No. 2 on Page 361, is a design for a Bookcase, which would look well in a library. The busts in the lower niches may be those of persons famed for literature and genius ; and the figures in the upper part may be suited to the chief subjects of the books contained in the bookcase. The inches may be formed by gluing up ribs of deal, or better if of the faulty mahogany, then veneer them in narrow slips, in the manner of a vase knife-case.

358

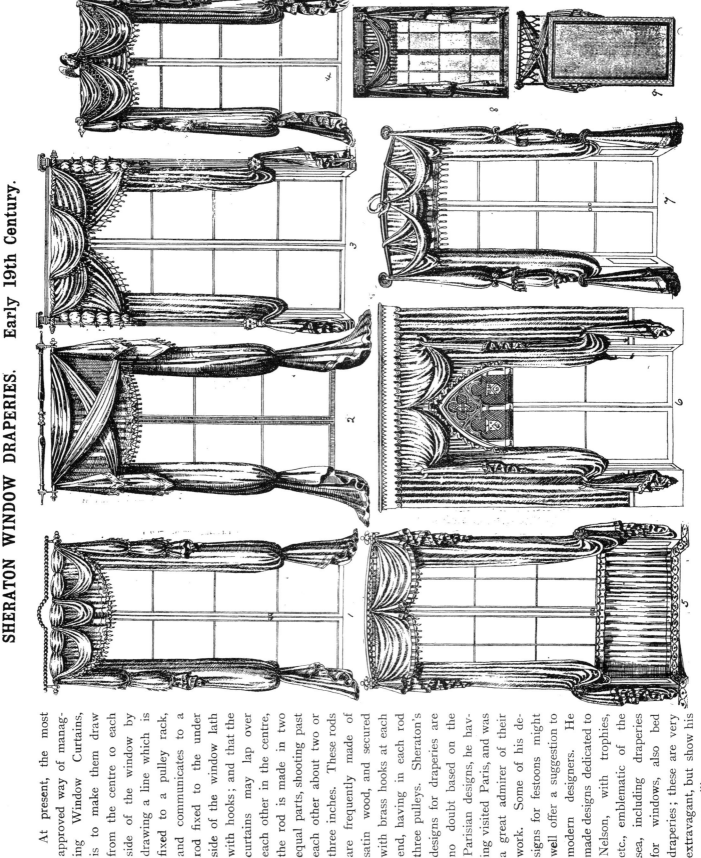

At present, the most approved way of managing Window Curtains, is to make them draw from the centre to each side of the window by drawing a line which is fixed to a pulley rack, and communicates to a rod fixed to the under side of the window lath with hooks; and that the curtains may lap over each other in the centre, the rod is made in two equal parts, shooting past each other about two or three inches. These rods are frequently made of satin wood, and secured with brass hooks at each end, having in each rod three pulleys. Sheraton's designs for draperies are no doubt based on the Parisian designs, he having visited Paris, and was a great admirer of their work. Some of his designs for festoons might well offer a suggestion to modern designers. He made designs dedicated to Nelson, with trophies, etc., emblematic of the sea, including draperies for windows, also bed draperies; these are very extravagant, but show his great versatility.

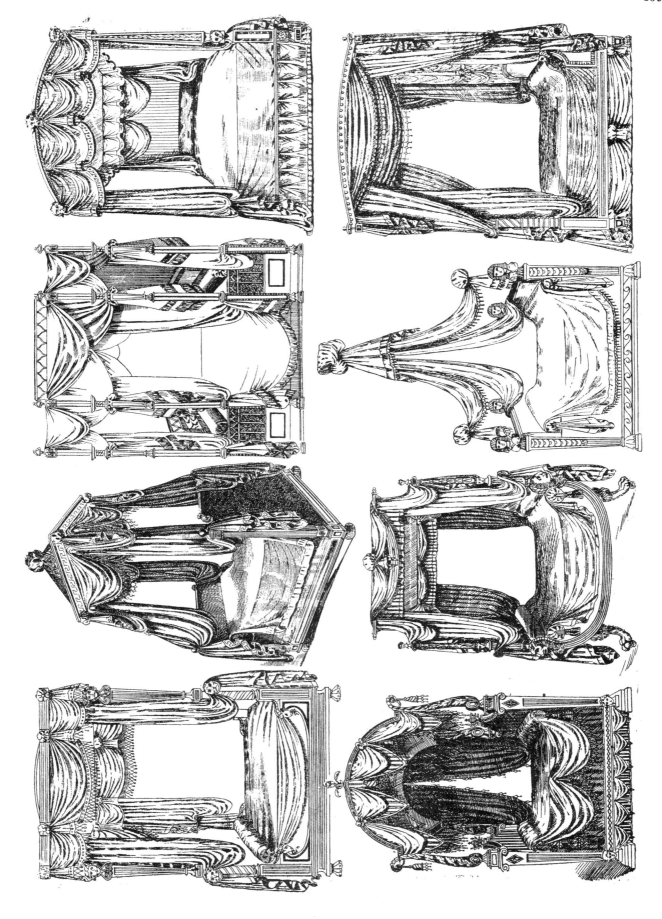

SHERATON BEDSTEADS.   Early 19th Century.

SHERATON BOOKCASES. Early 19th Century.

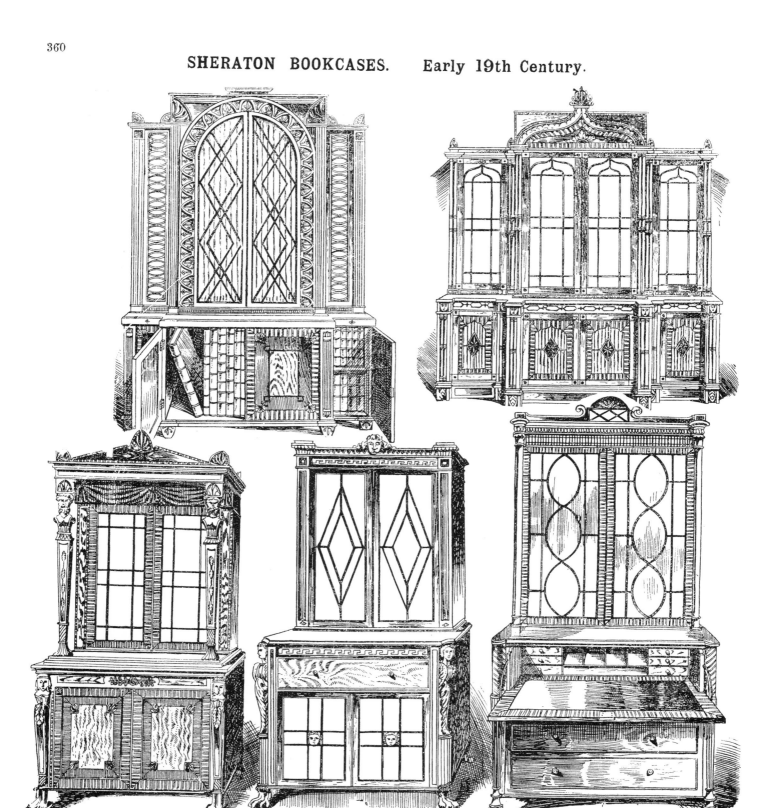

Triangular Basin Stand, No. 1 on Page 363.—Supposing the line cloth to be taken away, which it is supposed to be when it is not in use, the top would appear to be in shape to suit the basin itself, as in reality it is made to fit with it, and to shew a regular bead projecting quite round the whole.   To make this top rise to a convenient height, the back leg is glued up in the form of a long box, leaving a vacuity of about an inch and one-eighth square, into which an upright piece is fitted, as the design shews.   In this piece a groove is cut to admit of a suspar leg, that is hinged to it, and falls into notches made in the under side of the top ; and when this leg is pressed into the groove, the top will settle down to its place.   In raising it, it is stopped to any height by means of a rack and spring, fixed in the manner of a shaving stand glass.   In fixing the sliding

piece to the top, it will be advisable to take away the round to the depth of a veneer; and after a double tenon is let through the top, and wedged from the top side, to cover the whole by laying down a circular veneer, which will scarce be seen; and if the front corners be veneered also, there can be nothing objectionable in it. It is to be noticed that the back leg is straight down to the ground; and I think it will prove the best method, to dovetail the back angle together in half-inch mahogany, then to make a frame for the front, and to glue and screw the angular ends to the front frame, to be of three-quarter stuff; and lastly, to cut away the leg in an angle to fit on to this carcase, and glue it to and screw them from the inside. The shelf below must be fixed to the legs by

iron plates, as in common, and the pot cupboard, or it may be called the bottle cupboard, is made separately, with a tambour door, and screwed fast from the bottom of the shelf. Lastly, it may be noticed that the top of the legs are ornamented with a turned patera, glued on, which also serves to hide

the joints occasioned by the preceding manner of working.

The Octagon Library Table on Page 351, is suited to the centre of a large library room, and is furnished for the accommodation of four gentlemen to write at together. In the management of the doors of the niches, it is advisable to glue them up in styles of hard and dry mahogany, one inch thick and two inches in width; and, after being worked to their exact curve, to pin a slip of one inch thick mahogany lengthways, at top and bottom; or, if the doors be got out the full length, let a lath be ploughed into the ends of some kind of tough wood, and veneer be laid over it. The veneer being laid all over the ground, and the work suitably cleaned off, proceed to lay on the banding in thick veneer, to form the appearance of the stiles, with the square break in each corner, as shewn in the design. Lastly, by a plane made for the purpose, work two black beads together, and mitre them round, which will produce a good effect. This method forms a gently sunk panel, which in such situations, always looks well in mahogany work. It is needless to say that the same panelling continues uniform round the lower part. The diamond panel in the centre is composed of small reeds, let in flush with the veneer, after which a black line is let in. It is to be observed, with respect to the hollow doors in the niches, that, as their

opening in the centre is very oblique to the centre of the hinges on which they turn, the edges of the left hand doors must be bevelled towards the front, and those of the right in a reverse direction.

Sheraton, speaking of Tambour work, says that "in French it means a drum. Tambour Tables, among cabinet-makers, are of two sorts—one for a lady or gentleman to write at; and another for the former to execute needlework by. The Writing Tambour Tables are almost out of use at present, being both insecure and liable to injury. They are called Tambour from the cylindrical forms of their tops, which are glued up in narrow strips of mahogany and laid upon canvas, which binds them together, and suffers them, at the same time, to yield to the motion their ends make in the curved groove in which they run, so that the top may be brought round to the front, and pushed at pleasure to the back again when it is required to be open. Tambour tables are often introduced in small pieces of work when no great strength or security is requisite, as in Night Tables and Pot Cupboards. The Tambour Tables used by the ladies are on pillar and claws; and at the top of the stand or pillar is a wooden ball inclosed in a concave sphere, to which is fixed a circular rim of wainscot about a quarter of an inch thick and two inches broad. To this rim the ground for the needlework is fixed by lacing it over; and as the whole frame moves by the ball fixed as above, the work may be turned to any position, as the worker may require."

SHERATON WASHSTANDS, COMMODES, etc. Early 19th Century.

Washstands.

Dressing Commode.

Crib.

Camp Bedstead.

THOMAS HOPE and Others.   English Empire Style (?)   Early 19th Century.

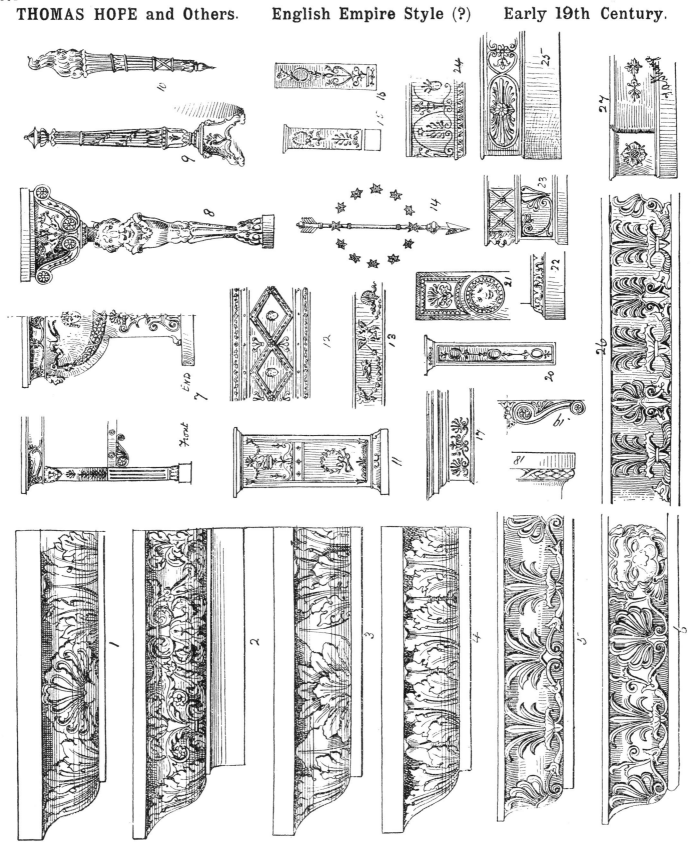

The following are a few particulars from Thomas Hope's work, published in 1807: Mahogany Chairs, inlaid in metal and ebony.   These species of inlaying in metal on a ground of ebony or dyed wood, seem peculiarly adapted to the nature of the mahogany furniture so much in use in that country (France), which they enliven, without preventing it, by any raised

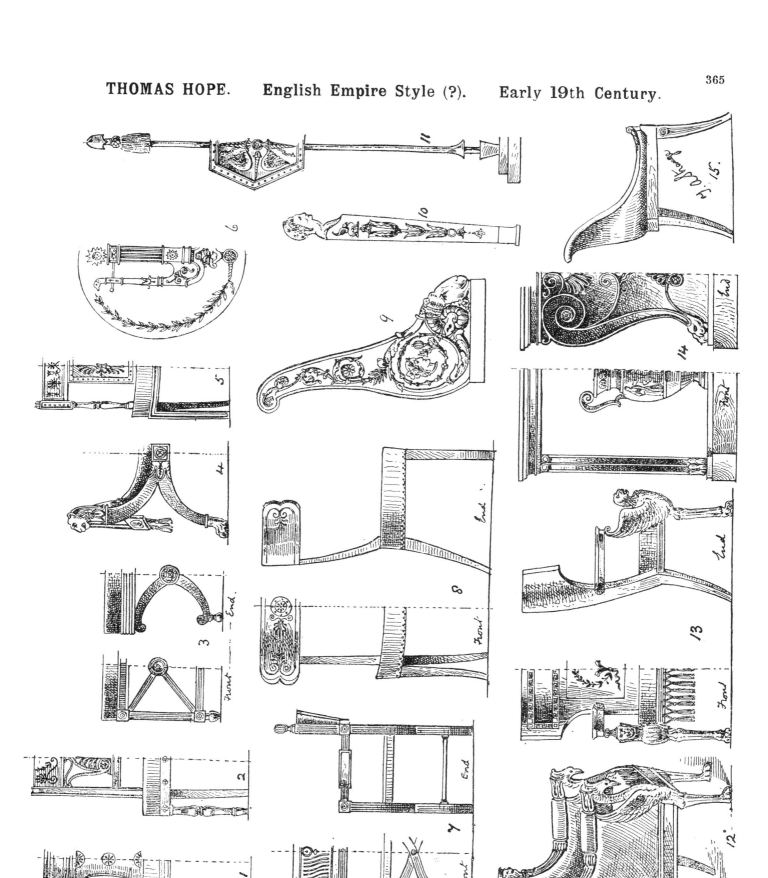

ornaments from being constantly rubbed, and kept free from dust and dirt. At Paris they have been carried to a great degree of elegance and perfection. The metal ornament, and the ground of stained wood in which it is inserted, being there

THOMAS HOPE. English Empire Style (?). Early 19th Century.

Large Writing Table
The tops of the pediment
contain the heads of the
patrons and patronesses of
Science
Apollo
& Minerva

Pedestal.

Cabinet.

Table.

Celleret ornamented
with amphora and
with figures allusive
of the liquid element.

Table.

State chair.

Sideboard
adorned with
emblems of
Bacchus and
of Ceres.

stamped together, and cut out, through dint of the same mechanical process, they are always sure of fitting each other to the greatest degree of nicety. Hope says : " The French Revolution commenced in 1792 ; Freedom, now consolidated in France, has restored the pure taste of the antique reproduction of ancient Greek forms for chairs, etc. The mouldings represent antique Roman fasces, with an axe in the centre ; trophies of lances, surmounted by a Phrygian cap of Liberty ; winged figures emblematical of freedom ; and antique heads of helmeted warriors arranged like cameo medallion." First consul, 1799 ; confirmed for life in 1802. Vases found in tombs have been placed in recesses, imitating the ancient columbaria, or receptacle of Cinerary urn. Indian or bearded Bacchus ; the scenic mask ; the Thyrfus, twined round with ivy leaves ; the

THOMAS HOPE and Others. English Empire Style (?). Early 19th Century.

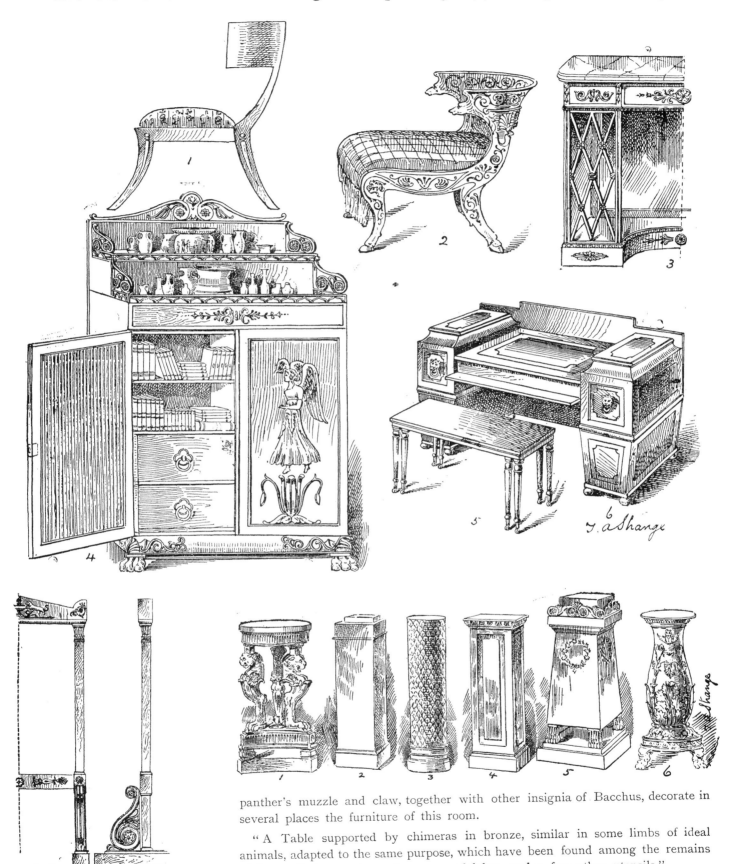

panther's muzzle and claw, together with other insignia of Bacchus, decorate in several places the furniture of this room.

"A Table supported by chimeras in bronze, similar in some limbs of ideal animals, adapted to the same purpose, which have been found among the remains of Pompeii, bronze lamp, bronze candelabra, and a few other utensils."

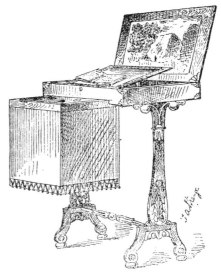

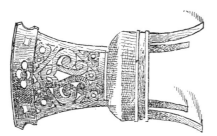

Plaques.—"Aurora visiting Cephalus on Mount Ida," by Flaxman; "The Owl, dedicated to Cephalus." The prevailing colours of both, as well as of the furniture, are that pale yellow and that bluish green which hold so conspicuous a rank among the Egyptian pigments, here and there relieved by masses of black and gold. In the front of a Table in the room dedicated to Aurora, females emblematic of the four horæ, or parts of the day, support its rails, the frieze of which contains medallions of the deities of night and sleep. On the table stands a clock carried by Isis, or the moon, adorned with her crescent; and the head of Jupiter, Serapis, or Pluto, emblematic of death.